Zoo
Regent's Park
Madame Tussaud's
The British Museum
St. Paul's Cathedral
The London Eye
Hyde Park
Buckingham Palace
Globe Theatre
Tower Bridge
The Thames Barrier
Houses of Parliament
Thames
GREENWICH
Greenwich

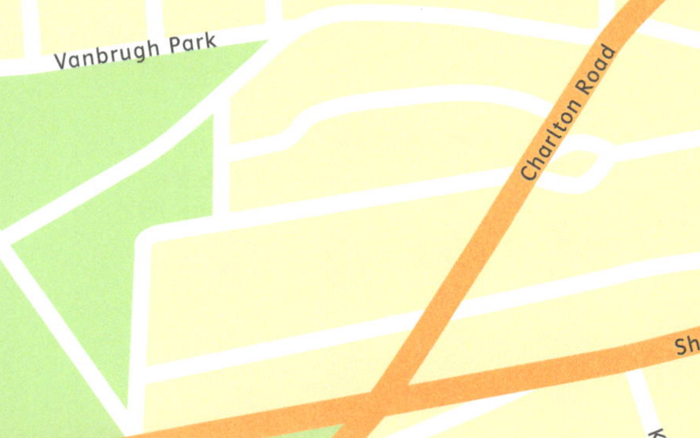

Kidbrooke Grove
Kidbrooke Park Road
Prince Charles Road
A2

Holly Richardson

- 11 years old
- has one sister, Amber (15)
- sees her dad at the weekend
- has two guinea pigs, Fluff and Honey
- likes animals and shopping

David (Dave) Preston

- 12 years old
- has no brothers or sisters
- has a cat, Sid
- likes computer games, science fiction movies and books

Thomas Tallis School

Blue Line 1

für Klasse 5

Das Lehrbuch versteht sich als Gesamtangebot. Welche Texte und Aufgaben verpflichtend sind, wird durch die schulinternen Curricula festgelegt.

1. Auflage ISBN 978-3-12-547871-8 (fester Einband) 1 13 12 11 10 | 28 27 26 25
1. Auflage ISBN 978-3-12-548871-7 (flexibler Einband) 1 10 9 8 7 | 28 27 26 25

Alle Drucke dieser Auflage sind unverändert und können im Unterricht nebeneinander verwendet werden.
Die letzte Zahl bezeichnet das Jahr des Druckes.

Herausgeber: Dr. Frank Haß, Kirchberg
Autorinnen und Autoren: David Brimage, Brighton; Jo Cummins, London; Elizabeth Daymond, Kiel; Timo Dorsch, Hamburg; Bettina Eisermann, Schneeberg; Leanne Garrity, London; Nicole Heidrich, Marktoberdorf; Patrick Hoke, Hamburg; Catrin Immel, Sinn; Melanie Ku, Köln; Andrew Mitchell, Jacksonville/IL; Howard Rayner, London; Karen Seekings, London; Lee Shutler, Margate; Louisa Stodd, Chichester; Clare Treleaven, Castellón
Beratung: Brunhilde Biek, Leonberg; Karin Braun, Dortmund; Wilma Brings, Bedburg; Amanda Chisnell, Lollar; Ulf Degen, Braunschweig; Tanja Frank, Ulm; Sandra Haberland, Recklinghausen; Wolfgang Hamm, Marktredwitz; Ulrike Heringhaus, Altheim; Michael Herrmann, Ludwigsfelde; Ines van Hove, Oldenburg; Christa Kathmann-Fuhrmann, Bonn; Dr. Margitta Kuty, Greifswald-Eldna; Grit Machut, Berlin; Michael Meisenzahl, Tauperlitz; Sibylle Olms, Everswinkel; Beatrix Pierce, Eppingen; Annegret Preker-Franke, Bielefeld; Christof Schmidt, Tübingen; Dr. Hubert Schwandt, Parchen; Dieter Vilimek, Helmstadt-Bargen

Für besondere Unterstützung danken wir herzlich Susan Bolton und Ken Jones von der Thomas Tallis School, London.

Redaktion: William Sears, Iris Seiler
Herstellung: Mechtild Frintrup, Andrea Schlegel

Umschlaggestaltung und Layout: know idea, Freiburg; Koma Amok, Stuttgart
Umschlagfoto: February Films (Elke Bock), London; Thinkstock (iStockphoto), München; iStockphoto (MARK BOND), Calgary, Alberta
Fotografen: Elke Bock, London; Andrew Kemp, London; Thomas Weccard, Ludwigsburg
Illustrationen: Kirill Chudinskiy, Köln; Christian Dekelver, Weinstadt; Tom Menzel, Scharbeutz/Klingberg; Yaroslav Schwarzstein, Hannover; Marcus Wilder, Hamburg; Steffen Wolff, Brohl-Lützing
Satz: Wiebke Hengst, Ostfildern; Eva Mokhlis, Stuttgart; Satzkiste GmbH, Stuttgart
Reproduktion: Schwabenrepro GmbH, Stuttgart
Druck: Firmengruppe Appl, aprinta druck, Wemding

Printed in Germany
ISBN 978-3-12-547871-8 (fester Einband)
ISBN 978-3-12-548871-7 (flexibler Einband)

Blue Line 1

Herausgeber: Dr. Frank Haß

Ernst Klett Verlag
Stuttgart • Leipzig

Inhalt

Unit 1: I'm from Greenwich

Unit 2: This is my school

L = Listening S = Speaking R = Reading W = Writing V = Viewing I = Intercultural

Kompetenzen / Themen / **Ich kann ...** Fertigkeiten Seite

Unit 3: My free time

Unit 4: Let's celebrate!

L = Listening S = Speaking R = Reading W = Writing V = Viewing I = Intercultural

Inhalt

L = Listening S = Speaking R = Reading W = Writing V = Viewing I = Intercultural

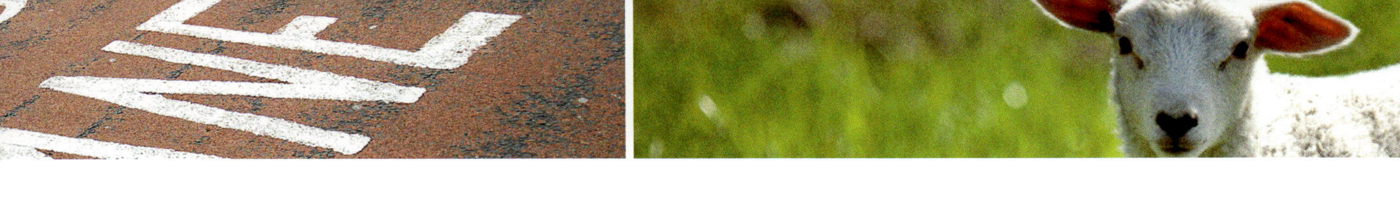

L = Listening S = Speaking R = Reading W = Writing V = Viewing I = Intercultural

So lernst du mit Blue Line

Hier zeige ich dir, wie du dich in deinem Buch gut zurechtfindest. Das Buch hat sechs Units (Kapitel). Jede Unit ist gleich aufgebaut.

Way in

Hier steigst du in das neue Thema ein. Dazu gibt es auch einen kurzen Film.

Im gelben Kasten siehst du, was du in der *Unit* lernst.

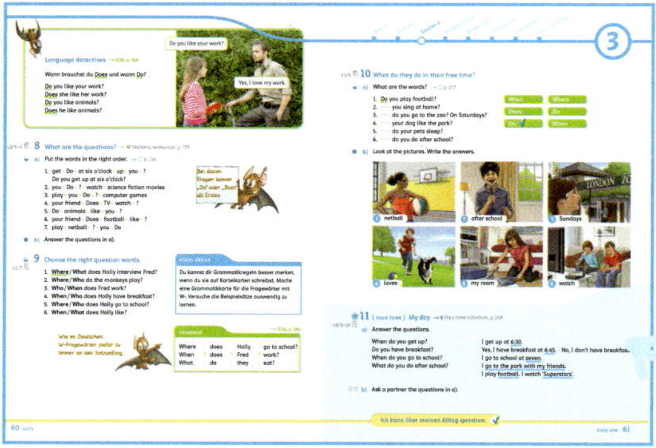

Stations

In jeder *Unit* gibt es zwei *Stations*, in denen du viele neue Dinge lernst. Diese Symbole zeigen dir, wie schwer die Übung ist und ob es im Anhang eine leichtere Variante gibt:

 p. 137,

In der *Your turn*-Aufgabe kannst du zeigen, dass du alles verstanden hast, und deine eigenen Ideen einbringen.

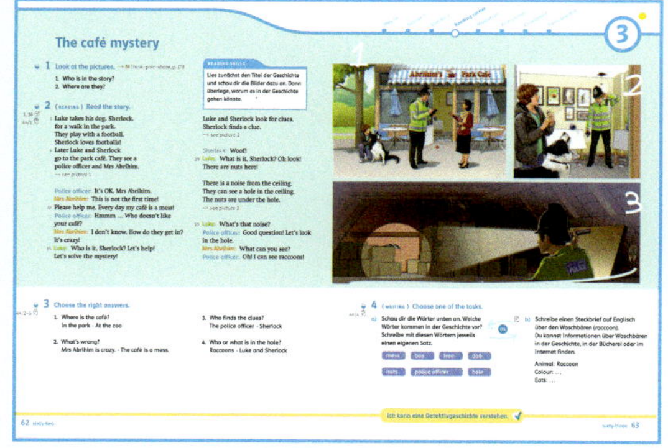

Reading corner

In der *Reading corner* gibt es verschiedene Geschichten, Dialoge und andere Texte. Vielleicht habt ihr Lust, sie nachzuspielen?

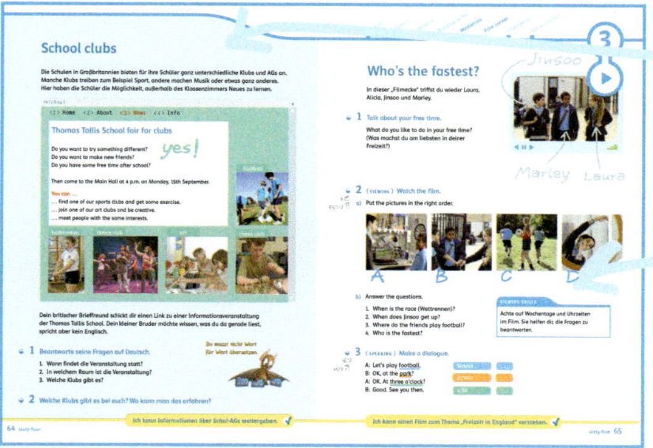

Mediation/Film corner

Auf der linken Seite geht es darum, englische Informationen auf Deutsch weiterzugeben oder umgekehrt. Das nennt man *Mediation*.

In der *Film corner* geht es um einen englischen Film.

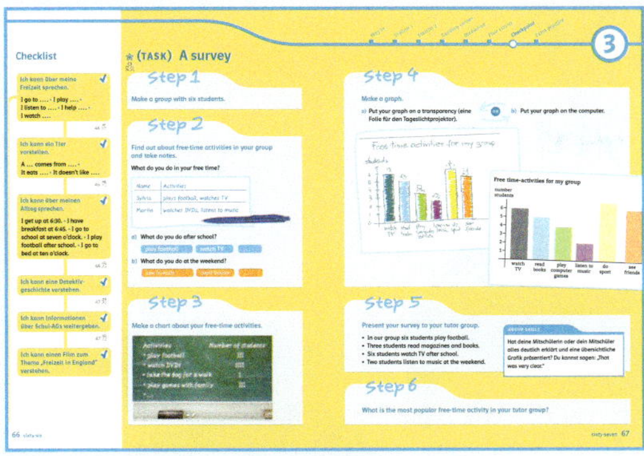

Checkpoint

Auf dieser Seite kannst du überprüfen, ob du in der *Unit* alles verstanden hast.
In der *Checklist* sind alle Lernziele noch einmal aufgelistet.

Die Abschluss-Aufgabe (*task*) sollt ihr zu zweit oder in der Gruppe lösen.

Extra practice

Hier findest du zwei Seiten mit Zusatz-Aufgaben, z. B. zur Vorbereitung auf die Klassenarbeit.

Skills

Auf einige *Units* folgt eine Doppelseite, auf der ihr eine bestimmte Fertigkeit (*skill*) besonders trainieren könnt, also z. B. das Hören, Lesen, Schreiben oder Sprechen.

Extra Grammar Methods Vocabulary

Im Anschluss an die sechs *Units* gibt es noch weitere nützliche Seiten:

Extra: Hier erwarten dich weitere Lesetexte: Gedichte, Geschichten und vieles mehr.

Grammar: Hier findest du alle Regeln und Erklärungen zur Grammatik sowie weitere Übungen.

Methods: Manche Übungen könnt ihr auf eine bestimmte Art und Weise bearbeiten.
Das erkennt ihr an diesem Symbol: → M.
Wie es genau funktioniert, kannst du hier nachlesen.

Vocabulary: Im *Vocabulary* findest du alle neuen Wörter in der Reihenfolge, in der sie in der *Unit* auftauchen, und die wichtigsten Arbeitsanweisungen.
Im *Dictionary* sind die Wörter noch einmal alphabetisch aufgelistet: zuerst Englisch-Deutsch und dann Deutsch-Englisch.

Ganz am Schluss des Buches findest du noch
- Sätze, die du im Unterricht sagen kannst, z. B. bei der Gruppenarbeit
- Lösungen zu den Übungen der *Extra training*-Seiten
- eine Liste mit den unregelmäßigen Verben

Symbol	Erklärung
○ ◒ ●	leicht/mittel/schwer (Niveaudifferenzierung)
remember	(Re)Aktivierung Grundschulwortschatz
✿	individualisierende Aufgabe (natürliche Differenzierung)
→ ○ p. 131	Verweis auf leichtere Parallelübung auf der *Diff corner*-Seite
OR	Aufgabe zur Auswahl (Wahldifferenzierung)
P	Hier entsteht ein Produkt für das Portfolio.
4/1	Verweis auf eine Übung im *Workbook*
→ G13, p. 172	Verweis auf den Grammatikanhang (*Grammar*)
→ M	Verweis auf die Methodenseite (*Methods*)
→ V	Verweis zum Wortfeld im Vokabular (*Vocabulary*)
	Partnerarbeit
	Gruppenarbeit
	Verweis auf die Lehrer-CD (Audio)
	Verweis auf die Lehrer-DVD (Film)
Find more online:	Code auf www.klett.de eingeben und Zusatzinformationen erhalten

1, 1

Welcome – Hello!

Hello! I'm Ben the bat! Nice to meet you. What's your name? I like English.

Hello! I'm Elena!
What's your name?
Hi Elena.
My name is Jonas.

1 (SPEAKING) **Ask a partner.** → M Double circle, p. 178

A: Hello! I'm Elena.
What's your name?
B: Hi Elena. My name is Jonas.

Hi! | Hello!

A: I like music. And you?
B: I like sport.

music | sport | animals | computers

A: OK, it's time to go. See you!
B: Yes, OK. Bye!

See you! | Goodbye! | Bye!

1, 2 2 (SONG) The welcome song → V Numbers, p. 187

Sprecht den „Countdown“ mit. Singt das Lied.

10 – 9 – 8 – 7 – 6 – 5 – 4 – 3 – 2 – 1 – Hello!

Blue, blue, blue is the colour of your shoes,
Red, red, red is the colour of your hat,
White, white, white is the colour of your shirt,
Green, green, green is the colour of your dress.

One, two, three, come with me,
Four, five, six, a colour mix,
Seven, eight, nine, you look so fine,
Ten, I like you!

Welcome to England!
Welcome to Greenwich!

Brown, brown, brown is the colour of your hair,
Grey, grey, grey is the colour of your skirt,
Black, black, black is the colour of your top,
Pink, pink, pink is the colour of your cap.

One, two, three, …

10 – 9 – 8 – 7 – 6 – 5 – 4 – 3 – 2 – 1 – zero!

3 Make a card.

Find or draw a picture.

Die häufigsten Arbeitsanweisungen findest du mit deutscher Übersetzung hinten im Buch auf S. 184.

Zoom in – In a park

1 (SPEAKING) Find and say.

1. colours	blue	...
2. animals	dog	...
3. activities	tennis	...
4. numbers	seven	...
5. people	boy	...

1, 3

2 (LISTENING) Listen and point.

Hör dir die sechs kurzen Szenen an.
Zeige auf die passende Stelle im Bild.
Die Geräusche können dir auch helfen.

3 (SPEAKING) I spy! → V Colours, p. 188

I spy with my little eye, something … red!

It's here!

It's a bus! I spy with my little eye, something yellow!

4 (SPEAKING) What can you do in the park?

I can play football.
I can buy ….
I can ….

Find more online:
fe76m3

Am Ende dieser Unit kann ich …
- mich vorstellen.
- über meine Familie sprechen.
- mich über mein Zimmer unterhalten.
- eine Bildergeschichte verstehen, zwei Personen miteinander bekannt machen und einen Film zum Thema „Wohnen in England“ verstehen.

1 1, 4 Unit 1

I'm from Greenwich

My name is Olivia Fraser.
What's your name?
This is my bike. It's cool!
Hi! I'm Luke Elliot.
I'm a football fan. I'm eleven.
How old are you?
This is my dog, Sherlock.
1
2

1 Who is in the photos?

1. **Olivia** is in photo 1.
2. … is in photo 2.
3. … is in photo 3.
4. … is in photo 4.

2 Who says it?

4/1

Fluff and Honey are my pets.
1. Holly

I'm eleven.
2. …

It's cool!
3. …

I'm from Greenwich.
4. …

I'm twelve.
5. …

I'm a football fan.
6. …

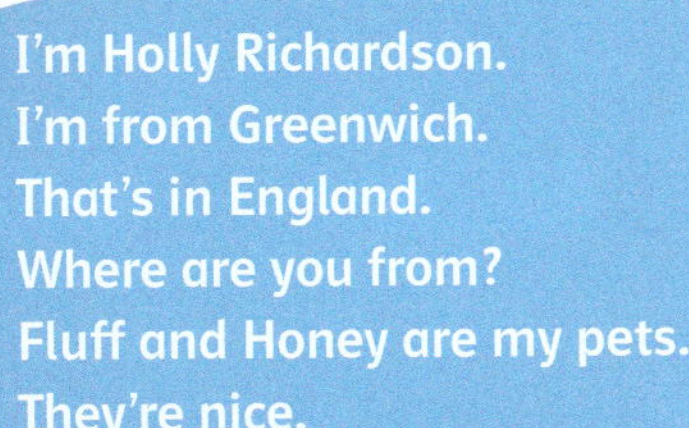

I'm Holly Richardson.
I'm from Greenwich.
That's in England.
Where are you from?
Fluff and Honey are my pets.
They're nice.

Hello. My name is Dave Preston.
I'm twelve. This is my cat, Sid.

3

4

3 (YOUR TURN) My card

4/2 a) Make a card. Find or draw a picture.
Tip: Write more on your card.
(Pet, football fan, …)

b) Read your sentences to a partner.

My name is Max.
I'm eleven.
I'm from Berlin.
That's in Germany.

So sagt man „Deutschland" auf Englisch: Germany!

Ich kann mich vorstellen. ✓

Hier lerne ich, über meine Familie zu sprechen.

Olivia and her family

1,5 **1** (LISTENING) Look at the photos. Then listen and point.

1,6 **2** (READING) Read about the Fraser family.

Hi! I'm with my family in this photo. We're in the garden. It's a nice photo. **1**

I'm here, and this is Lucy. She's my sister. She's five. I have no brothers. (Phew!) **2**

This is our father. His name is Desmond. He's cool! Claire is Lucy's mother. She's here too. She's OK. Claire is Dad's friend. **3**

And this is a photo of my mother. Her name is Janet. Bye! **4**

3 Complete the sentences.

1. Olivia is with her family.
2. Lucy is her — .
3. Desmond is her — .
4. Janet is her — .
5. Claire is her dad's — .
6. Olivia: I have no — .

sister	mother	friend
brothers	family ✓	father

4 (SOUNDS) Listen, read and say.

1, 7
5/1

In this photo I can spy
my mother (my brother, my father)
with my little eye!

[ð]
Nimm die Zungenspitze zwischen die Zähne und summe wie eine Biene.

5 (WRITING) What are the words?

a) Write the words. → ○ p. 128

5/2a) 

1. sis – er → **sister**
2. mot – er
3. bro – – er
4. fa – – er
5. fami – –
6. fr – – nd

Schreibe die Wörter in dein Heft ab. Welche Buchstaben fehlen hier?

b) Find the words. → V Family, p. 189

5/2b) 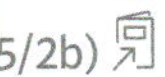

1. My father's brother is my uncle.
2. My mother's sister is my ....
3. My father's mother is my ....
4. My mother's father is my ....
5. My mother and my father are my ....

parents · uncle ✓ · grandmother · aunt · grandfather

Language tip → G1, p. 160
Lucy's mother
My father's brother

6 (SONG) The family song

1, 8
5/3

Singt das Lied: den Refrain („chorus") alle, die Strophen in Gruppen.

This is my dad, football is his game,
This is my mum, she's a music fan.
This is my brother, he's a crazy kid,
Together we are a family.

We're in the garden, everyone is here,
Mum and Dad and my brother too.
We live here, our name is on the door,
Together we are a family.

(Chorus): Mum and Dad, my brother and me,
This is my family.
Mum and Dad, my brother and me,
Together we are a family.

Hey, it's my friend!
Hi, come in and meet my family!
Hi, nice to meet you! Hello there!

(Chorus)

Language detectives → G2, p. 161

Nimm die Sätze unter die Lupe:
Wann verwendest du am, is und are?

He is my dad.
They are nice.

I am here.
We are sisters.

This is my bike.
It is cool.

7 Put in am, is or are.

1. We are sisters.
2. I — here.
3. She — nice.
4. He — my dad.
5. They — nice.
6. It — cool.

STUDY SKILLS

Ihr könnt die Regel auf einem Poster darstellen. Macht eine Tabelle und ordnet die Wörter in die richtige Spalte ein.

am	is	are
	he	

8 Match the words. Compare with your partner. → M Peer correction, p. 178

6/4 

1. he – Desmond 2. they –

he ✓ they she we it

the photo Desmond ✓ my mum and dad Lucy and I Claire

9 What can Olivia say?

6/5a) a) Make sentences. → ○ p. 128

1. I **am** / **is** Olivia Fraser.
2. Lucy and I **is** / **are** sisters.
3. Lucy **am** / **is** five.
4. Desmond **am** / **is** my dad.
5. Janet and Desmond **is** / **are** my mum and dad.
6. Claire **am** / **is** my dad's friend.

6/5b) b) What can Lucy say? Finish the sentences.

1. I .... 2. Olivia .... 3. Desmond and Claire .... 4. Janet ....

10 What can Lucy say?

GRAMMAR → G2, p. 161

So bildest du Kurzformen:
I am → I'm

he is → he's
she is → she's
you are → you're

I'm Ben.

a) Put in the short forms (Kurzformen). → ○ p. 128

7/6a) 7/7

She's · I'm · He's

1. This is my family.
   This is my mum. She's nice.
2. This is my dad. —— cool.
3. This is my sister, Olivia. —— eleven.
4. Janet is Olivia's mum. —— nice too.
5. This is me. —— five!

b) Put in we're or they're.

7/6b)

1. My mum and dad are OK.
2. Olivia and I are sisters.
3. Olivia and my mum are in the garden.

We are → we're
They are → they're

11 (YOUR TURN) My family → V My family, p. 194

a) Draw your family tree, or bring a picture of your family.

b) Tell a partner about your family.

/8–8/1–2

This is my family.
This is my mum. She's cool.
This is my dad. He's nice.
This is my sister. She's eight.
(This is my brother. He's ten.)
This is my mum's friend. He's nice.
(This is my dad's friend. She's OK.)

cool · OK · ...

eight · nine · ...

STUDY SKILLS

Versuche, die Sätze über deine Familie auswendig zu lernen.
Lies deine Sätze so oft vor, bis du sie vorlesen kannst, ohne zu stocken.

Ich kann über meine Familie sprechen. ✓

Hier lerne ich, mich über mein Zimmer zu unterhalten.

Luke's bedroom

1 (LISTENING) **Look at the bedroom. Listen and point.**

1, 9

2 (SPEAKING) **Match the numbers with the words.**

9/1

Number 1 is a table.
Number 2 is a —— .

box • mobile • T-shirt • chair • poster • table ✓ • football • book • bed

3 (READING) **Read about Luke's bedroom.**

1, 10

It's Saturday. Luke is at home. He's in his bedroom.

Luke: Yes? Who is it?
Dave: It's me! Are you ready, Luke?
Luke: Hi Dave. I'm under the bed. I can't find my new mobile, Dave.
Dave: There is a red mobile on the table.
Luke: My new mobile is blue. Where is it?
Dave: Is it in a box? There are two black boxes here, next to your books.
Luke: No, Dave.
Dave: Your room is a mess! What's that?
Luke: It's my mobile, Dave. It's on the chair, under the T-shirt!

4 **Finish the sentences.**

1. Luke is **under the bed.**
   under the table • **under the bed**
2. Luke can't find ....
   his new mobile • his football
3. His new mobile is ....
   blue • black
4. There are two boxes ....
   next to the books • on the bed
5. There is a T-shirt ....
   on the table • on the chair
6. The mobile is ....
   under the bed • under a T-shirt

9/2 5 Who or what is in the room?

a) Look at Luke's room. Who or what is it? → ○ p. 129

1. It's red and white. It's on the chair.
   It's a T-shirt.
2. It's red. It's on the table.
   It's ....
3. It's under the T-shirt. It's blue.
4. He's black and white. He's next to Luke.
5. It's black and white. It's on the table.
6. He's under the bed.

b) Make more sentences.

Language tip → G3, p. 162

There is **a** book.
There is **one** book.
There are **two** book**s**.

9/3 6 Look at the room again.

a) Make sentences about the room. → ○ p. 129

There is	one	T-shirt • dog • table • bed • ...
There are	two • three • five • six	books • chairs • footballs • mobiles • posters • ...

b) Make more sentences about the room. → V Room things, p. 191

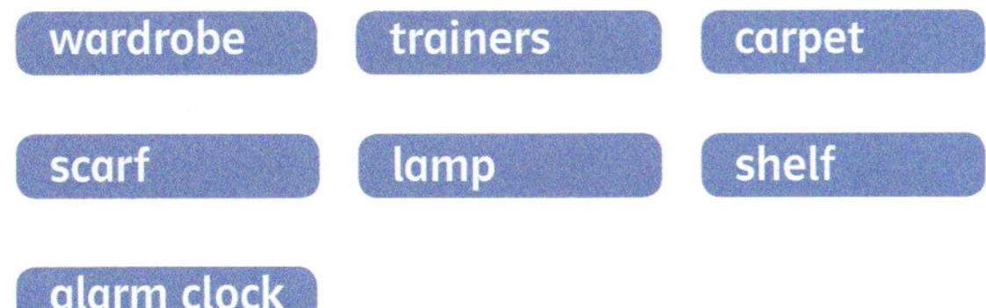

7 (GAME) Make a quiz about Luke's room.

Are the sentences right or wrong?

A: There are three books on the table.
B: That's wrong! There are **two** books on the table!
There are two footballs in the room.
A: That's right!

Language detectives → G4, p. 163

Luke is from Greenwich.

Is Luke from Greenwich?

Schau dir die beiden Sätze an.
Was ändert sich bei der Frage?
Wo steht das Verb (is oder are)?

Are you ready, Luke?

Is the mobile on the chair?

8 Make questions.

10/4–5

1. —— you a football fan?
   Are you a football fan?
2. —— you eleven?
3. —— you from Greenwich?
4. —— your room a mess?
5. —— Luke from Germany?
6. —— Sherlock a cat?
7. —— your name Ben?

Are you ...?
Is your room ...?
Is Luke ...?

9 Who, what or where?

11/6

a) Make questions about Luke. → ○ p. 130

1. Where is Luke? – He's under the bed.
2. —— is under the T-shirt? – Luke's new mobile.
3. —— is Dave? – He's Luke's friend.
4. —— is on the table? – Luke's red mobile.
5. —— is Sid? – He's Dave's cat.
6. —— is Sherlock? – He's next to the bed.

b) Make questions. Find the right answers.

1. —— is that? – —— his mobile.
2. —— are Luke's mum and dad? – —— in the garden.
3. —— is Irina Elliot? – —— Luke's sister.

GRAMMAR → G4, p. 163

Wenn du eine Frage mit Fragewort stellst, steht das Fragewort am Anfang. Dann kommt das Verb (is oder are).
Who is it? → **Wer** ist das?
What is that? → **Was** ist das?
Where are they? → **Wo** sind sie?

Vorsicht! Im Deutschen ist das genau anders herum!
Who = Wer
Where = Wo

11/7 10 What are the words?

a) Look at the picture.

Who

What

Where (2x) ✓

Is (2x)

Are

Find the words. → ○ p. 130

1. Where is Luke? – He's on the bed.
2. —— is that on the table? – It's a red mobile.
3. —— is next to the bed? – It's Sherlock, Luke's dog.
4. —— is Luke's T-shirt? – It's on the bed.
5. —— Dave in the room? – No, Luke is with Sherlock.
6. —— there posters in the room? – Yes, there are football posters.
7. —— the room a mess? – No, it's OK.

b) Make questions. Find the answers.

1. —— Luke's trainers?　2. —— the alarm clock?　3. —— Luke's footballs?

11 (YOUR TURN) My room → V In my room, p. 195

11/8

a) Draw your bedroom. Write the words.

b) Ask a partner.

A: What's in your room?
B: There are two beds, a chair and a table in my room.
A: Are there posters in your room?
B: Yes, there's a football poster in my room. (No, there are no posters in my room.)
A: Where's the poster?
B: It's next to my bed.
A: Is your room a mess?
B: Yes, it's a mess! (No, it's OK!)

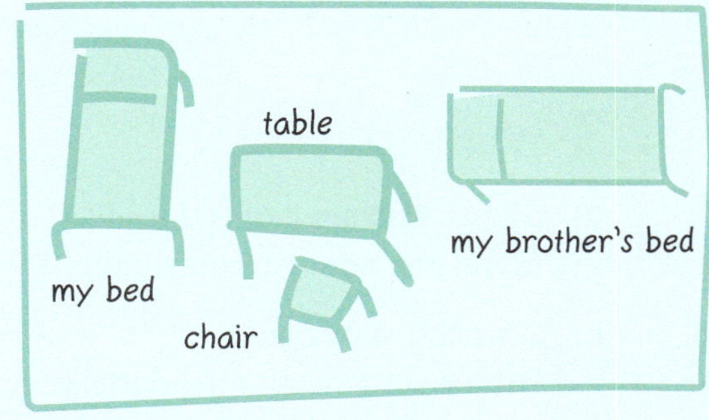

a bed | two chairs | ...

cat | music | ...

my brother's bed | my sister's bed | ...

Ich kann mich über mein Zimmer unterhalten. ✓

Olivia's tree house

1 What do you know about Olivia? Talk with a partner. → M Think-pair-share, p. 178

(Was weißt du über Olivia? Überlege und sprich dann mit einer Partnerin oder einem Partner.)

1, 11

2 (READING) Read the story.

1

It's Saturday. Olivia and her dad are in the garden. Lucy is there too. Claire is in the house. Olivia's dad is in the tree. There's wood and there's a ladder.

2

Olivia and her dad are busy.

3

Later …

The tree house is ready! It's cool!

3 What is it?

12/1–2

a) Guess: Who or what is the noise?
(Rate: Wer oder was macht das Geräusch?)

b) Read the story again.
Put the sentences in the right order.

A There's a funny noise.
B It's ready!
C It's Saturday and the Frasers are in the garden.
D Is it the wind or a dog?
E They're busy with the tree house.
F Holly is on the ladder.

READING SKILLS

Wenn du eine Bildergeschichte auf Englisch liest, dann überspringe beim ersten Lesen die Wörter, die du nicht kennst. Sieh dir die Bilder an und sage in zwei bis drei Sätzen, worum es in der Geschichte geht.

Hast du mich schon in der Bildergeschichte entdeckt?

What? Who's there?
Holly!

4

Then …
Olivia is in the new tree house. Holly is on the ladder.

5

In the night …
Olivia and Holly are in the tree house. There's a funny noise. What is it?

6

Is it Lucy?
There's no one on the ladder.
Is it a dog? Is it the wind?

4 (LISTENING) Who or what is it?

1, 12

(Hör das Ende der Geschichte: Was war das Geräusch?)

5 Choose one of the tasks.

12/3

a) Sucht euch eine Szene aus der Geschichte aus und macht ein Standbild dazu. Die anderen beschreiben die Szene und finden heraus, welche es ist. → M Freeze frame, p. 180

That's Desmond and that's Olivia!
That's Olivia in the tree house!

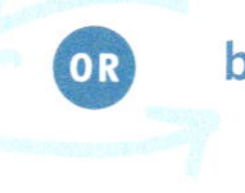

OR

b) Zeichne eine Skizze von deinem Traum-Baumhaus und beschrifte es. Erkläre dein Traum-Baumhaus den anderen mithilfe deiner Skizze.

In my tree house there's … !
It's ….

Ich kann eine Bildergeschichte verstehen. 

Jayden and Moritz

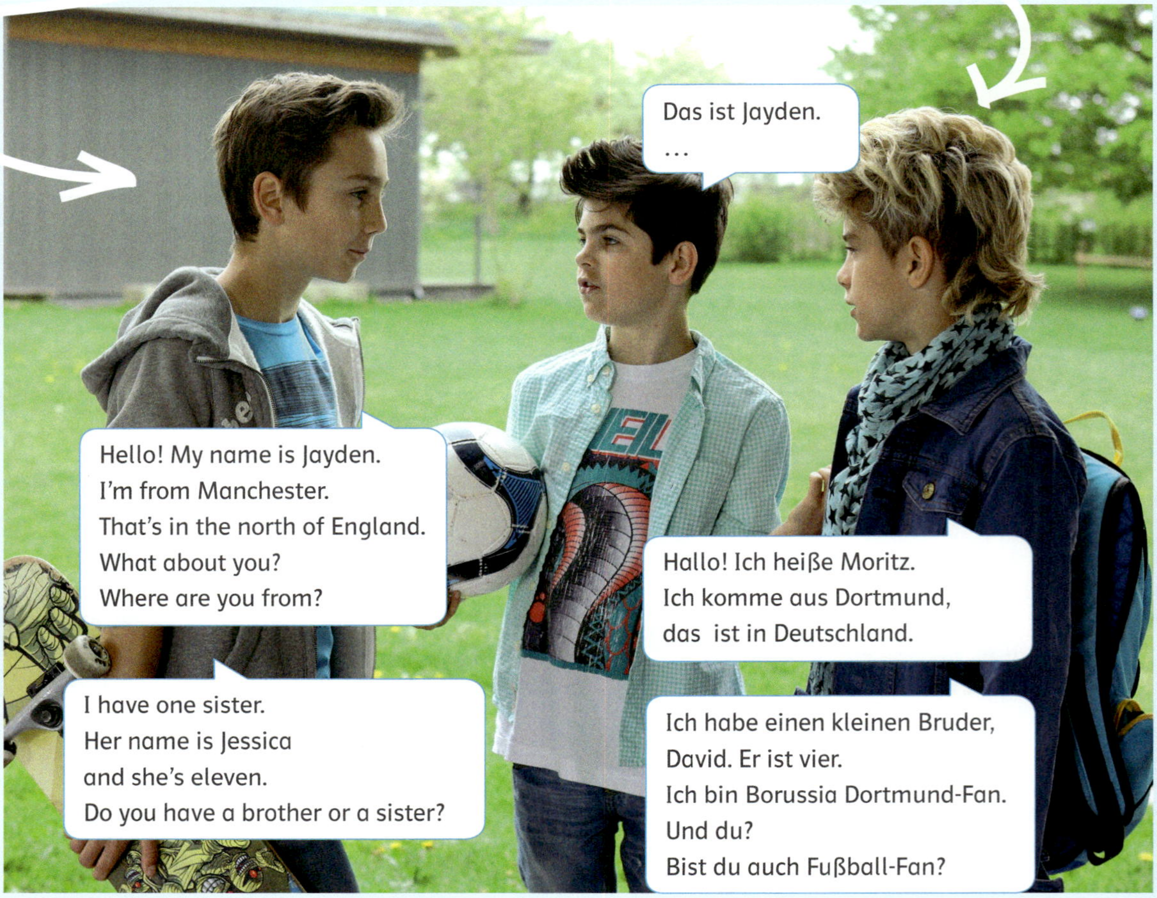

Das ist Jayden.
...

Hello! My name is Jayden.
I'm from Manchester.
That's in the north of England.
What about you?
Where are you from?

Hallo! Ich heiße Moritz.
Ich komme aus Dortmund,
das ist in Deutschland.

I have one sister.
Her name is Jessica
and she's eleven.
Do you have a brother or a sister?

Ich habe einen kleinen Bruder,
David. Er ist vier.
Ich bin Borussia Dortmund-Fan.
Und du?
Bist du auch Fußball-Fan?

1 Stelle Jayden auf Deutsch vor.

Moritz möchte Jayden kennenlernen. Stell ihn auf Deutsch vor.

Das ist ....
Er kommt aus ....
Er möchte wissen, ...
Er ....

2 Stelle Moritz auf Englisch vor.

Sprich nun mit Jayden und stelle Moritz vor.

This is ....
He is ....
He has ....
And you?

MEDIATION SKILLS

In solchen Situationen brauchst du nicht Wort für Wort zu übersetzen.
Es genügt, die wichtigsten Informationen in der anderen Sprache weiterzugeben.

Ich kann zwei Personen miteinander bekannt machen. 

Around the house

In dieser „Filmecke“ triffst du Laura und ihre Freundin aus Greenwich.

1 Talk about the rooms of a house. → V Rooms, p. 193

Which words do you already know for the rooms of a house or a flat? (Welche Wörter für die Zimmer in einem Haus/einer Wohnung kennst du schon?)

2 (VIEWING) Watch the film.

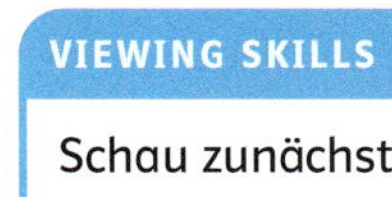

VIEWING SKILLS

Schau zunächst einmal auf die Bilder. Kümmere dich nicht um Wörter, die du nicht verstehst.

2 13/1–2

a) Put the pictures in the right order.

in the kitchen

in a bedroom

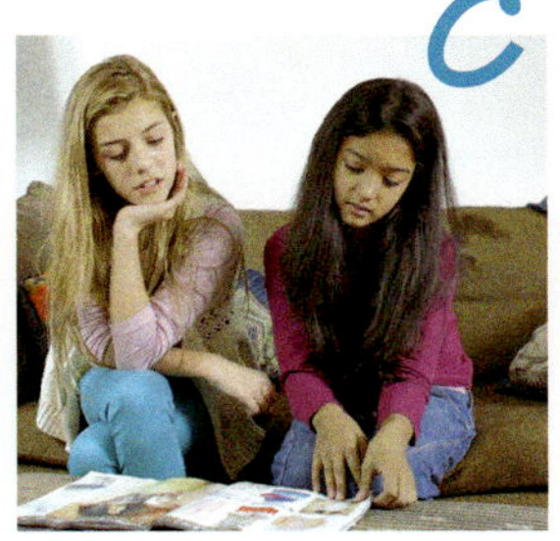

in the living room

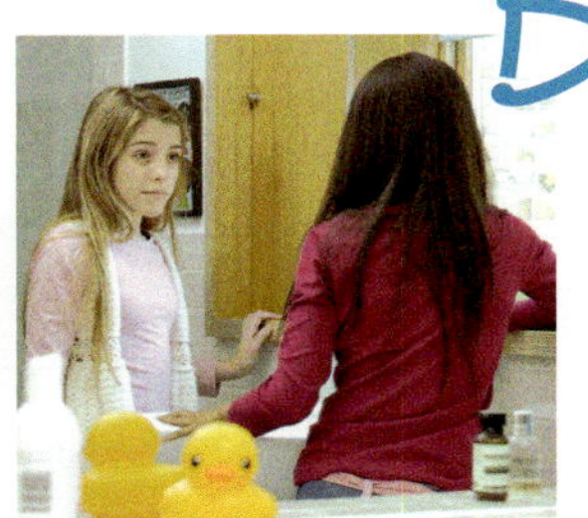

in the bathroom

b) Finish the sentences.

1. Laura is ....
2. They can't find ....
3. It's ....

with her mum • with Parule
a mobile • Laura's hair straightener
in Nathan's room • in the kitchen

3 (SPEAKING) Make a dialogue.

A: I can't find my mobile.
B: Well, look in the bathroom.
A: Thanks!

book | T-shirt | ...
living room | kitchen | ...

CULTURE

Warum sucht Laura nicht im Keller? Viele englische Häuser haben keinen Keller! Wie ist es bei dir zu Hause?

Ich kann einen Film zum Thema „Wohnen in England“ verstehen. ✓

Checklist

Ich kann mich vorstellen. 

Hello/Hi! • My name is .... •
I'm .... • I'm from .... •
I'm a ... fan. • This is my ....

14

Ich kann über meine Familie sprechen. 

This is my family. •
This is my .... • I have a .... •
I have two/three/ ....

14

Ich kann mich über mein Zimmer unterhalten. 

What's in your room? • There are ... in my room. • Are there ...? • Where's the ...? • It's next to .... • Is your room a mess? • Yes, it's a mess! • No, it's OK.

14

Ich kann eine Bildergeschichte verstehen. 

15

Ich kann zwei Personen miteinander bekannt machen.

15

Ich kann einen Film zum Thema „Wohnen in England“ verstehen. 

(TASK) A presentation

Step 1

Collect ideas for a presentation about you.

My family	Me	My room	Pets/bike/...
My dad	ten	two beds	dog, Timi
My mum	from ...	football posters	bike
My brother	football fan	...	...
...	...	...	...

Step 2

Write sentences.

My name is ....
I'm ten. I'm from ....
This is my family.
This is my brother. He's ....
This is my room.
There are two beds in my room. ...
I have a dog. His name is ....
...

Step 3

Collect pictures.

My dog

My bike

My room

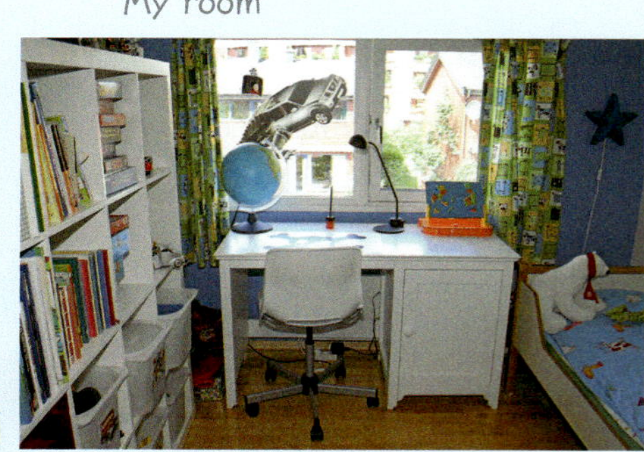

Step 4

Present yourself, your home and your family.

Use your pictures and your sentences.

My name is ....
I'm ....
This is my ....

SPEAKING SKILLS

- Übe zuerst deinen Vortrag mit einer Partnerin oder einem Partner.
- Sprich frei vor der Klasse oder verwende deine Notizen von Step 1 oder deinen Text von Step 2.
- Sprich klar und deutlich.
- Schau deine Klasse an.

Step 5

Ask for and give feedback.

Ask about your presentation.

How was my presentation?
It was very interesting!
I'd like to know more about your pet.

GROUP SKILLS

- Wenn du ein Feedback gibst, sage zuerst immer etwas Positives.
- Hat deine Mitschülerin oder dein Mitschüler klar und deutlich gesprochen?
- Hast du alles verstanden?
- Hat deine Mitschülerin oder dein Mitschüler beim Präsentieren die Klasse angeschaut?

Extra practice

○ **1** (WRITING) **Write the answers.** (nach 13/3)

Hello.
What's your name?
How old are you?
Where are you from?

Hi!
My name is — .
I'm — .
I'm from — .

○ **2** (WRITING) **Write the words.** (nach 14/3)

1. Irina is his s– – – – – . → **Irina is his sister.**
2. Anna is his m– – – – – .
3. Jack is his f– – – – – .
4. Jamie is his b– – – – – – .
5. The Elliots are a nice f– – – – – .

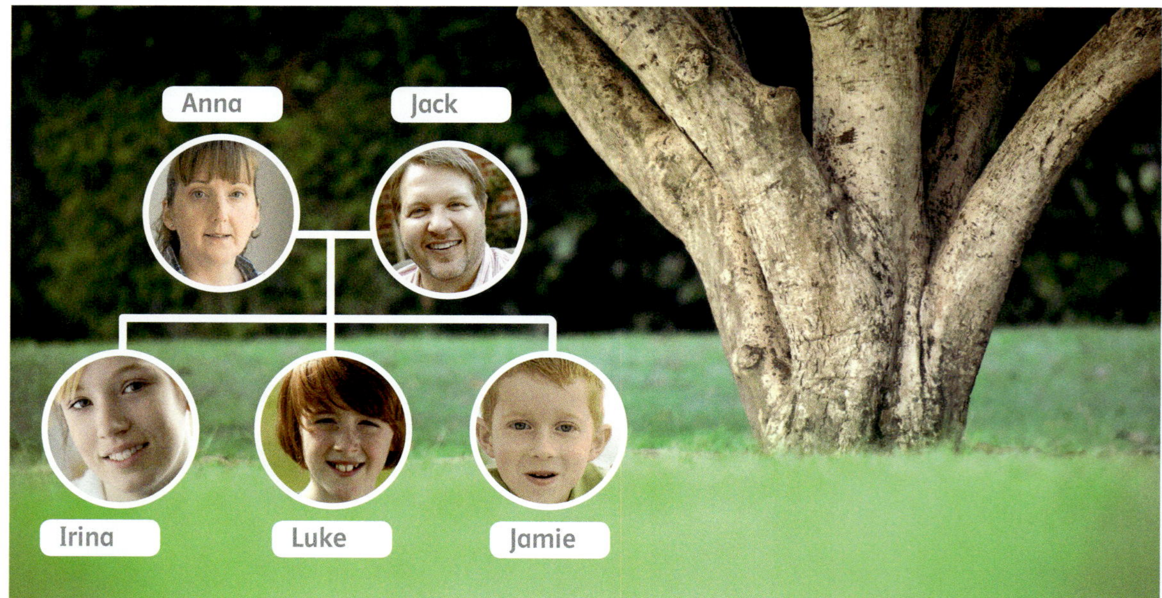

○ **3** **Find the words.** (nach 19/5)

1. Where's your football? It's under the chair.
2. "Where are you, Luke?" " — under the bed!"
3. This is Lucy. — Olivia's sister.
4. This is Desmond. — my dad.
5. This is Janet — my mum.
6. Dave is my friend. — cool.

I'm | He's | He's | It's ✓ | She's | She's

○ 4 Say the colours. (nach 19/5)

Number 1 is red.
Number 2 is ___ .

1 2 3 4 5 6

black | red ✓ | white | blue | yellow | green

○ 5 Make questions. (nach 21/11)

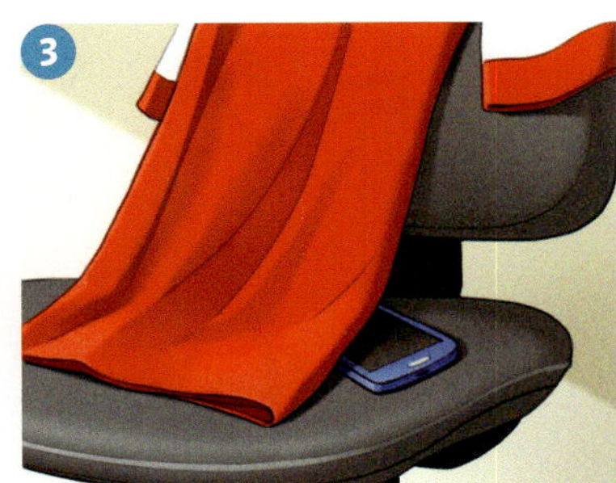

1. Where is Holly? – She's in her bedroom.
2. Where are ___ ? – They're under the bed.
3. Where ___ ? – It's under the T-shirt.
4. Where ___ ? – He's next to Holly.
5. Where ___ ? – They're in Luke's bedroom.
6. Where ___ ? – She's on her bike.

is | are
Olivia | Luke and Sherlock
the mobile | Dave
Holly ✓ | Fluff and Honey

○ 6 Find ten words. (nach 22/3)

Luke's home and family

1 What can you see in the picture?

Bevor du dir einen Text anhörst,
schaue die Bilder dazu an.
Was kannst du auf dem Bild sehen?

1, 13

2 Find the rooms.

Listen to the sounds in the house.
Where are they?

1. In the dining room.

garden | Irina's bedroom | bathroom | kitchen | living room | dining room ✓ | Luke's bedroom

Achte auf die Geräusche.
Sie können dir helfen,
den Text besser zu verstehen.

1, 14

3 Who is it?

Listen to the people in Luke's house.
Who is it?

1. That's Luke.

Luke's mum | Luke ✓ | Jamie | Luke's dad | Irina

Finde heraus, um wen es geht.
Es macht nichts, wenn du nicht
jedes Wort verstehst.

1, 15
19/2–3

4 Choose the right word.

1. We can play a cool football game • **a computer game.**
   We can play **a computer game**.
2. This game is cool • nice!
3. Hello. This is • I am Holly.
4. Is Luke here • there?
5. Is this your T-shirt • your football?

Wenn du den groben Zusammenhang
verstanden hast, kannst du auf die
Details achten. Achte auf die
Satzanfänge und finde heraus,
wie der Satz weitergeht.

Find more online:
fe76m3

Am Ende dieser Unit kann ich ...
- über meine Schule sprechen.
- Aufforderungen im Klassenzimmer verstehen und ausdrücken.
- sagen was ich an der Schule mag oder nicht mag.
- eine Fotostory verstehen, Informationen einer Schul-Website weitergeben und einen Film zum Thema „Schule in England“ verstehen.

3 1, 16 Unit 2

This is my school

I go to Thomas Tallis School (TTS). I'm in Year 7.
My school uniform is blue.
THOMAS TALLIS S
1

1 (SPEAKING) Talk about the photos.

20/1

a) What is the name of Holly's school?

b) What are the places in photos 2–5? Who is in photo 4?

c) Talk about the school with a partner.

I like ...   I don't like ...

2 (LISTENING) Where are Luke and Dave?

1, 17

Luke and Dave are ...

1. in the classroom. • in the cafeteria.
2. in the classroom. • in the playground.

LISTENING SKILLS

Achte auf die Hintergrundgeräusche. Sie können dir Hinweise darauf geben, wo die Szenen stattfinden.

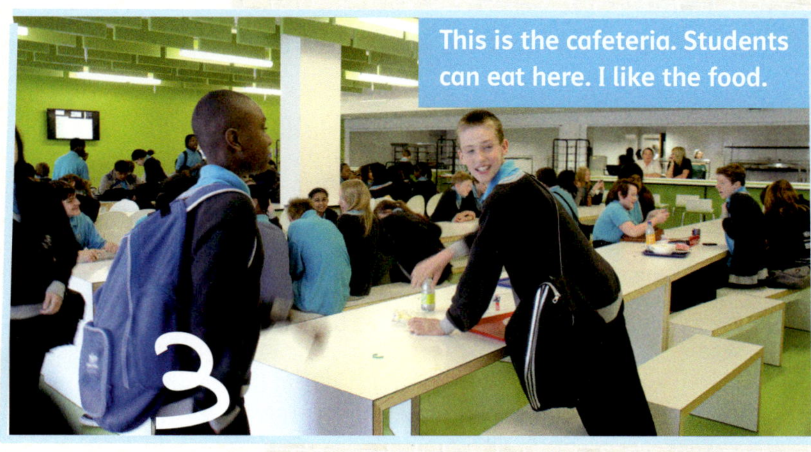

This is the cafeteria. Students can eat here. I like the food.
3

4
This is Mrs Warren. She's a caretaker.

This is my classroom. I'm in tutor group 7RS. My tutor is Mr Swindon. He's a Maths teacher.
5

3 (YOUR TURN) My school → V At school, p. 202

20/2

a) Write about your school.

I go to Albert-Schweitzer-Schule.
I'm in tutor group 5c.
My tutor is Mr Baier.
My English teacher is Mrs Hartmann.
My favourite place is the playground.
We can play games. That's cool.

b) Read your text to your tutor group.

CULTURE

An vielen Schulen in England tragen die Schülerinnen und Schüler eine Uniform. Nicht alle mögen das, aber manche finden es gut, dass sie sich nicht entscheiden müssen, was sie anziehen. Was meinst du?

classroom	cafeteria	...
talk	eat	...
nice	OK	...

Ich kann über meine Schule sprechen. ✓

Hier lerne ich, Aufforderungen im Klassenzimmer zu verstehen und auszudrücken.

A new student

1 Look at the pictures and find out.

Who is in the pictures?
What classroom things can you see?

2 (READING) Read about the new student in Holly's tutor group.

1, 18

1
Hello 7RS! This is Jahangir Azad, a new student. Don't talk, please! Can you close the window, Holly?
JAHANGIR AZA
It's Wednesday.

2
Call me Jay. I'm a music fan. I'm a good singer.
Are you a football fan, Jahangir? I like football.
Really?

3
This new boy is crazy.
Jay is a good singer.
She's the girl … the girl … for me!

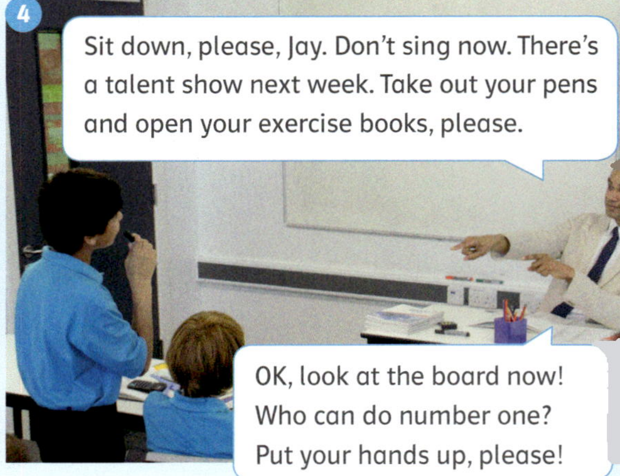

4
Sit down, please, Jay. Don't sing now. There's a talent show next week. Take out your pens and open your exercise books, please.
OK, look at the board now! Who can do number one? Put your hands up, please!

3 Right or wrong?

21/1

a) Are the sentences right or wrong? → ○ p. 131

1. It's Saturday. (Photo 1)
   That's wrong.
2. Jay is a new student. (Photo 1)
   That's ….
3. Luke is a football fan. (Photo 2)
4. Jay is a football fan. (Photo 2)
5. Jay can't sing. (Photo 3)
6. "Close your exercise books, please." (Photo 4)

b) Correct the wrong sentences.

4 (LISTENING) What are the words?

21/2
1, 19
a) Look at the words and pictures. Listen and say.

1 a ruler
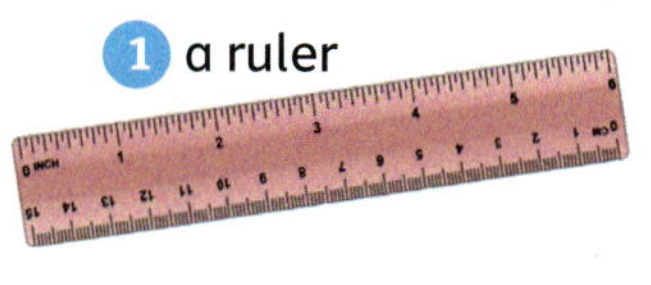

2 an eraser
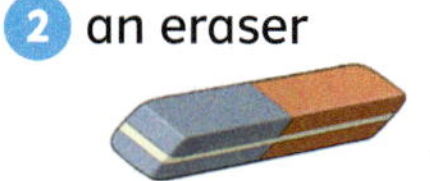

3 a pen

4 a pencil
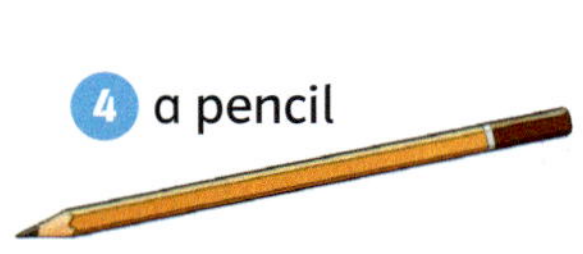

5 a bag

6 an exercise book

Language tip → G5, p. 164
a pen
an exercise book

1, 20
b) Look at the pictures again. Listen and point.

5 (SPEAKING) Make dialogues. → V School things, p. 197

21/3a)
a) Make dialogues with a partner.
Use the words from exercise 4. → ○ p. 131

A: Can I have your pencil, please?
B: Yes, here you are.
A: Thank you!

21/3b)
b) Make dialogues with other words.

calculator | pencil case | glue | felt-tip | pencil sharpener

6 (SOUNDS) Listen, read and say.

1, 21

Jay is a new student with a new uniform.
He's a music fan. He's with his tutor group.

7 (SONG) This is our classroom

1, 22

Singt das Lied. Zeigt auf die erwähnten Gegenstände oder haltet sie hoch.

This is our classroom, with things for you and me.
So have a look around now, and tell me what you see!

We have chairs, we have tables, there's a carpet for us all.
We have pens and we have pencils, there's a board on the wall.
We have a door and we have windows, with curtains we can pull,
But where is our teacher? I know she's in the school!

(Chorus): This is our classroom, we come here every day,
Here we all learn English. It's easy, hooray!

English is fun, put your hands up now! English is fun, now look at the board!
All together now! *(Chorus)*

English is fun and that's what it's all about!

Language detectives → G6, p. 165

A: Call me Jay. B: Don't call me Jay. A: Sing now. B: Don't sing now.

Welchen Satz sagt Jay, welchen Satz sagt Mr Swindon? Schau auf Seite 34 nach.
Was bedeutet das Wort don't?

8 (WRITING) Write Mr Swindon's sentences.

a) Write sentences with don't. → ○ p. 132

22/4
22/5a)

1. Talk, please.
   Don't talk, please.
2. Open your exercise book.
   Don't — your exercise book.
3. Write on the board, please.
   Don't — on the board, please.
4. Look at your books.
   Don't — at your books.
5. Play with your mobile.
   Don't — with your mobile.
6. Sing that song, please.
   Don't — that song, please.

b) Make more sentences. Then write the sentences with don't.

22/5b)

1. Play — .
2. Close — .
3. Take out — .
4. Eat — .

your pens, please | in the cafeteria | in the classroom | the window, please

9 Choose the right words.

1. **Play / Don't play** football in the classroom, Luke!
2. **Eat / Don't eat** in the cafeteria, Jay. The food is good!
3. **Read / Don't read** the question, Holly. What's the answer?
4. Shhh! **Talk / Don't talk**, please!
5. **Look / Don't look**! Your pencil is under the chair.
6. **Write / Don't write** your name on your exercise book, Jay.

23/6–7 ## 10 Look at the pictures.

a) Complete the sentences. → ○ p. 132

1. —— with my mobile.
   Don't play with my mobile.
2. —— at the board.

Look
Don't play ✓

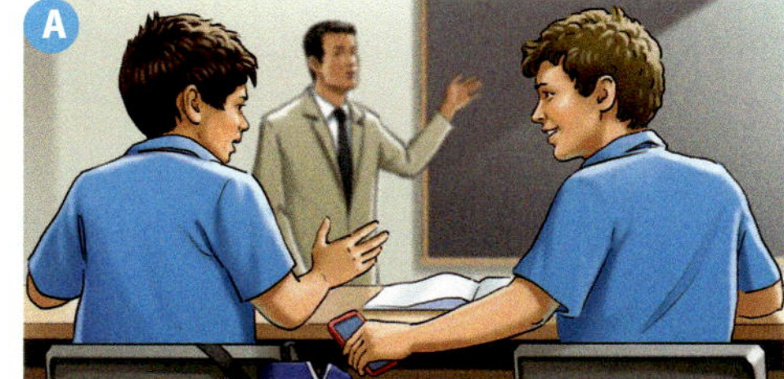

3. —— at this photo.
4. —— the window.

Don't open
Look

5. —— to the playground.
6. —— to this song. It's cool.

Go
Listen

b) Make your own sentences for picture C.

11 (YOUR TURN) Simon says → V At school, p. 202

8–24/2

One student in your group is Simon.
"Simon says: 'Sit down'." – You sit down.
"Simon says: 'Look at the board'." – You look at the board.
"Open your books." (with no "Simon says …")
– **Don't** open your books!

… open your books!
… say your name!
… put your hands up!
… look at the window!
…

Führe nur die Befehle aus, die mit „Simon says" beginnen. Machst du einen Fehler, bist du raus! Wer am Ende übrig bleibt, darf in der nächsten Runde Simon sein.

Ich kann Aufforderungen im Klassenzimmer verstehen und ausdrücken. ✓

At break

1 (READING) Read the dialogue.

1, 23

Jay: What's the next lesson?

Luke: It's English with Ms Kapoor.

Jay: Hmm. English isn't my favourite subject. It isn't easy.

Dave: You're right! I don't like English. I'm not very good at spelling.

Luke: I like English. Ms Kapoor is nice. Her jokes are funny.

Dave: My favourite subject is Design Technology. It's interesting. We have DT on Tuesday. Tuesday is my favourite day.

Luke: Design Technology? Hey, Dave, can you spell that?

Dave: Er, D-E-S- … er …

Luke: Wrong! It's T-H-A-T!

Dave: Ms Kapoor's jokes aren't like that, Luke. *Her* jokes are funny!

2 Who is it? Say the names.

1. English isn't his favourite subject. – It's Jay.
2. He isn't very good at spelling. – It's ....
3. His favourite subject is Design Technology.
4. His jokes aren't funny.
5. Her jokes are funny.

3 Look at Jay's timetable.

Say the days of the week.

School timetable

	Mon	Tue	Wed	Thu	Fri
Registration					
Lesson 1	Maths	DT	Maths	French	English
Lesson 2	Art	Maths	PE	Science	Music
Break					

CULTURE

An englischen Schulen gibt es zweimal am Tag eine Anwesenheitskontrolle, die man „registration" nennt. Wie ist es bei dir in der Schule?

4 (LISTENING) Listen and say the days.

1, 24

"Monday, Tuesday … Wednesday!"

5 (WRITING) Put the days in the right order. Start with Monday. → M Peer correction, p. 178

25/1

Tuesday | Friday | Wednesday | Sunday
Thursday | Saturday | Monday

6 (SPEAKING) Make a dialogue.

25/2

a) Talk with a partner. → ◯ p. 133

A: What's your favourite subject?
B: My favourite subject is Maths.
It's interesting.
What's your favourite subject?

English | PE | German
easy | cool | …

b) Talk about more subjects. → V School subjects, p. 199

History | Geography | IT | Biology | RE

boring | difficult | fun

7 (RAP) The alphabet

1, 25 a) Listen and say the letters.

1, 26 b) Listen and say the rap.

25/3–4

A to the H to the J to the K,
Let's all go out and play.

B to the C to the D to the E,
Come over here and stand by me.

G to the P to the T to the V,
You can spell your A B C.

I to the Y – can you fly?

R and O are all alone,
But not U and Q and W.

F L M N S X Z,
Now you're set to go ahead!

STUDY SKILLS

So kannst du einen Text auswendig lernen: Lies dir eine Zeile durch. Decke ein Wort ab und lies die Zeile noch einmal. Decke ein zweites und dann ein drittes Wort ab. Kannst du den Text immer noch sagen?

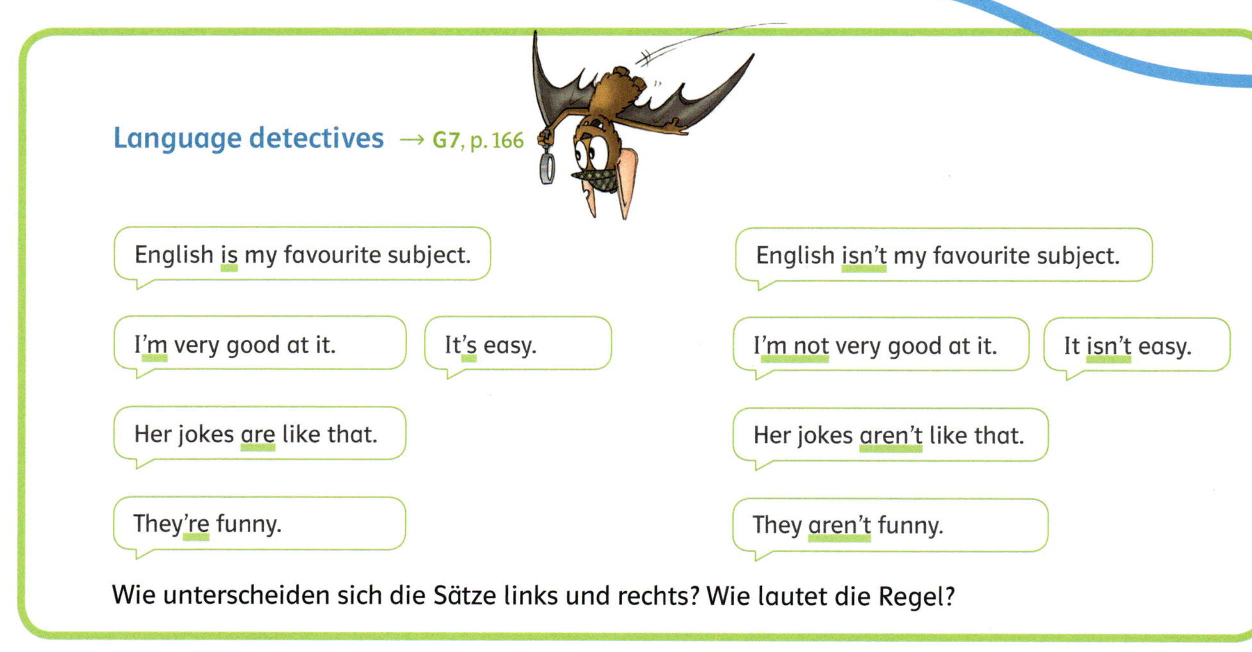

Language detectives → G7, p. 166
English is my favourite subject.
English isn't my favourite subject.
I'm very good at it.
It's easy.
I'm not very good at it.
It isn't easy.
Her jokes are like that.
Her jokes aren't like that.
They're funny.
They aren't funny.
Wie unterscheiden sich die Sätze links und rechts? Wie lautet die Regel?

8 Make sentences about the boys and girls.

26/5

Dave	is	eleven.
Jay	isn't	good at spelling.
Olivia		a girl.
Holly		a new student.
Luke		a football fan.
		a boy.
		twelve.

Weißt du noch, wie alt die Kinder sind? Wenn nicht, kannst du im Buch zurückblättern.

9 (SPEAKING) Talk about yourself.

26/6a)

a) Tell a partner about yourself. → ○ p. 133

I'm — .
I'm not — .

ten	eleven	...
at ... school	in tutor group ...	...
English	German	...
good at football	good at spelling	...

And you?

26/6b)

b) Talk about your partner.

This is ....
He's .... / She's ....
He isn't .... / She isn't ....

10 Look at the pictures and the sentences.

a) Find the right sentences. → ○ p. 133

27/7

1. Dave isn't eleven.

They aren't good singers. • Dave: "I'm not good at spelling." • French isn't easy. • Luke isn't good at computer games. • Dave isn't eleven. ✓

b) Make the sentences for this picture.

27/8

1. Mrs Warren isn't ___.
   She's ___ .
2. The students ___ .

a teacher | a caretaker | from TTS | from Berlin

11 (YOUR TURN) My school life → V Subjects at our school, p. 203

Write about your school life.

My favourite subject is English. It's interesting.
Maths isn't my favourite subject. It isn't easy.
My favourite day is Wednesday.
We have English and PE. I like PE.
My friends at school are David and Erkan.
My tutor is Mr Weber.
My favourite teacher is Mrs Michels.

Science | Music | ...

OK | cool | ...
Tuesday | ...

Ich kann sagen, was ich an der Schule mag oder nicht mag.

The Thomas Tallis talent show

1 Guess the student. → M Think-pair-share, p. 178

Who can do football tricks? Who can sing? Who can play the saxophone?

2 (READING) Read about the talent show.

1, 27

I can't. I have a music lesson.

You can't sing, Luke! What's your talent?

It's lunch break.

What is Luke's talent?

She's … the girl … the girl … for me!
Jay is cool!
4
Football tricks and music! This is cool too.
Who's the winner? Luke or Jay?
5
This is good music.
Wow!
6

It's the talent show.

Luke's tricks are cool.

Olivia is in the talent show too.

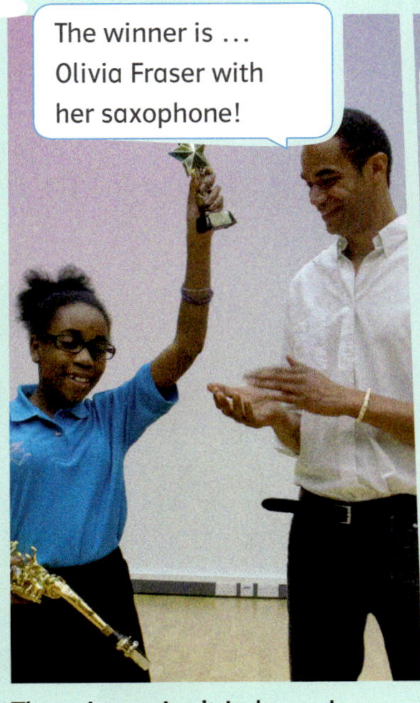

The winner isn't Luke or Jay …

8
Well done, Olivia!
You're a star.
Thank you!
Your music is cool.

Later …

3 Who is it? Say the names.

28/1–2

1. Who can do football tricks? – Luke.
2. Who can play the saxophone?
3. Who is in the talent show?
4. Who is the teacher at the talent show?
5. Who can sing?
6. Who is the winner?

4 Choose one of the tasks.

a) Olivias Mutter konnte nicht dabei sein. Schreibe ihre SMS („text message“) an Olivia.

Hi Olivia, …

Your music is …. | Bye! | Well done! | You're a ….

OR

b) Stell dir vor, statt Olivia hat Jay oder Luke gewonnen. Was sagt Mr. Swindon dann am Schluss? Schreibe einen neuen Text für die Sprechblase in Bild 7.

Ich kann eine Fotostory verstehen. ✓

A new school

INTERNET

<1> Home <2> About <3> News <4> Info

Information...

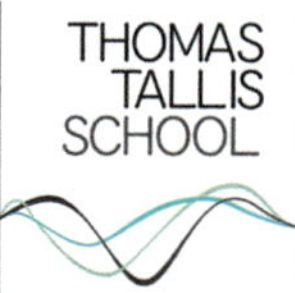

... for new students

Welcome to Thomas Tallis School!
Students must be at school by 8.30 a.m.
Classes start at 8.50 a.m. They finish at 3.10 p.m.

The cafeteria is open five days a week, from Monday to Friday.
Lunchtime is from 1.10 p.m to 2.10 p.m.

The TTS school uniform
You must buy school pullovers
and polo shirts (with the school logo) from the school shop.

You can buy these items in any shop:
- black trousers (no jeans!)
- black skirts
- black shoes (no trainers!)
- black socks

All mobile phones must be switched off!
Do not use your mobile in school.

1 Beantworte die Fragen deiner kleinen Schwester zur Thomas Tallis School.

1. Wann kann man in der Cafeteria essen?
2. Was bedeuten „a.m.“ und „p.m.“?
3. Wie sieht die Uniform der Thomas Tallis School aus?
4. Darf man Handys mit in die Schule bringen?
   Welche Regeln gibt es dazu?

2 Sprich über deine Schule.

Was ist an deiner Schule in Deutschland anders als an der Thomas Tallis School?
Was ist gleich?

Ich kann Informationen einer Schul-Website weitergeben. ✓

Making friends

In dieser „Filmecke“ triffst du Laura wieder und Alicia, Marley und Jinsoo.

VIEWING SKILLS

Achte auf Gestik (z. B. Handbewegungen) und Mimik (Gesichtsausdrücke). Was verraten diese dir über die Personen?

Jinsoo

Marley Alicia

CULTURE

Es gibt an der Thomas Tallis School eine Art Uniform für den Sportunterricht. Alle tragen die gleichen Shorts und die gleichen T-Shirts.

1 Talk about school rules.

What's against the rules at your school? (Was ist an deiner Schule nicht erlaubt?)

mobile phones | chewing gum | jeans | ...

2 (VIEWING) Watch the film.

4
29/1–2

a) Put the pictures in the right order.

A

B

C

b) Who says it?

1. “Football is for boys!”
2. “I like Jinsoo. He's nice!”
3. “No chewing gum at school.”
4. “Alicia put it in there.”

3 (SPEAKING) Make a dialogue about the film.

29/3

A: I like Jinsoo in the film. He's nice.
B: Yes, that's right.
A: I don't like Alicia in the film. She isn't nice.

Laura | teacher | ...
cool | funny | ...

Ich kann einen Film zum Thema „Schule in England“ verstehen.

Checklist

Ich kann über meine Schule sprechen. 

I go to .... • I'm in .... • My tutor is .... • My favourite place is .... • We can ....

30

Ich kann Aufforderungen im Klassenzimmer verstehen und ausdrücken. 

Look at ..., please. • Please go .... • Don't ..., please.

30

Ich kann sagen, was ich in der Schule mag oder nicht mag. 

My favourite subject is .... • It's .... • ... isn't my favourite subject. • My favourite day is .... • We have ... and .... • My tutor is .... • My favourite teacher is ....

31

Ich kann eine Foto-story verstehen. 

31

Ich kann Informationen einer Schul-Website weitergeben. 

31

Ich kann einen Film zum Thema „Schule in England“ verstehen. 

(TASK) A leaflet

Step 1

Get into groups. (Bildet Gruppen.)

Make a leaflet (eine Broschüre) about your school in a group of two or three.

Step 2

Make a model for the leaflet.

Step 3

Collect ideas and write sentences.

a) Choose headings (Titel) for the pages.

Welcome – students – teachers – places – subjects – clubs – ...

b) Write one or more sentences under the headings.

Welcome! This is Albert-Schweitzer-Schule.
We have Maths on Tuesday and Thursday.
Here you can see tutor group 5c. Our tutor is Mrs Geist.
There is a cafeteria. The food is nice.
There isn't a uniform at Albert-Schweitzer-Schule.
We have a circus club. It's cool!

GROUP SKILLS

Jeder darf seine Ideen einbringen, nachfragen und Verbesserungsvorschläge machen. Ihr entscheidet gemeinsam. Entscheidet, wer von euch Hilfe holt, wenn es nötig ist.

Step 4

Check your sentences and find pictures.

a) Read your sentences. Show them to your friends or a teacher.

b) Correct your sentences.

c) Find pictures or photos for the pages.

STUDY SKILLS

Beim Schreiben ist es sehr wichtig, dass ihr hinterher überprüft, ob alles korrekt ist:

- Habt ihr alle Wörter richtig geschrieben?
- Wie ist es mit der Groß- und Kleinschreibung?

Step 5

Make your leaflet.

Put the text and the pictures together.
Make your leaflet like this or with a computer.

Step 6

Show your leaflet.

Show your leaflet to the other students in your tutor group.

I don't understand ... .
I like ... .
Can you say more about ..., please?

Step 7

Give feedback to the other groups.

Extra practice

○ **1** (WRITING) **Complete Holly's sentences.** (nach 33/3)

1. I go to Thomas Tallis School.
2. I'm in —— .
3. Students can eat in the —— .
4. My favourite place is the —— .
5. I'm in —— 7 RS.
6. My —— is Mr Swindon.

playground | Year 7 | cafeteria
tutor group | tutor | go ✓

○ **2** (WRITING) **What is it?** (nach 35/4)

1. Number 1 is a pencil.
2. Number 2 is an —— .
3. Number 3 is a —— .
4. Number 4 is a —— .
5. Number 5 is a —— .

chair | ruler | eraser
pen | pencil ✓

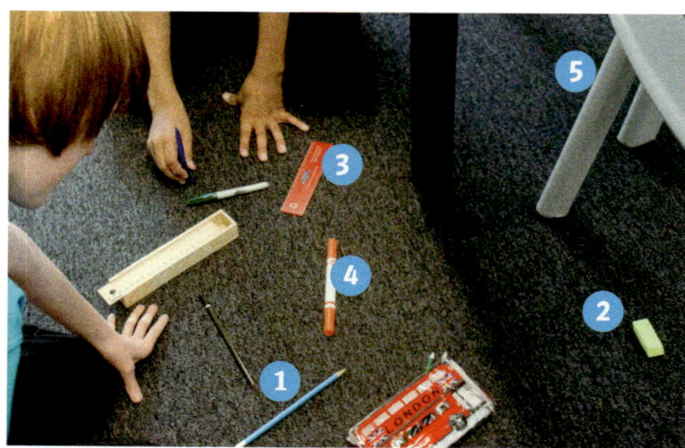

○ **3** **What can Mr Swindon say?** (nach 37/10)

1. "Look at …
2. "She's the girl for me!"
3. "Put your hands …
4. "Sit down …
5. "Take out …
6. "Shh! Don't …

A … talk, please."
B … now, Jay."
C … your exercise books."
D "Don't sing now."
E … up, please!"
F … the board, please!"

4 What are the words? (nach 39/6)

PE	Music
Maths	English ✓
Art	DT

1. Dave: I don't like English.

2. Olivia: I like — !

3. Dave: — with Mrs Robbins is cool.
4. Luke: My favourite subject is — .
5. Olivia: I have — on Tuesday.
6. Holly: Mr Swindon is my — teacher.

5 Match the sentences with the pictures. (nach 41/11)

1. Holly isn't at school. That's picture C.
2. Luke isn't a music fan. That's picture — .
3. Olivia and Jay aren't twelve.
4. Mr Swindon isn't an Art teacher.
5. Lucy isn't Holly's sister.
6. Mrs Warren isn't a teacher.

A

B

C
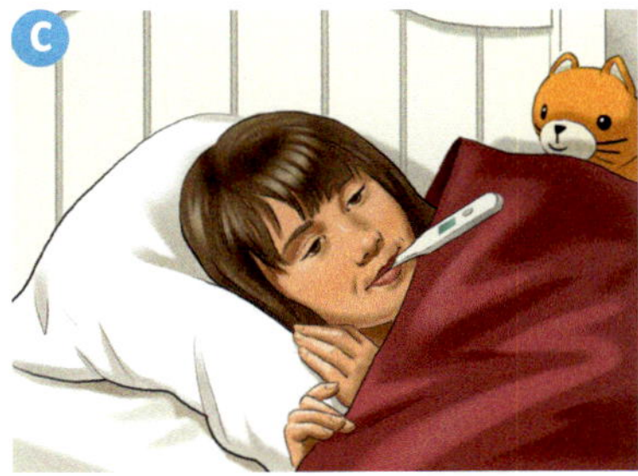
D

E

F

6 (WRITING) Write the words. (nach 43/3)

1. sch– –l → school
2. t– –cher
3. talent sh– –
4. playgr– –nd
5. c– –etaker
6. cla– –r– –m

1, 28 Tallis Talk

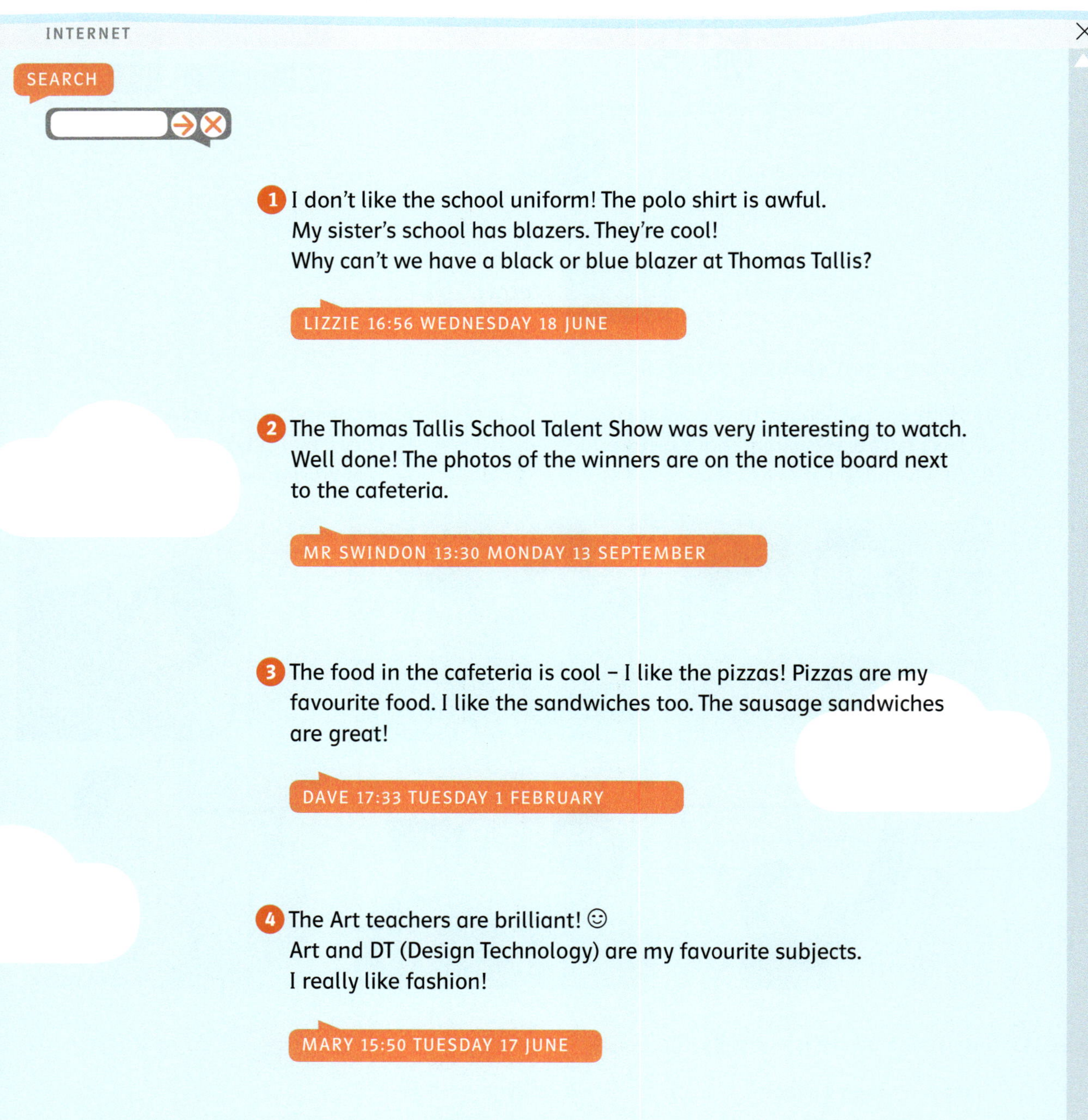

1 I don't like the school uniform! The polo shirt is awful. My sister's school has blazers. They're cool! Why can't we have a black or blue blazer at Thomas Tallis?

LIZZIE 16:56 WEDNESDAY 18 JUNE

2 The Thomas Tallis School Talent Show was very interesting to watch. Well done! The photos of the winners are on the notice board next to the cafeteria.

MR SWINDON 13:30 MONDAY 13 SEPTEMBER

3 The food in the cafeteria is cool – I like the pizzas! Pizzas are my favourite food. I like the sandwiches too. The sausage sandwiches are great!

DAVE 17:33 TUESDAY 1 FEBRUARY

4 The Art teachers are brilliant! ☺ Art and DT (Design Technology) are my favourite subjects. I really like fashion!

MARY 15:50 TUESDAY 17 JUNE

1 Before you read: Look at the texts.

Schau dir als Erstes die Überschrift an. Verrät sie dir schon, worum es geht?

Where can you read this?
Choose the right picture.

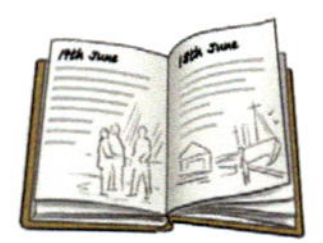

2 Read the texts.

Versuche nicht, jedes Wort zu verstehen, sondern schau nach positiven (z. B. „like“) oder negativen (z. B. „don't like“) Wörtern im Text.

a) Are the texts positive or negative?
Make a chart.

	positive	*negative*
Text 1		
Text 2		

b) Find the words in the texts.
Guess what they mean.

Manchmal kannst du die Bedeutung eines Wortes aus dem Zusammenhang erschließen. Oder es gibt ein ähnliches Wort im Deutschen.

- blazer
- notice board
- sandwich
- brilliant

„Blazer“ – hmm! Lizzie erwähnt auch die „school uniform“. Das muss ein Kleidungsstück sein. Gibt es im Deutschen nicht auch Blazer?

1-35/6
3 Read the texts again.

What are the right German words?

1. awful
   hässlich • furchtbar • alt
2. watch
   ansehen • mögen • finden
3. sausage
   Käse • Ei • Wurst
4. fashion
   Kunst • Möbel • Mode

Wenn du ein Wort gar nicht erschließen kannst oder nicht sicher bist, kannst du auch ein Wörterbuch zu Hilfe nehmen.

Find more online: fe76m3

Am Ende dieser Unit kann ich ...
- über meine Freizeit sprechen.
- ein Tier vorstellen.
- über meinen Alltag sprechen.
- eine Detektivgeschichte verstehen, Informationen über Schul-AGs weitergeben und einen Film zum Thema „Freizeit in England" verstehen.

5 1, 29 Unit 3

My free time

After school on Wednesdays I listen to music or watch TV. I love 'Superstars'.

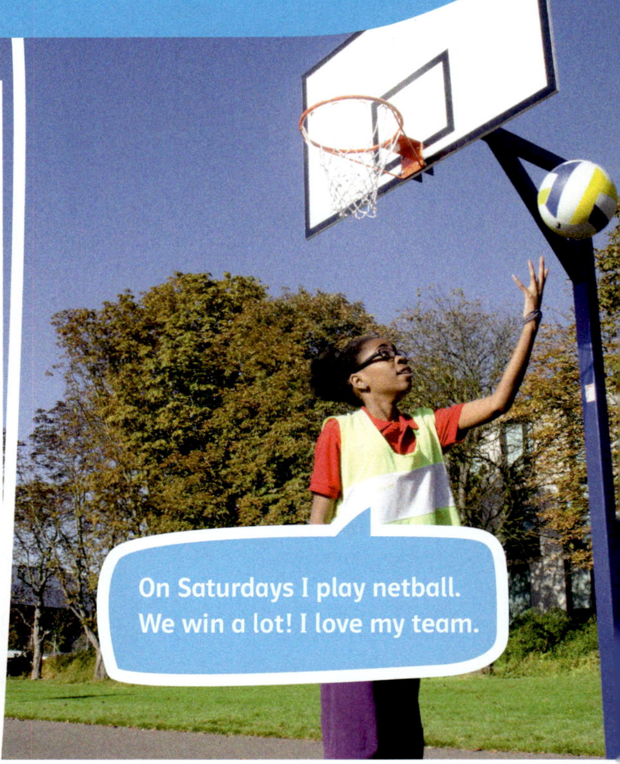

On Saturdays I play netball. We win a lot! I love my team.

1 Who is it?

36/1

a)
1. Luke: I play football.
2. Dave: I go to the —— .
3. Holly: I love —— .
4. Jay: I listen to —— .
5. Olivia: I play —— .
6. Jay: I watch —— .

football ✓ | music | netball | TV | cinema | animals

b)
1. She loves her team. – That's Olivia.
2. She helps at a shelter. – That's —— .
3. He likes science fiction movies.
4. He loves 'Superstars'.
5. She wins a lot.
6. He's captain of the team.

CULTURE

Olivia und Luke sind nicht in Sportvereinen, sondern Mitglieder in Schulsportmannschaften. Alle englischen Schulen haben Sportmannschaften. Wo machst du Sport? Wie ist es an deiner Schule?

I have football practice at lunchtime on Thursdays. I'm captain of the school team.

CINEMA
At the weekend I go to the cinema. I like science fiction movies.

After school I help at an animal rescue shelter – I love animals!

2 (YOUR TURN) My free time → V Free-time activities, p. 209

36/2

Say what you do in your free time.

On Mondays After school At the weekend …	+	I listen to I go to I help I play I watch …	+	my family. football. the cinema. music. with my friends. TV. …

Ich kann über meine Freizeit sprechen. ✓

At the zoo

1,30 **1** (LISTENING) **Look at the photos and point. What animals do you hear?**

2 **What other animals do you know?**

37/1 **3** (WRITING) **Make animal words.**

a) Look at the photos. Make words. → ○ p. 134

mon key → monkey

sna ti ele gir pen + phant ke affe guin

b) Finish the words. → V Animals, p. 205

li…, flam…, zeb…, croc…, cam…

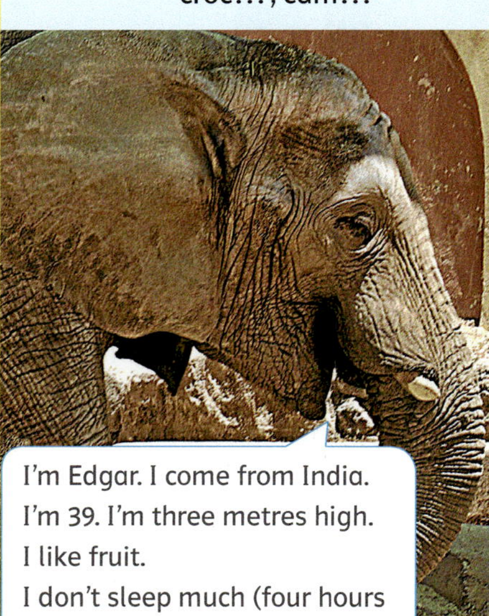

I'm Edgar. I come from India.
I'm 39. I'm three metres high.
I like fruit.
I don't sleep much (four hours a day).

Name: Tom
Age: 6
Food: meat (7 kilograms a day)

- 93 centimetres high
- sleeps 18 hours a day
- runs 40 kilometres an hour

Name: Lizzy
Age: 11
Food: mice
She doesn't eat fruit.

- 2 metres long
- sleeps for 5 months in winter

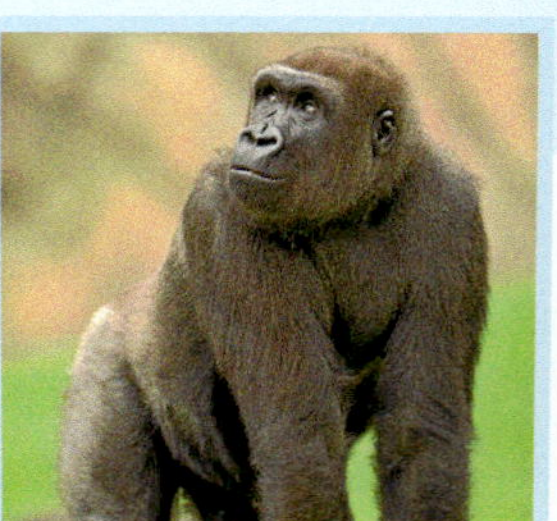

Du sagst: It eats 7 kilograms. (tiger)
Aber der Tiger hat einen Namen: Tom.
Dann sagst du „he": He eats 7 kilograms.

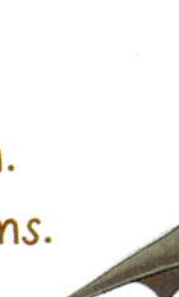

1, 31 37/2 **4** (READING) **Find the right animals.**

a) Which boxes are about the tiger, the snake or the elephant? → ○ p. 134

6 – That's the tiger.

4 hours a day | 3 metres high | 5 months | 6 

40 kilometres an hour | 7 kilograms | 11

b) Which facts are on page 54 but **not** in a)?

5 (LISTENING) **What are the numbers?** → V Numbers 11 – 100, p. 205

1, 32 a) Listen and say the numbers.

1, 33 b) Listen and write the numbers.

13 thirteen	**21** twenty-one	**30** thirty
14 fourteen	**22** twenty-two	**40** forty
15 fifteen	**23** twenty-three	**50** fifty
16 sixteen	**24** twenty-four	**60** sixty
17 seventeen	**25** twenty-five	**70** seventy
18 eighteen	**26** twenty-six	**80** eighty
19 nineteen	...	**90** ninety
20 twenty	**29** twenty-nine	**100** a/one hundred

6 (SPEAKING) **Say the next numbers.**

37/3–4

1. 10 – 15 – 20 – 25 – ...
2. 8 – 16 – 24 – ...
3. 92 – 82 – 72 – ...

7 (SOUNDS) **Listen, read and say.**

1, 34

The zoo is nice.
Her name is Lizzy. [z]

The snake sleeps in winter.
They are Sam and Sally. 
[s]

8 (GAME) **Crack the code! (Knack den Code!)**

a) Use this code. Write the name of an animal in numbers.
Snake is "49 – 44 – 31 – 41 – 35".

b) Say your numbers to your group.
Who can crack the code?

A	B	C	D	E	F	G	H	I	J	K	L	M
31	32	33	34	35	36	37	38	39	40	41	42	43

N	O	P	Q	R	S	T	U	V	W	X	Y	Z
44	45	46	47	48	49	50	51	52	53	54	55	56

Language detectives → G8, p. 167

I like fruit.

He likes tigers.

They like trees.

LONDON ZOO
She likes animals.

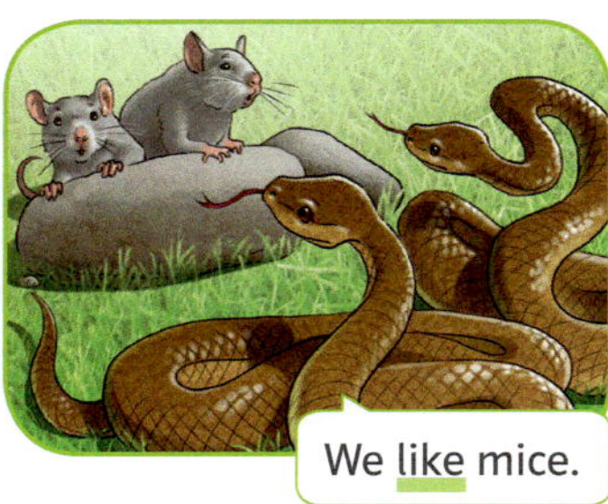
We like mice.

Wann endet das Verb auf s und wann nicht?

9 Complete the sentences with like or likes.

38/5–6

1. I — penguins.
   I like penguins.
2. We — Edgar!
3. He — fruit.
4. We — the animal song.
5. I — Lizzy.
6. Holly — her pets.
7. She — the zoo.

10 (SPEAKING) Play the game.

Lena: I like monkeys.
Lukas: Lena likes monkeys. I like tigers.
Katrin: Lena likes monkeys. Lukas likes tigers. I like …

Spielt in Gruppen. Kannst du dir alles merken?

11 Complete the sentences. → M Peer correction, p. 178

38/7

a) Put in the verbs. → p. 134

1. Edgar — from India. (come)
   Edgar comes from India.
2. Lizzy — mice. (eat)
3. Tom — 18 hours a day. (sleep)
4. Elephants — fruit. (eat)
5. Snakes — in winter. (sleep)
6. Tigers — 40 kilometres an hour. (run)
7. They — seven kilograms of meat a day. (eat)

b) Write your own sentences.

1. Monkeys ….
2. Holly ….
3. Penguins ….

3

Language detectives → G9, p. 168

She doesn't like snakes.

It doesn't sleep at night.

I don't like fish.

They don't eat bananas.

Lies die vier Sätze. Was sind die Unterschiede?

/8–10 12 Make sentences about the animals.

a) Choose the right words. → ○ p. 135

I come from Africa. I eat
bananas. I don't like fish.
I play with my friends.

We don't eat fruit, we eat meat!
We sleep eighteen hours a day
and run 40 kilometres an hour.
We come from India.

Mary, the monkey

1. Mary comes / **doesn't come** from Africa.
2. She **eats / doesn't eat** bananas.
3. She **likes / doesn't like** fish.
4. She **plays / doesn't play** with the penguins.

Tom and Tim, the tigers

5. Tom and Tim **eat / don't eat** meat.
6. They **sleep / don't sleep** four hours a day.
7. They **run / don't run** 40 kilometres an hour.
8. They **come / don't come** from Germany.

b) Write about Jack, the giraffe.

come from Africa | not eat meat | sleep four or five hours

13 (YOUR TURN) My animal profile → V Animals, p. 210

0/1–2 a) Make your own animal profile.

Animal: monkey
Name: Mary
Age: 6
Comes from: Africa
Eats: bananas
Doesn't like: fish
Colour: brown

b) Present your profile to your tutor group.

My animal is a monkey.
Her name is Mary and she is six.
She comes from Africa. Mary eats
bananas. She doesn't like fish.
She is brown.

Ich kann ein Tier vorstellen. 

Zookeeper Fred's busy Saturdays

1 (READING) Read about Fred.

1, 35

Holly interviews the zookeeper Fred for the Thomas Tallis school magazine.

Holly: When do you get up on Saturdays?
Fred: I get up at six o'clock. Then I have breakfast. I go to the zoo at seven o'clock.
Holly: Wow! What do you do first at the zoo?
Fred: First I feed Edgar, the elephant.
Holly: Does he eat a lot?
Fred: Yes! Then I feed the giraffes, the monkeys and the penguins. After that I work on the computer. In the afternoon I clean the cages.
Holly: Do you like your work?
Fred: Yes, I love my work. Do you like the zoo?
Holly: Yes! I love animals.

2 Find out about Fred.

41/1

a) Choose the right answers. → ○ p. 135

1. Fred **gets up** at …
   six o'clock. • 6:30. • eight o'clock.
2. At **seven o'clock** Fred …
   has breakfast. • goes to the zoo. • interviews Holly.
3. First Fred **feeds** …
   the penguins. • the giraffes. • Edgar.
4. In the afternoon Fred **cleans** …
   the cages. • the animals. • his room.

Suche die fett gedruckten Wörter im Dialog. Dort findest du die richtige Antwort.

b) What else does Holly find out about Fred?

3 (SPEAKING) What time is it?

1 

What time is it?
It's nine twenty.

2 

3 

4 

5 

6 

4 (LISTENING) Listen to Fred and write the times.

1, 36
41/2–3

1. It's 7:30.

It's nine o'clock.

5 (SPEAKING) Say the times.

→ V What time is it?, p. 211

a) 41/4a)

1. 8:30 → ○ p. 136
   It's eight thirty.
2. 11:45
3. 2:15
4. 7:30
5. 6:50
6. 4:28

b) 41/4b)

1. 8:30
   It's half past eight.
2. 10:00
3. 8:15
4. 12:30
5. 5:45
6. 1:05

nine oh five
five past nine

nine thirty
half past nine

nine fifteen
quarter past nine

nine forty-five
quarter to ten

nine twenty
twenty past nine

nine fifty
ten to ten

6 What does Holly do?

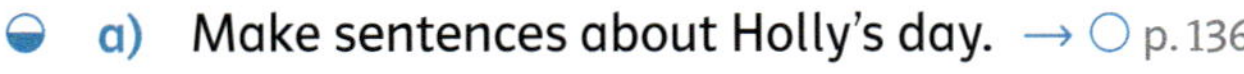

a) Make sentences about Holly's day. → ○ p. 136

1. 7:30 • gets up
   Holly gets up at seven thirty.
2. 8:00 • has breakfast
   She … .
3. 8:30 • goes to school
4. 4:45 • cleans the cage
5. 5:00 • feeds her pets
6. 5:15 • plays on the computer

CULTURE

In England fängt die Schule später an als in Deutschland (gegen 9 Uhr). Der Unterricht dauert jeden Tag bis etwa 16 Uhr. Wenn man nach der Schule nach Hause kommt, gibt es „tea".
Das kann entweder Tee und Kuchen oder Abendessen sein.

b) Make sentences about Holly's evening. → V Daily routines, p. 206

1. 5:30 • have tea
2. 6:00 • watch 'Superstars'
3. 8:00 • call her dad
4. 10:00 • go to bed

7 (SONG) I'm going to the zoo

1, 37

Singt das Lied und macht die Bewegungen mit.

I want to dance with the elephants,
Give a high-five to the monkey gang.

I'm going to the zoo.

I want to go skiing with the penguins,
Climb a tree with a panda.

I'm going to the zoo.

I want to go fishing with a grizzly bear,
I want to play chess with a gorilla.

I'm going to the zoo.

I want to go surfing with a crocodile,
Play hide-and-seek with a chameleon.

I'm going to the zoo.

I want to play ball with a seal,
Go roller skating with a giraffe.

I'm going to the zoo.

Language detectives → G10, p. 169

Wann brauchst du Does und wann Do?

Do you like your work?
Does she like her work?
Do you like animals?
Does he like animals?

42/5–6 

8 What are the questions? → M Walking sentences, p. 179

a) Put the words in the right order. → ○ p. 136

1. get • Do • at six o'clock • up • you • ?
   Do you get up at six o'clock?
2. you • Do • ? • watch • science fiction movies
3. play • you • Do • ? • computer games
4. your friend • Does • TV • watch • ?
5. Do • animals • like • you • ?
6. your friend • Does • football • like • ?
7. play • netball • ? • you • Do

Bei diesen Fragen kommt „Do" oder „Does" als Erstes.

b) Answer the questions in a).

9 Choose the right question words.

42/7

1. **Where / What** does Holly interview Fred?
2. **Where / Who** do the monkeys play?
3. **Who / When** does Fred work?
4. **When / Who** does Holly have breakfast?
5. **Where / Who** does Holly go to school?
6. **When / What** does Holly like?

STUDY SKILLS

Du kannst dir Grammatikregeln besser merken, wenn du sie auf Karteikarten schreibst. Mache eine Grammatikkarte für die Fragewörter mit W-. Versuche die Beispielsätze auswendig zu lernen.

Wie im Deutschen: W-Fragewörter stellst du immer an den Satzanfang.

GRAMMAR → G10, p. 169

Where	does	Holly	go to school?
When	does	Fred	work?
What	do	they	eat?

43/8 10 What do they do in their free time?

a) What are the words? → ○ p. 137

1. Do you play football?
2. ___ you sing at home?
3. ___ do you go to the zoo? On Saturdays?
4. ___ your dog like the park?
5. ___ do your pets sleep?
6. ___ do you do after school?

What	Where
Does	Do
Do ✓	When

b) Look at the pictures. Write the answers.

1 netball

2 after school

3 Sundays

4 loves

5 my room

6 watch

11 (YOUR TURN) My day → V Free-time activities, p. 209

3/9–10 a) Answer the questions.

When do you get up?	I get up at 6:30.
Do you have breakfast?	Yes, I have breakfast at 6:45. • No, I don't have breakfast.
When do you go to school?	I go to school at seven.
What do you do after school?	I go to the park with my friends.
	I play football. I watch 'Superstars'.

b) Ask a partner the questions in a).

Ich kann über meinen Alltag sprechen. ✓

The café mystery

1 Look at the pictures. → M Think-pair-share, p. 178

1. Who is in the story?
2. Where are they?

2 (READING) Read the story.

1, 38
44/1

Luke takes his dog, Sherlock, for a walk in the park. They play with a football. Sherlock loves footballs! Later Luke and Sherlock go to the park café. They see a police officer and Mrs Abrihim.
→ see picture 1

Police officer: It's OK, Mrs Abrihim.
Mrs Abrihim: This is not the first time! Please help me. Every day my café is a mess!
Police officer: Hmmm ... Who doesn't like your café?
Mrs Abrihim: I don't know. How do they get in? It's crazy!
Luke: Who is it, Sherlock? Let's help! Let's solve the mystery!

Luke and Sherlock look for clues. Sherlock finds a clue.
→ see picture 2

Sherlock: Woof!
Luke: What is it, Sherlock? Oh look! There are nuts here!

There is a noise from the ceiling. They can see a hole in the ceiling. The nuts are under the hole.
→ see picture 3

Luke: What's that noise?
Police officer: Good question! Let's look in the hole.
Mrs Abrihim: What can you see?
Police officer: Oh! I can see raccoons!

READING SKILLS

Lies zunächst den Titel der Geschichte und schau dir die Bilder dazu an. Dann überlege, worum es in der Geschichte gehen könnte.

3 Choose the right answers.

44/2–3

1. Where is the café?
   In the park • At the zoo
2. What's wrong?
   Mrs Abrihim is crazy. • The café is a mess.
3. Who finds the clues?
   The police officer • Sherlock
4. Who or what is in the hole?
   Raccoons • Luke and Sherlock

1

2

3

4 (WRITING) Choose one of the tasks.

44/4

a) Schau dir die Wörter unten an. Welche Wörter kommen in der Geschichte vor? Schreibe mit diesen Wörtern jeweils einen eigenen Satz.

mess | box | tree | dad | nuts | police officer | hole

OR

b) Schreibe einen Steckbrief auf Englisch über den Waschbären (raccoon). Du kannst Informationen über Waschbären in der Geschichte, in der Bücherei oder im Internet finden.

Animal: Raccoon
Colour: …
Eats: …

Ich kann eine Detektivgeschichte verstehen. ✓

School clubs

Die Schulen in Großbritannien bieten für ihre Schüler ganz unterschiedliche Klubs und AGs an. Manche Klubs treiben zum Beispiel Sport, andere machen Musik oder etwas ganz anderes. Hier haben die Schüler die Möglichkeit, außerhalb des Klassenzimmers Neues zu lernen.

INTERNET

<1> Home <2> About <3> News <4> Info

Thomas Tallis School fair for clubs

Do you want to try something different?
Do you want to make new friends?
Do you have some free time after school?

yes!

Then come to the Main Hall at 4 p.m. on Monday, 15th September.

You can …
… find one of our sports clubs and get some exercise.
… join one of our art clubs and be creative.
… meet people with the same interests.

football

badminton

dance club

art

chess club

Dein britischer Brieffreund schickt dir einen Link zu einer Informationsveranstaltung der Thomas Tallis School. Dein kleiner Bruder möchte wissen, was du da gerade liest, spricht aber kein Englisch.

1 Beantworte seine Fragen auf Deutsch.

1. Wann findet die Veranstaltung statt?
2. In welchem Raum ist die Veranstaltung?
3. Welche Klubs gibt es?

Du musst nicht Wort für Wort übersetzen.

2 Welche Klubs gibt es bei euch? Wo kann man das erfahren?

Ich kann Informationen über Schul-AGs weitergeben. ✓

Who's the fastest?

In dieser „Filmecke“ triffst du wieder Laura, Alicia, Jinsoo und Marley.

1 Talk about your free time.

What do you like to do in your free time? (Was machst du am liebsten in deiner Freizeit?)

2 (VIEWING) Watch the film.

6
5/1–2

a) Put the pictures in the right order.

A

B

C

D

b) Answer the questions.

1. When is the race (Wettrennen)?
2. When does Jinsoo get up?
3. Where do the friends play football?
4. Who is the fastest?

VIEWING SKILLS

Achte auf Wochentage und Uhrzeiten im Film. Sie helfen dir, die Fragen zu beantworten.

3 (SPEAKING) Make a dialogue.

45/3

A: Let's play football.
B: OK, at the park?
A: OK. At three o'clock?
B: Good. See you then.

tennis	...
school	...
4:30	...

Ich kann einen Film zum Thema „Freizeit in England“ verstehen. ✓

Checklist

Ich kann über meine Freizeit sprechen. ✓

I go to .... • I play .... • I listen to .... • I help .... • I watch ....

46 

Ich kann ein Tier vorstellen. ✓

A ... comes from .... • It eats .... • It doesn't like ....

46 

Ich kann über meinen Alltag sprechen. ✓

I get up at 6:30. • I have breakfast at 6:45. • I go to school at seven o'clock. • I play football after school. • I go to bed at ten o'clock.

46 

Ich kann eine Detektivgeschichte verstehen. ✓

47 

Ich kann Informationen über Schul-AGs weitergeben. ✓

47 

Ich kann einen Film zum Thema „Freizeit in England" verstehen. ✓

(TASK) A survey

Step 1

Make a group with six students.

Step 2

Find out about free-time activities in your group and take notes.

What do you do in your free time?

Name	Activities
Sylvia	plays football, watches TV
Martin	watches DVDs, listens to music

a) What do you do after school?

play football | watch TV | ...

b) What do you do at the weekend?

see friends | read books | ...

Step 3

Make a chart about your free-time activities.

Activities	Number of students
• play football	III
• watch DVDs	IIII
• take the dog for a walk	I
• play games with family	III
• ...	

Step 4

Make a graph.

a) Put your graph on a transparency (eine Folie für den Tageslichtprojektor).

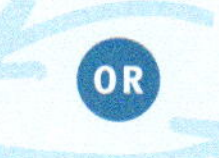

b) Put your graph on the computer.

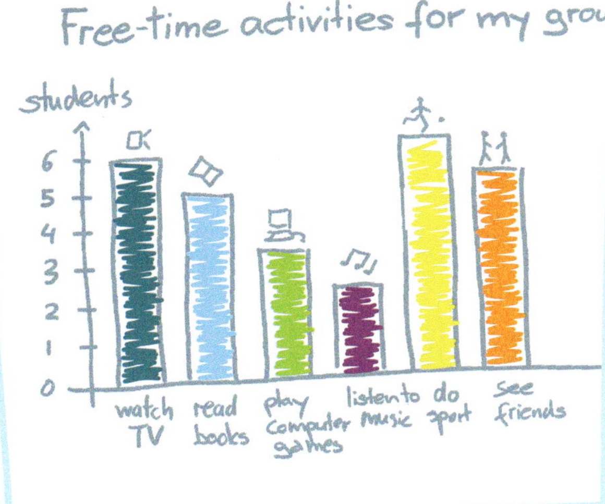

Step 5

Present your survey to your tutor group.

- In our group six students play football.
- Three students read magazines and books.
- Six students watch TV after school.
- Two students listen to music at the weekend.

GROUP SKILLS

Hat deine Mitschülerin oder dein Mitschüler alles deutlich erklärt und eine übersichtliche Grafik präsentiert? Du kannst sagen: „That was very clear."

Step 6

What is the most popular free-time activity in your tutor group?

Extra practice

○ 1 Complete the sentences. (nach 53/2)

1. After school I listen to — .

2. On Saturdays I play — .

3. I go to the — .

4. I have — practice on Saturdays.

5. I — at an animal rescue shelter.

help | music | netball | football | cinema

○ 2 Match the numbers with the words. (nach 55/6)

a) Match the numbers.

1. 38 That's thirty-eight.
2. 21
3. 42
4. 100
5. 15
6. 64

thirty-eight ✓ | a hundred | fifteen | sixty-four | fifty | forty-two | twenty-one

b) Welches Zahlwort hast du nicht gebraucht?

○ 3 Match! (nach 56/11)

1. Tom, the tiger
2. Tigers
3. Edgar, the elephant
4. Elephants
5. Holly Richardson
6. She

comes from India.
loves animals.
helps at an animal rescue shelter.
eat meat.
like fruit.
runs 40 kilometres an hour.

○ 4 What time is it? (nach 59/6)

It's eleven forty-five.
It's ten forty-five.

It's four o'clock.
It's two o'clock.

It's seven fifteen.
It's seven twenty.

It's twelve thirty.
It's one thirty.

It's two thirty-five.
It's three twenty-five.

It's nine forty.
It's nine fourteen.

○ 5 Match the questions with the answers. (nach 61/10)

	help at home on Saturdays?	play football on Saturdays?	watch TV on Saturdays?
Luke	✓	✓	✗
Holly	✗	✗	✓

Find Luke's and Holly's answers.

1. Do you help at home on Saturdays, Luke?
2. And do you play football on Saturdays?
3. Do you watch TV, Luke?
4. Holly, do you play football on Saturdays?
5. Do you watch TV?
6. Do you help at home on Saturdays, Holly?

a) No, I don't play football.
b) Yes, I watch TV with my mum.
c) Yes, I help my mum and dad.
d) No. I don't help on Saturdays.
e) Yes. We play football on Saturdays.
f) No, I don't watch TV on Saturdays!

○ 6 (WRITING) Put the words in two groups. (nach 63/3)

Animals	Free time
tiger	netball

netball ✓ · giraffe · football · music · cinema · tiger ✓ · café · penguin · snake · monkey

Find more online: fe76m3

Am Ende dieser Unit kann ich ...
- über Feste sprechen.
- über Geburtstage sprechen.
- ein Einkaufsgespräch führen.
- einen dramatischen Text verstehen, Informationen über ein Stadtfest weitergeben und einen Film über eine Party verstehen.

7 2, 1

Unit 4
Let's celebrate!

1 Find out about special days.

50/1–2

a) Match the texts with the photos.

1. Olivia: The Notting Hill Carnival is in London, in August. I like the carnival. People dance a lot.

   Olivia's special day is the Notting Hill Carnival. That's photo E.

2. Holly: Halloween is in October. In the evening I wear a scary costume. We go to people's houses and say "Trick or treat!"
3. Luke: I like Christmas. It's in December. We eat together and we get presents.
4. Dave: Red Nose Day is in March. People wear a red nose on this day and collect money for other people.
5. Jay: Eid is a special day for Muslims. We eat together. We get new clothes and sweets.

b) Talk about special days in Germany.

We have .... • We don't have ....

2,2 **2** (SPEAKING) **Listen and say the months.**

May	April	June	November	December	February
March	August	July	September	October	January

3 (WRITING) **Put the months in the right order.** → M Peer correction, p. 178

January, February, …

4 (YOUR TURN) **My special day** → V Special days, p. 218

50/3 a) Write about your special day.

I like Christmas.
It's in December.
We get presents.

Christmas	Eid	…
February	October	…
We eat together.	We dance.	…

b) Talk about your special day with your group.

Ich kann über Feste sprechen. ✓

Hier lerne ich, über Geburtstage zu sprechen.

Birthday parties

remember 1 **What birthday words do you know? Look at the pictures for help.**

2 **(READING) Read about birthday parties.**

2, 3 50/1

Luke: Jay's birthday party is this weekend, right?

Olivia: Yes, I have a great present for him. And I have a cool costume too.

Luke: Oh right, it's a fancy dress party. What's your costume?

Olivia: It's a big surprise … When's your birthday, Luke?

Luke: It's on 7th July. I can have a barbecue party in the garden. My dad always makes a chocolate cake for me. And Sherlock doesn't forget my birthday. He always gives me a birthday card.

Olivia: That's nice! My birthday is on 28th February. I never have a party in the garden! But I often invite my friends to the cinema.

Luke: The cinema? That's cool!

3 **Find out about the birthdays.**

a) Match a photo with a person in the text.

1

1. Photo 1 is **Luke's birthday**.

2

3

4

b) Find a sentence from the text.

1. Luke: My dad always makes a chocolate cake for me.

Language tip → G11, p. 170

I – me – my

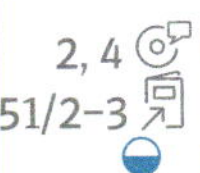
2, 4
51/2–3

4 (LISTENING) When are their birthdays?

a) What's right? → ○ p. 137

26th December · 20th April

1. Olivia's birthday is **on 28th February.**
2. Holly's birthday is ….

21st March · 21st May

3. Dave's ….
4. Jay's ….

My birthday is on 29th February.
When is your birthday?
Say dates like this: on the twenty-ninth of February.
Write: on 29th February.

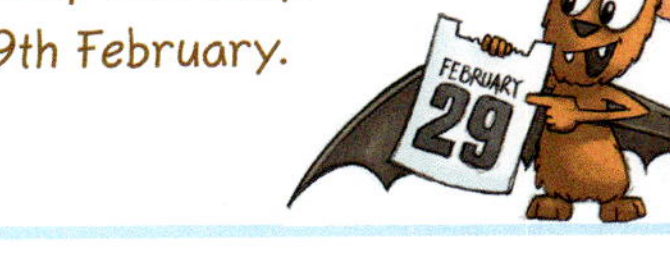

1st first
2nd second
3rd third
4th fourth → V Ordinal numbers, p. 213

b) Listen again. What do Holly and Dave do on their birthdays? → V Birthday activities, p. 214

picnic in the park • sleepover • theme park • fast food restaurant • favourite meal: burgers • favourite ice cream: strawberry

5 (WRITING) Match the numbers. → M Peer correction, p. 178

a) Write the number. → ○ p. 138

13th	7th
23rd	5th
31st	12th

thirteenth ✓ · thirty-first · twenty-third · twelfth · seventh · fifth

b) Write the next number.

1. 10th – 20th – 30th – 40th – **fiftieth**
2. 1st – 3rd – 5th – …
3. 3rd – 9th – 15th – …
4. 92nd – 82nd – 72nd – …

6 (SONG) The birthday song

2, 5

Singt das Lied in Gruppen (je zwei Zeilen pro Gruppe).

Today is a special day, we're going to a party.
We will eat a chocolate cake, everyone's invited.

(Chorus): Happy birthday, it's your birthday, let's all celebrate!
Happy birthday, it's your birthday, let's all celebrate, celebrate!

Today is a special day, we'll have a party in the garden.
We will have a barbecue, everyone's invited. *(Chorus)*

Today is your birthday, let's celebrate, let's celebrate!
Today is your birthday! *(Chorus)*

Language detectives → G12, p. 171

I often have a barbecue in the garden.

My dad always makes a chocolate cake for me.

I never have a party in the garden.

But I often invite my friends to the cinema.

Was ist richtig?
Wörter wie never, often, always stehen
a) nach dem ersten Wort in einem Satz.
b) in der Mitte des Satzes.
c) vor dem Verb (z. B. „have", „makes").
d) am Ende eines Satzes.

7 Put the words in the right places.

52/4a)–b)

1. Sherlock forgets Luke's birthday. (never)
   Sherlock never forgets Luke's birthday.
2. Sherlock gives Luke a card. (always)
3. Luke has a barbecue party in the garden. (often)
4. Luke has a party at the cinema. (never)
5. Luke's friends come to his house. (often)
6. Luke's dad makes a chocolate cake. (always)

Finde das Verb im Satz. Setze „never", „always" oder „often" vor das Verb.

8 (WRITING) Write sentences. → M Bus stop, p. 181

a) Put the words in the right order. → ○ p. 138

1. always • a party • Olivia • has
   Olivia always has a party.
2. her friends • Olivia • invites • often
3. Olivia • never • the cake • makes
4. always • gets • nice presents • Olivia
5. never • her friends' birthdays • forgets • Olivia
6. writes • Olivia • birthday cards • always

b) Write more sentences about Olivia's birthday.

52/4c)

Olivia …
She …

a barbecue party | with her friends | often | never
in the garden | the cinema | goes to | has

53/5 9 What can you do on a birthday?

a) Make sentences about Jay's birthday. → ○ p. 138

1 always

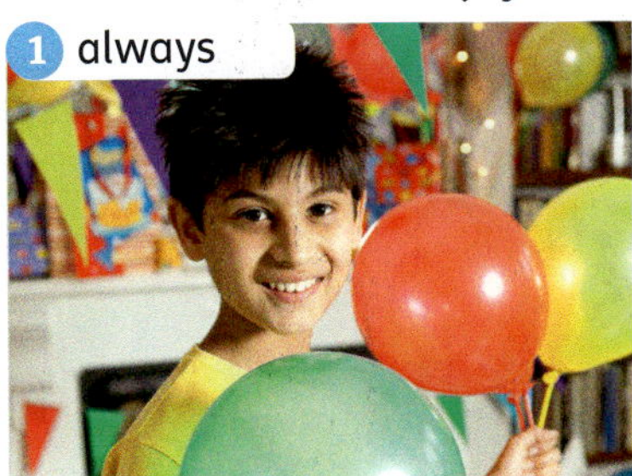

Jay • has a party
Jay always has a party.

2 always

Jay's mum • makes a cake

3 always

Jay • gets presents from his friends

4 never

Jay's dad • dances

5 often

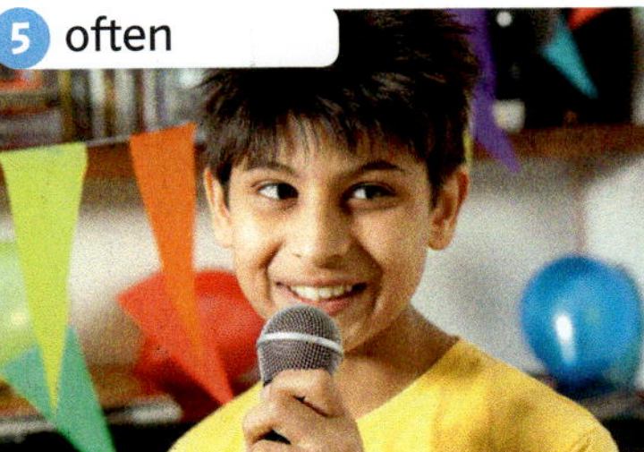

Jay • sings for his friends

6 often

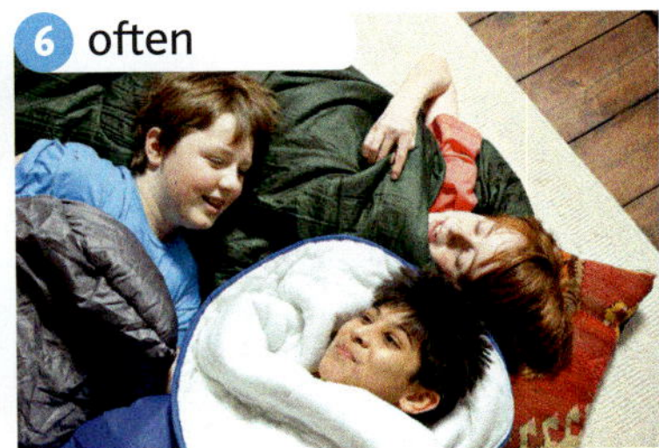

Jay and his friends • sleep in the living room

b) What do you know about birthdays around the world?

- I know something about birthdays in .... People ....
- I know a girl/a boy from .... She/He ....

10 (YOUR TURN) Birthdays → V Special days, p. 218

6–54/2 a) Ask a partner.

When is your birthday?

What do you do on your birthday?

My birthday is on 5th June. On my birthday I often play games.

On my birthday I ...

never | often | always

eat cake | have a party at home | sing | dance | play games | go to the cinema | watch movies | get presents | wear a costume

b) Tell your tutor group about your partner.

"Hannah's birthday is on 5th June.
She often plays games.
She never wears a costume on her birthday."

Ich kann über Geburtstage sprechen. ✓

Shopping for a birthday party

remember **1** What do you need for a birthday party? Look at the pictures for help.

2 (READING) Read the dialogues.

2, 6

Let's see … We have crisps, a bar of chocolate and candles.
We don't have coke or balloons, Mum.
You're right. Can you go to the corner shop, please?

Mr Safi: Hello Jay. How can I help you?
Jay: Hi. Can I have a bottle of coke, please?
Mr Safi: Here you are. Anything else?
Jay: Do you have a packet of balloons?
Mr Safi: Yes, here you are.
Jay: Thanks. How much is it?
Mr Safi: The coke is 99p, and the balloons are £1.50. That's £2.49, please.
Jay (gives Mr Safi £5): Here you are. Thanks.
Mr Safi: You're welcome. Here's your change.
Jay: Thank you. Bye!

CULTURE

In Großbritannien bezahlt man mit **pounds** (£) und **pence** (p).

3 Check the sentences.

a) Right or wrong? → ○ p. 139

1. Jay and his mum don't have chocolate. That's wrong.
2. Jay goes to the corner shop.
3. The corner shop doesn't have balloons.
4. The coke is 99p.
5. The balloons are £1.59.
6. Jay gives Mr Safi £3.49.
7. Jay gets his change.

b) Correct the wrong sentences.

1. Jay and his mum don't have coke or balloons.

4 (LISTENING) Listen. Point at the right picture on page 76.

2,7

5 How much is it? → ○ p. 139

55/1a) 55/2

Look at the pictures again. Make sentences.

1. A bottle of coke is 99p. 2. …

a bottle of | a bar of | a packet of

6 (SPEAKING) Make dialogues. → V Food, p. 215

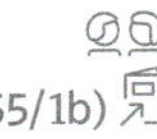

55/1b)

a can of | a box of | …

1. A: Can I have a can of peaches, please?
   B: Here you are. That's 65p.

7 (SOUNDS) Listen, read and say.

2, 8 55/3

1. chocolate
2. joke
3. oranges
4. There are three chairs in the room.
5. Here's your change.
6. Fluff and Honey are in the cage.

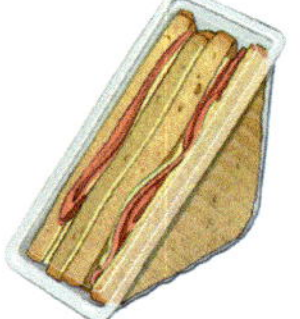

8 (CHANT) Say the chant.

2, 9

Cheese or chocolate, cheese or chocolate.
What do you choose? Cheese or chocolate?

Cheese, please. I love cheese.

Sandwiches or oranges, sandwiches or oranges.
What do you choose? Sandwiches or oranges?

Oranges, please. I love oranges.

MR SAFI'S CORNER SHOP

 56/4

9 (SPEAKING) Make dialogues. → G10, p. 169

a) Partner A: Ask Mr Safi for these things.
Partner B (Mr Safi): Give the right answer. → ○ p. 140

1. bananas
2. fish
3. pencils
4. balloons
5. oranges
6. sandwiches
7. chocolate
8. footballs
9. CDs
10. DVDs

1. A: Hi! Do you have bananas?
   B: Yes, they're here.
2. A: Hi! Do you have fish?
   B: No, sorry! We don't have fish.

● b) Ask for more things.

nuts | peaches | lemonade
water | pasta | ...

Suche die Sachen im Bild. Wenn sie nicht im Angebot sind, sagst du "No, sorry!" Vielleicht kannst du dem Kunden etwas Anderes anbieten?

57/5 **10** Make a dialogue about Jay's present.

a) What does Jay do?
Look at the pictures and make questions and answers. → ○ p. 141

1. play computer games? ☺

2. read books? ☹

3. have a pet? ☹

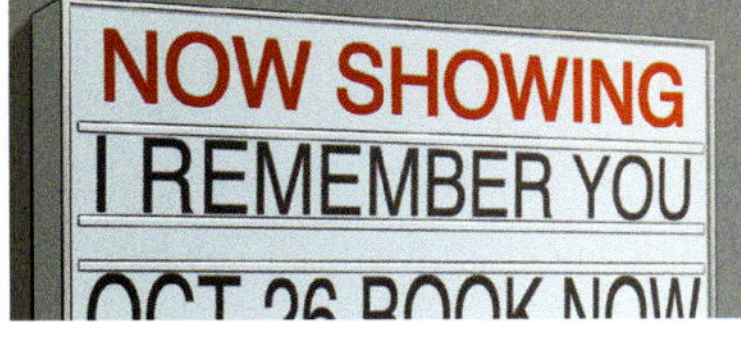

4. go to the cinema? ☺

5. like football? ☹

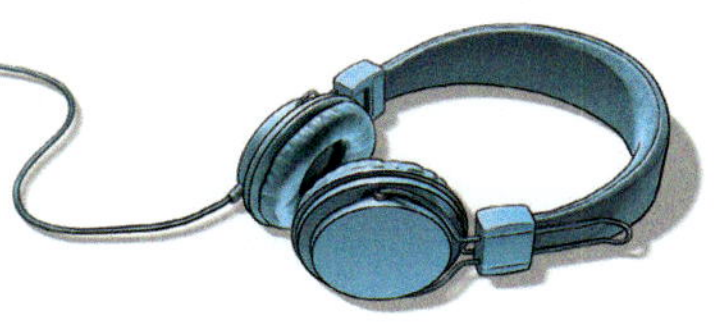
6. listen to music? ☺

1. Olivia: Does Jay play computer games?
Holly: Yes, he plays games.

2. Olivia: Does he read books?
Holly: No, he doesn't read books.

b) What can Holly and Olivia give Jay?
Make their dialogue.

Let's buy a present … | CD? | … | How much is … | DVD?

11 (YOUR TURN) Shopping → V Shopping, p. 219

57/6 a) Write a shopping list with three things.

a packet of crisps
a sandwich
…

b) Act the shopping dialogue with a partner.

Mr Safi: Hello. How can I help you?
You: Hi. Can I have a packet of crisps, please?
Mr Safi: Here you are. Anything else?
You: Yes. Can I have a sandwich, please? (Yes)

(No)
You: No, thank you. How much is it?
Mr Safi: That's £3.70, please.
You: Here you are.
Mr Safi: Here's your change.
Thank you. Bye.
You: Bye.

STUDY SKILLS

Wenn du etwas nicht verstehst, bitte um Wiederholung:
- Sorry, can you say that again, please?
- Pardon?

Ich kann ein Einkaufsgespräch führen. ✓

A fancy dress party

1 Look at the picture.

a) Match the costumes with the children.

1. Holly is the **witch.**
2. … is the smurf.
3. … is Superman.
4. … is the alien.
5. … is the carnival dancer.

b) What's your favourite costume?

2 (READING) Read the play.

2, 10
58/1–2

Narrator: It's Jay's birthday and he invites his friends to a fancy dress party.
Jay: Hello. Welcome to my birthday party!
Dave: Thanks for your invitation, Jay. Happy birthday! I like your costume. You are scary!
Jay: Look at Holly and Luke. Their costumes are cool too.
Holly: Hey Dave! I'm a witch.
Dave: Really? I'm Superman. Who is that?
Holly: I don't know. I think it's Olivia. It's a pirate costume.

Dave: Here's Luke now.
Luke: Hello you three. I like your costumes.
Jay: Are you a smurf, Luke?
Luke: Yes! I'm blue. Let's dance!
Jay's mum: Your costumes are so cool! Can I take a photo?
Holly: Yes, but where is Olivia?
All: Olivia! Can you come here, please?
Narrator: The pirate doesn't look. Can Olivia hear them? The doorbell rings. It's Olivia.
Olivia: Hi! Happy birthday, Jay! You look brilliant.
Holly: But who is the pirate?
Dave: Yes, let's go and ask.
Narrator: They want to ask the pirate but the pirate isn't there. The friends look in the house but they can't find the pirate. Holly goes into the garden and sees the pirate under a tree. She talks to the pirate and it is …

3 Who is the pirate?

1. Luke's brother, Jamie
2. Holly's sister, Amber
3. Jay's brother, Shahid

4 Put the sentences in the right order.

58/3

A Jay, Holly and Dave see the pirate.
B There's a birthday party at Jay's house.
C Dave, Luke and Holly dance.
D The pirate isn't there.
E Jay's mum wants to take a photo.
F Olivia comes to the party.

STUDY SKILLS

Bildet Gruppen. Entscheidet, wer welche Rolle liest. Übt mit der CD. Welche Wörter werden betont? Wann geht der Sprecher mit der Stimme hoch oder runter? Sprecht die Sätze wie auf der CD nach.

5 Choose one of the tasks.

a) Read the play in class.

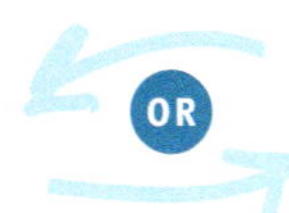

b) Record the play and listen to it in class.

Ich kann einen dramatischen Text verstehen. ✓

Greenwich Summer Festival

INTERNET

×

GREENWICH
SUMMER
FESTIVAL

Greenwich Summer Festival takes place every year in July or August. It's in the park near the Naval College. It is free.

There are two music stages. Rock bands play on one stage. On the other stage an orchestra plays classical music.

If you like theatre, go to the big tent where you can see plays and circus shows. In the evening you can watch movies on the big screen.

Hungry? Try the food at the street stalls. There are sausages, burgers, salads and lots more!

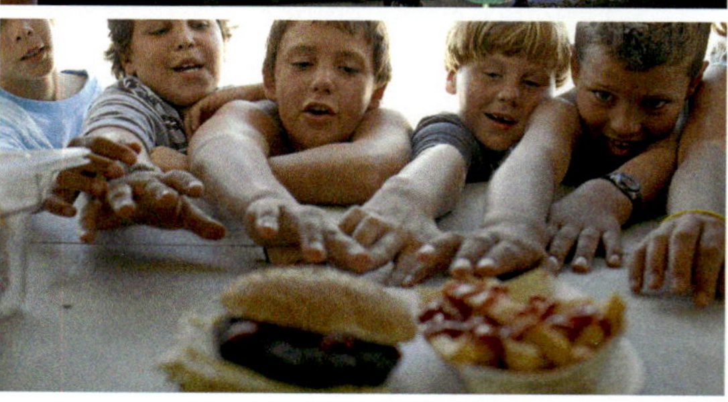

1 Informiere deine Eltern über das Greenwich Summer Festival.

Deine Eltern möchten zum Greenwich Summer Festival gehen.
Du hast dich darüber schon im Internet informiert und erklärst ihnen,

1. wann es stattfindet,
2. wo es stattfindet,
3. was es kostet,
4. was man dort machen kann,
5. was man dort essen kann.

Ich kann Informationen über ein Stadtfest weitergeben. 

The sleepover

In dieser „Filmecke" triffst du wieder Laura, ihre Familie, Alicia, Parule and Emily.

1 Talk about you and your friends at home.

What do you do when your friends are at your house?
(Was macht ihr, wenn deine Freunde bei dir zu Hause sind?)

VIEWING SKILLS

Überlege dir, was du schon über die Figuren im Film weißt. Wer ist mit wem befreundet?

2 (VIEWING) Watch the film.

8
59/1–2

a) Put the pictures in the right order.

A

B

C

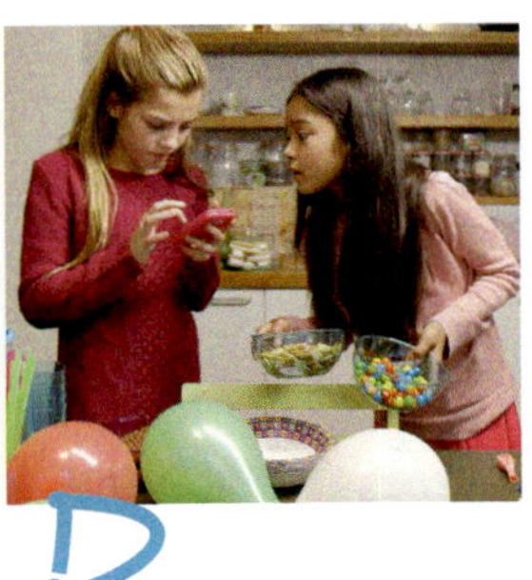
D

b) Who is it?

1. She has a present.
2. She helps Laura with the snacks.
3. She's funny.
4. He goes to the party.

3 (SPEAKING) Make a dialogue.

59/3

A: It's Sally's birthday. Let's buy a present for her.
B: OK. Does she like books?
A: No, she likes computer games.
B: OK. Let's go to the shops.

DVDs | clothes | ...

Ich kann einen Film über eine Party verstehen. ✓

Checklist

Ich kann über Feste sprechen. 

My special day is .... • It's in .... • I / We / My family ....

60

Ich kann über Geburtstage sprechen. 

My birthday is on .... • On my birthday I always/often/never ....

60

Ich kann ein Einkaufsgespräch führen. 

Good morning/Hello/Hi. • Can I have ... , please? • How much is/are ... ? • Here you are. • You're welcome .... • Thank you. Bye.

60

Ich kann einen dramatischen Text verstehen. 

61

Ich kann Informationen über ein Stadtfest weitergeben. 

61

Ich kann einen Film über eine Party verstehen. 

(TASK) Let's plan a party.

Step 1

Find a partner. → M Milling around, p. 179

Find a partner who has a birthday in the same month as you.

A: My birthday is in June. When is your birthday?
B: My birthday is in June too.

Step 2

Collect ideas for your birthday party.

You and your partner want to celebrate your birthdays together and make plans for a party with a theme. Talk with your partner. Make a list.

What theme would you like?

I'd like a stars party.

When can we have our party?

What music can we have?

Let's have it on 15th June.

What food can we have?

Where can we have the party?

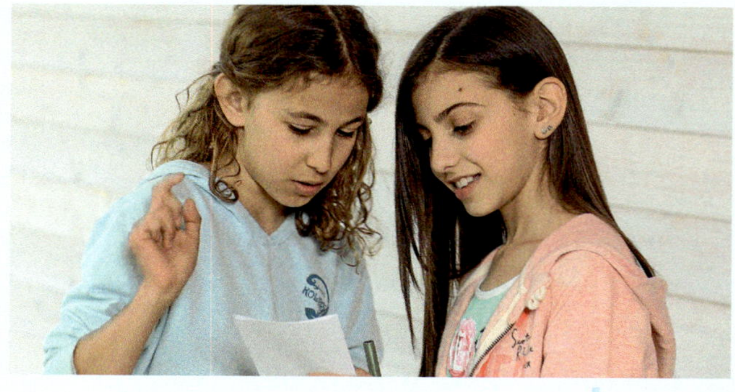

Our birthday party

theme:	stars
food:	pizza, chocolate, birthday cake
music:	favourite stars
date:	15th June
time:	4 p.m.
place:	at Hannah's house

Step 3

Make an invitation.

Theme: Stars
Please come as your favourite star.
Place: Hannah's house
Date and time: 15th June at 4 p.m.
Pizza and cake for everyone!
Love from Hannah and Michelle

Ihr könnt diesen Text als Vorlage für eure Einladung nehmen.

Step 4

Organize a gallery walk. → M Gallery walk, p. 180

a) Put your invitations on the wall.

b) Find your favourite invitation.

c) Talk about your favourite invitation.

My favourite invitation is Hannah's and Michelle's invitation.
- It has all the information.
- I can understand it.

GROUP SKILLS

Wenn du Feedback zu einem Produkt wie z. B. einer Einladung gibst, achte auf den Inhalt, die Sprache und die Gestaltung.
Folgende Fragen helfen dir dabei:
- Enthält die Einladung alle wichtigen Informationen?
- Ist sie verständlich geschrieben?
- Ist sie toll gestaltet?

Extra practice

○ 1 (WRITING) Match the pictures with the days. (nach 70/1)

1. It's Halloween.

2. It's —— .

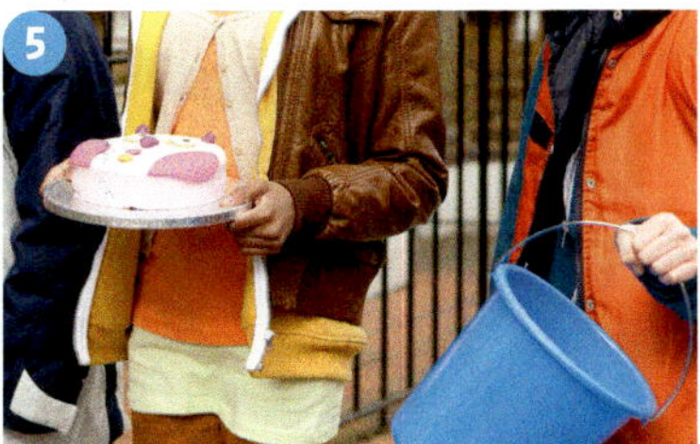

Christmas | Halloween ✓ | Red Nose Day | Eid | the Notting Hill Carnival

○ 2 (WRITING) Write the next month. (nach 71/3)

1. April, May, June
2. October, November, ——
3. January, February, ——
4. December, January, ——
5. May, June, ——
6. August, September, ——

Oft ist nur ein Buchstabe anders als im Deutschen!

○ 3 Find the words. (nach 72/3)

1. Luke's birthday is on 7th July.
2. He often has a —— party in the garden.
3. Sherlock always gives him a birthday —— .
4. His dad always makes a chocolate —— .
5. Sherlock is a —— dog.
6. Luke never has a party at the —— .

card | cake | cinema | July ✓ | nice | barbecue

4 What does Holly do on Sundays? (nach 75/9)

1. Holly + gets up at nine o'clock.
   Holly often gets up at nine o'clock.
2. She ++ has breakfast.
3. She ++ plays with Fluff and Honey.
4. She – cleans their cage.
5. She + makes a cake with her mum.
6. She + watches TV.

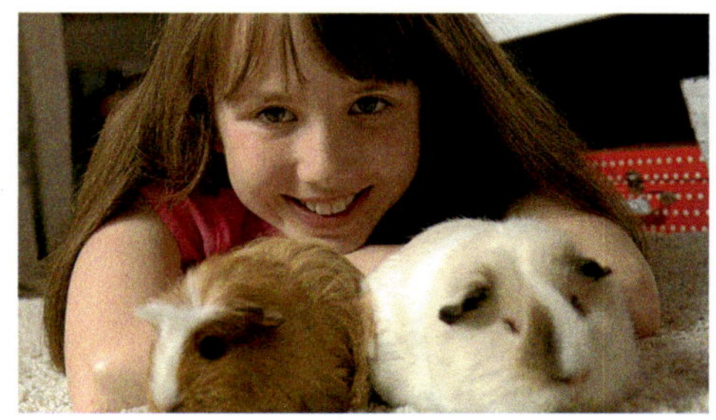

– = never + = often ++ = always

5 (WRITING) Write a shopping list. (nach 77/5)

a) Write a shopping list with four things.

b) You have five pounds. Can you buy the things on your shopping list?

6 Find ten words. (nach 80/4)

birthdayfriendpartybrilliantcostumethinkscarysorryinvitationhappy

Hier geht es um das Schreiben.

Jay's special day

Es gibt Internet-Plattformen, über die man Menschen auf der ganzen Welt Grußkarten schreiben kann. Schreibe wie Jay eine Karte über ein besonderes Fest. Willst du deine Karte auch verschicken?

16th May

Hello!
My name is Jay and I'm twelve.
I'm from Greenwich, London.
My special day is Eid.
It's in May this year.
We get lots of great cards.
We always eat carrot pudding.
We often sing songs.
And what about you? Do you celebrate a special day?

Bye for now, Jay

So kannst du eine Mind-Map machen:

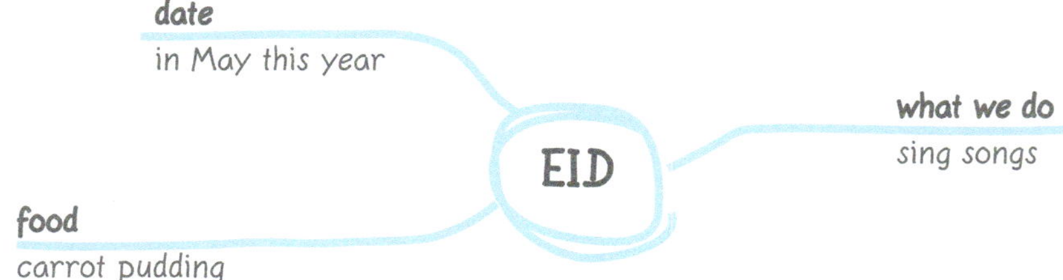

-65/4

1 Write a card.

a) Choose your topic.

> Folgende Fragen können dir bei der Wahl des Themas helfen:
> - Welches Thema findest du interessant?
> - Was weißt du über dieses Thema schon?

b) Collect information.

> Notiere dir zunächst deine Ideen. Du kannst auch deine Familie oder Freunde fragen. Deine Notizen kannst du in beiden Sprachen machen.

c) Make a mind map.
Du kannst die Oberbegriffe von Jays Mind-Map übernehmen. Manche Wörter musst du vielleicht nachschlagen. Was heißt z. B. „Weihnachtsschmuck" auf Englisch?

> das **Weihnachten** Christmas; **fröhliche Weihnachten!** merry Christmas!; **etwas zu Weihnachten bekommen** to get something for Christmas; **was hast du ihr zu Weihnachten geschenkt?** what did you get her for Christmas?

> der **Schmuck** ① (*Juwelen*) jewellery ['dʒuːəlri] (GB), jewelry (USA), ⚠ *‚schmuck' bedeutet im amerikanischen Englisch ‚Idiot'!* ② (*Dekoration*) decoration [ˌdekəˈreɪʃən]

> Wenn du ein Wort im Wörterbuch nachschlägst, nimm nicht gleich das erste Wort, sondern lies den ganzen Wörterbucheintrag.

d) Write a draft.

Welche Sätze kannst du aus Jays Karte übernehmen?

> Wenn du einen Entwurf schreibst, schreibe nur in jede zweite Zeile. Die Zwischenzeilen kannst du im nächsten Schritt für deine Korrekturen nutzen.

e) Check your draft.

> Gib deinen Text deiner Partnerin oder deinem Partner. Findet sie oder er deinen Text verständlich? Ist alles richtig?

f) Write your card.

> Schreibe nun deine Karte in schöner, gut lesbarer Schrift.

Find more online: fe76m3

Am Ende dieser Unit kann ich ...
- meinen Wohnort vorstellen.
- über mein Wochenende sprechen.
- mich über einen Tagesausflug unterhalten.
- Auszüge aus einem Tagebuch verstehen, touristische Informationen über Greenwich weitergeben und einen Film zum Thema „Einkaufen“ verstehen.

9 2, 11

Unit 5

Where I live

I live in Greenwich. It's an old town and it's in London. Our house is in Brook Lane. Holly's flat is in our road too.

This is the Cutty Sark. It's a famous old ship in Greenwich.

1 Name the place.

1. It's an old town and it's in London. **It's Greenwich.**
2. Luke often goes there with Dave.
3. The sandwiches there are great.
4. Sherlock loves it.
5. It's a famous ship.
6. Luke and Holly live in this road.

2 (LISTENING) Listen to Holly.

2, 12
66/1–2

a) Which places does Holly talk about?

park | swimming pool | shopping centre | Brook Lane

b) What's her favourite place in Greenwich?

3

There's a café in Greenwich. They have great sandwiches.

4

My favourite place in Greenwich is the park. I often go to the park with Sherlock. He loves it!

5

There's a swimming pool in Greenwich. I often go swimming there with Dave.

3 (YOUR TURN) Where I live

→ V In town, p. 225

66/3

Tell a partner about where you live.
What's your favourite place?

I live in Dortmund.
My flat is in Konrad-Adenauer-Straße.
There's a park and a nice café.
My favourite place is the shopping centre.

CULTURE

In Großbritannien fahren die Autos auf der linken Straßenseite. Darum muss man zuerst nach rechts schauen, wenn man über die Straße geht. Fallen dir noch weitere Unterschiede auf?

house | swimming pool | zoo | ... | shopping centre

Ich kann meinen Wohnort vorstellen. 

Hier lerne ich, über mein Wochenende zu sprechen.

It's Monday morning!

1 (READING) Read the dialogue.

2, 13

Olivia: I'm tired! I played netball yesterday. It was a really exciting game!

Jay: Hey! I saw Ray-B at the shopping centre on Saturday.

Luke: Ray-B? Really?

Jay: Yes. He opened a new sports shop. My brother bought his new CD. It's great.

Luke: Wow! I went to the cinema with my sister on Saturday evening. We watched *Lucky Number*. It was brilliant.

Olivia: Cool. I went shopping with my mum on Saturday and we had a pizza in the afternoon. And I did my homework last night.

Jay: How was your weekend, Holly?

Holly: I had a great weekend. I can tell you at break.

2 Complete the sentences.

67/1

1. … played netball.
   Olivia played netball.
2. … saw Ray-B at the shopping centre.
3. … opened a new sports shop.
4. … bought Ray-B's new CD.
5. … watched *Lucky Number* at the cinema.
6. … went shopping.
7. … had a great weekend.

Holly | Ray-B | Jay's brother | Jay | Olivia ✓ | Olivia and her mum | Luke and his sister

3 (LISTENING) Listen to Dave and Jay.

2, 14

a) Choose the right answer. → ○ p. 142

1. On Saturday evening Dave
   played football. • watched TV. • listened to music.
2. In the afternoon he
   helped his dad • cleaned his room • went to the shopping centre.
3. On Sunday he
   did his homework. • watched a DVD. • played a computer game.

b) What is Dave's idea at the end?

Höre gut zu und schreibe die Antwort als Stichwort. Bei Nummer 1 reicht es, „football", „TV" oder „music" zu schreiben.

4 Make a mind map. → M Think-pair-share, p. 178

67/2

a) These places are in Greenwich.

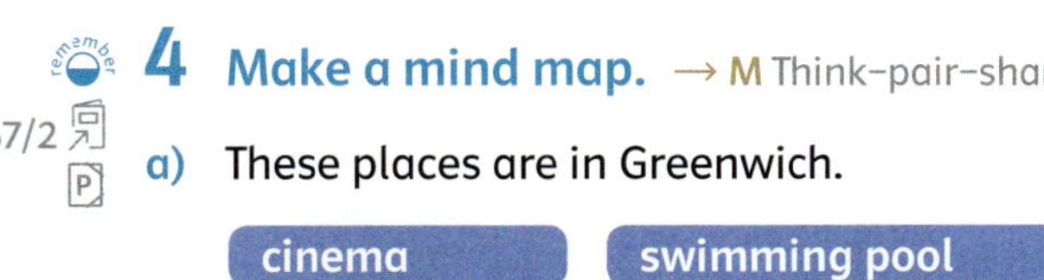

What other places in a town do you know?

b) Make a 'town' mind map with places and activities.

watch movies | go swimming | play games | buy clothes | ...

swimming pool — park — town — shopping centre — cinema

5 (WRITING) What can you do in your town at the weekend?

67/3

a) Look at your mind map in exercise 4 and write sentences. → ○ p. 142

I can + go swimming / play games / buy clothes / watch movies / ... + in the park. / at the shopping centre. / at the cinema. / at the swimming pool. / ...

67/4

b) Write more sentences. → V Town, p. 220

station | library | department store | river | market | museum | supermarket

6 (SOUNDS) Listen, read and say.

2, 15

1. How old is this town?
2. My house is in a big road.
3. Don't close the window now!
4. Let's go to the playground.

7 (GAME) Amber went shopping.

Amber went shopping. She bought apples.
Ben went shopping. He bought balloons.
Claire went shopping. She bought chocolate.

Wenn euch nichts einfällt, könnt ihr die Wortlisten hinten im Buch benutzen.

Language detectives → G13, p. 172

Jay: "Ray-B opened a new shop last Saturday."
Olivia: "I played netball yesterday."
Luke: "We watched a movie at the weekend."

Was ist mit den Verben („open", „play" und „watch") passiert?
Was drückt die neue Verbform aus?
Was bedeuten diese Wörter?

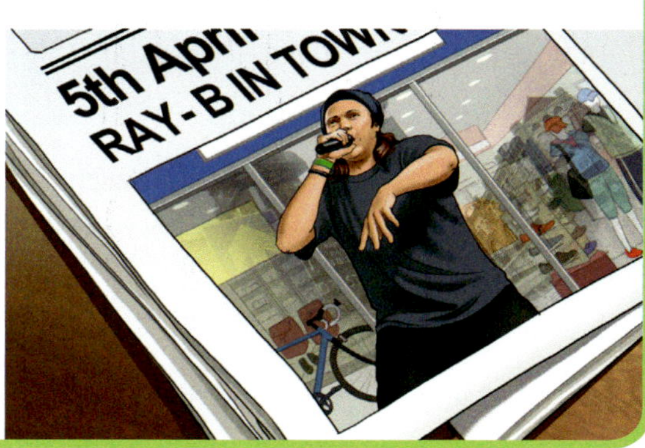

68/5 **8** **What did they do at the weekend?**

a) Complete the sentences. → ○ p. 143

1 
Olivia • on Sunday
Olivia played netball on Sunday.

2 
Luke • on Saturday

3 
Dave • on Sunday

4 
Dave's mum • on Saturday

5 
on Saturday • Jay

6 
Olivia • on Saturday

worked | talked to her mum | watched a movie | played netball ✓ | played computer games | listened to Ray-B's songs

b) What about your weekend?
play … watch …
talk to … …

Hier musst du -ed an das Verb anhängen!

9 Match the sentences. Find the word.

1. Olivia: I played netball yesterday. — I did it on Sunday. I
2. Jay: Ray-B is cool. — We saw the tigers. N
3. Olivia: I saw my mum on Saturday. — Dave was at the swimming pool too. N
4. Holly: We went swimming yesterday. — Shahid and I listened to his new songs. O
5. Luke: That homework was easy! — Oh! I had it at break! G
6. Holly: We went to the zoo in March. — It was a great game! M
7. Dave: Where's my chocolate? — We had a pizza together. R

What's the word? M —

10 Complete the sentences.

a) Choose the right words. → ○ p. 143

68/6
9/8–9

1. Olivia: I had a pizza with my mum in the afternoon.
   I had a pizza with my mum in the afternoon.
2. Olivia: I — my homework last night.
3. Jay: My brother — Ray-B's new CD.
4. Luke: I — to the cinema on Saturday evening.
5. Luke: The movie — brilliant.

bought · went · had ✓ · was · did

Manche Verben haben eine unregelmäßige Vergangenheitsform. Die musst du auswendig lernen.
have → had
do → did
see → saw

b) Write about *your* movie.

68/7

I saw — at the cinema / on TV.
I watched it with — . It was — !

11 (YOUR TURN) My weekend → V Activities in town, p. 226

-70/1

a) Write sentences about last weekend.

On Saturday In the morning In the afternoon In the evening On Sunday morning …	+ I +	played · watched · listened to · went (to) · bought · talked to · …	+ computer games · football · music · a DVD · TV · swimming · shopping · the cinema · the park · the shopping centre · my brother · my friends · …

b) Tell a partner about your weekend.

On Saturday morning I went shopping.

Ich kann über mein Wochenende sprechen. ✓

Hier lerne ich, mich über einen Tagesausflug zu unterhalten.

Day trip to Margate

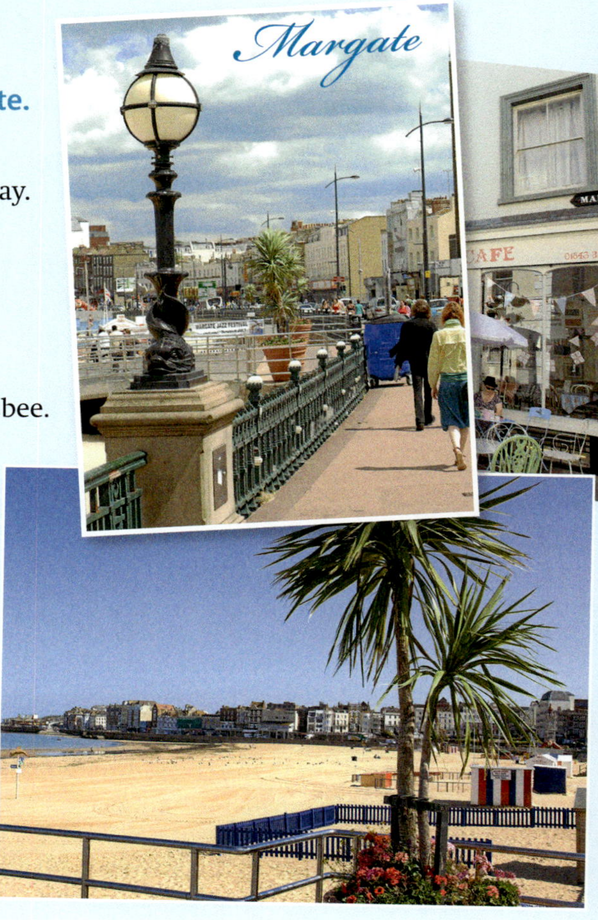

1 (READING) Read about Holly's day in Margate.

2, 16 71/1

Jay: What did you do at the weekend, Holly?
Holly: I went to Margate with my dad on Sunday.
Jay: Margate? Where's that?
Holly: It's at the seaside.
Jay: How did you go there? By train?
Holly: No, we went by car.
Jay: What did you do there?
Holly: We walked on the beach and played frisbee. It was nice.
Jay: Cool! Did you have fish and chips?
Holly: Dad had fish. I'm a vegetarian. I had chips. They were great! We went to the shops after that and I bought postcards.
Jay: Did you send me a postcard?
Holly: No, Jay! I don't know where you live!

71/2

2 Check the sentences.

a) Are the sentences right or wrong? → ○ p. 144

1. Holly went to Margate with her dad on Saturday. That's wrong!
2. They went by train.
3. They played frisbee on the beach.
4. Holly had fish and her dad had chips.
5. She bought posters.
6. She doesn't know where Jay lives.

b) Correct the wrong sentences.

CULTURE

Egal wo man in England wohnt – das Meer ist nie weit weg. Darum isst man auch oft *fish and chips*. Wie weit ist es von dir bis zum Meer?

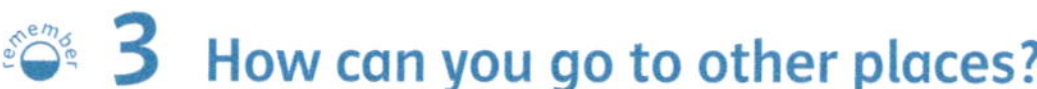

3 How can you go to other places?

train

What other transport words (Verkehrsmittel) do you know?

4 (LISTENING) Which picture is it?

2, 17 a) Look at the pictures and listen to the sounds. Which picture is it?

A by train · B by car · C by bike · D on foot · E by bus

2, 18 b) Listen to the sentences. Which picture is it?

5 (SPEAKING) Ask the students in your tutor group. → M Milling around, p. 179

Make a chart.

A: How do you go to school?
B: I go to school ....

by bus	on foot	by bike	by ...
𝍸 I	III		

6 (WRITING) How do they go to school?

a) Write about your chart. → ○ p. 144

71/3 a)–b)

Six students go to school ....
... students go .... No students go ....

b) How would you like to go to school? Use these words. → V Transport, p. 221

71/3 c)

submarine · tram · helicopter · plane · boat · motorbike · skateboard · underground

I go to school by bus but I'd like to go by ....

7 (SONG) A postcard from Margate

2, 19

Singt das Lied in Gruppen.

(Chorus): This is a postcard from Margate,
It's where I am.
A postcard from Margate,
I really like it here.
A postcard from Margate,
I want to have a nice time here.
A postcard from Margate,
From Margate with love.

I took my bags and I went on a trip,
To Margate in England, in England.
I'd like to visit friends, and have a cup of tea,
Maybe in the park, it's nice to be here! *(Chorus)*

You lovely old town, here I come again,
You've always been the best part of England.
I'd like to play frisbee on the beach,
And I'd like to stay a little longer! *(Chorus)*

Language detectives → G14, p. 173

Did you like Margate, Holly? – Yes, it was great.
Did you have fish and chips? – No, I'm a vegetarian.

Wie bildest du eine Frage in der Vergangenheit?

Did you send me a postcard?

No, Jay.

8 Ask questions about last weekend.

a) Put the words in the right order. → ○ p. 145

72/4a)

1. Jay • did • to Margate • go • ?
   Did Jay go to Margate?
2. go with • Holly • her mum • did • ?
3. to the shops • Holly and her dad • go • did • ?
4. have • did • fish and chips • Holly's dad • ?
5. by bus • did • go • they • ?
6. Margate • like • Holly • did • ?

Suche zuerst das Wort „did". Das steht immer als Erstes.

b) Answer the questions.

72/4b)

9 (SPEAKING) Ask a partner. → M Double circle, p. 178

72/5

A: Did you	go shopping / swimming play football / netball / … watch TV / a DVD …	yesterday?

B: Yes, it was great / cool / … !
No, I was busy / tired / … .

10 Complete the dialogue.

73/6

Jay is with his brother, Shahid. Put in the right question words.

How | Where | What

1. ___ did you do yesterday, Shahid? – **I went to London**, Jay.
   What did you do yesterday, Shahid?
2. ___ did you go there? – I went **by bus**, Jay.
3. ___ did you do in London? – **I bought a new T-shirt.**
4. ___ did you buy it, Shahid? – I bought it **at a sports shop**.
5. ___ did you do in the afternoon? – **I went to the cinema**.
6. ___ did you watch? – **Lucky Number**. It's a cool movie!

GRAMMAR → G14, p. 173

Wenn es ein Fragewort gibt, stellst du es vor das Wort **did**:

Where **did** you go on Sunday?

73/7 **11** (SPEAKING) **What did Dave and Jay do yesterday?**

a) Look at the picture. Ask questions and answer them. → ○ p. 145

Where did / What did / When did / Did	+	Jay / Jay and Dave / they	+	go yesterday? / do? / have for lunch? / have fun? / play?

A: Where did Jay go yesterday?
B: He went to Dave's house.

had fun
had two pizzas
played computer games
played in Dave's room
played in the afternoon

b) Write about Jay's day.

Jay went to Dave's house yesterday.
They ....

12 (YOUR TURN) **My day trip** → V Activities in town, p. 226

73/8 a) Think of a day trip to a town. It can be a fantasy trip. Make notes.

My day trip

Sunday morning – went to the zoo with my family – by car – saw tigers and elephants – had a nice day

STUDY SKILLS

Wenn du dir Notizen machst, schreibst du keine ganzen Sätze, sondern nur die wichtigsten Wörter auf. Manchmal hilft es dir, wenn du Antworten auf diese Fragen findest: **When?**, **Where?**, **What?**, **Who?**, **How?**.

b) Ask a partner about her or his day trip.

Where did you go?	I went to ....
When did you go there?	I went on ....
How did you go there?	I went by ....
What did you do there?	I ....
Did you like it?	Yes, it was nice. / It was OK.
...	...

Ich kann mich über einen Tagesausflug unterhalten. ✓

Adventure on the Cutty Sark

1 What can you find in an attic? → M Think – pair – share, p. 178

2 (READING) Read about Dave's afternoon in the attic.

2, 20

"Sid!" Dave can't find his cat. Is Sid in the attic? "Sid?" There are a lot of boxes. Dave opens the boxes and finds a very old book. "Diary of Jim Preston, 1885," he reads. "Wow! He was my great-great-grandad!" He opens the book …

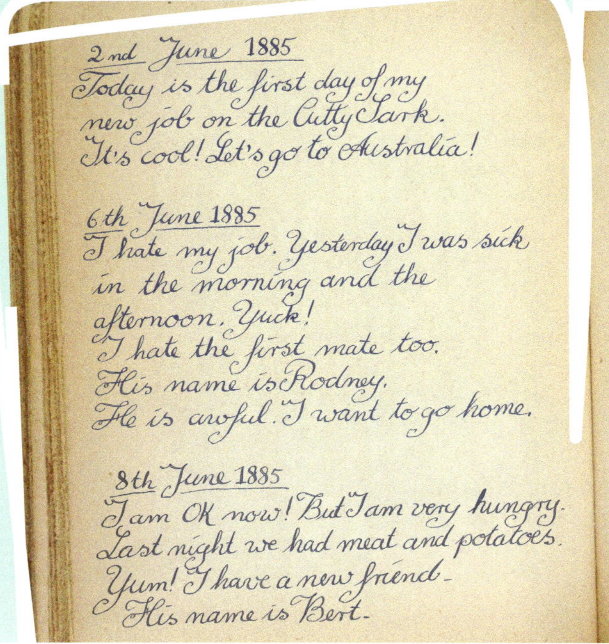

2nd June 1885
Today is the first day of my new job on the Cutty Sark. It's cool! Let's go to Australia!

6th June 1885
I hate my job. Yesterday I was sick in the morning and the afternoon. Yuck!
I hate the first mate too.
His name is Rodney.
He is awful. I want to go home.

8th June 1885
I am OK now! But I am very hungry.
Last night we had meat and potatoes.
Yum! I have a new friend.
His name is Bert.

3 Finish the sentences.

1. In the box in the attic there was ….
2. The Cutty Sark went to ….

STUDY SKILLS

Viele Wörter kannst du sofort verstehen, weil sie im Deutschen genauso oder ähnlich sind: *job* – Job, *hungry* – hungrig, *man overboard* – Mann über Bord.
Wenn du aber doch einmal unsicher bist, kannst du die unbekannten Wörter auch in der Wortliste hinten im Buch nachschauen.

11th June 1885
Yesterday there was a storm.
The waves were very big.
I was scared. Then there was a shout.
"Man overboard!"
The first mate was
in the water!
Some men helped him
with a rope.
Rodney was very
scared.

12th September 1885
Australia! There are beautiful
beaches here.
We saw a big shark in the water
and I didn't want to go swimming!
Bert and I were very busy.
We put bags of wool on the ship.
The wool is from sheep.
There are a lot of sheep in Australia.
Life on the Cutty Sark isn't easy,
but it's exciting!

12th September 1885

"Miaow!" says Sid.
"There you are, Sid!" says Dave.
"Look at this diary. It's cool!

4 Find it in the diary.

 4/1–2

1. A new friend
   That's 8th June.
2. Sharks and wool
3. The Cutty Sark is cool.
4. Storm!
5. Rodney is awful!

5 Choose one of the tasks.

 74/3

a) What did Dave write in his diary that night? Write a text.

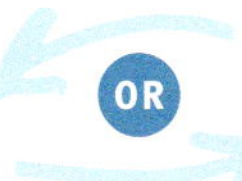

b) What did Dave tell Luke on the phone that night? Act a phone call.

went to the attic this morning – there was a diary in a box – Jim Preston's diary – was my great-great-grandad! – worked on the Cutty Sark – went to Australia – saw sharks and sheep – life was exciting

Ich kann Auszüge aus einem Tagebuch verstehen. 

Sights in Greenwich

The **Cutty Sark** is a very beautiful old ship. It was the fastest ship in the world.
120 years ago the Cutty Sark went from Greenwich to Australia.

The **Royal Observatory** is an interesting museum with old clocks and maps of the world.
The Meridian Line is there too. One side of the line is in the east and the other side is in the west.

1 Lies die Texte über Greenwich.

Welche der zwei Sehenswürdigkeiten würdest du gern in Greenwich anschauen? Warum gerade diese?

2 Spielt den Dialog zu dritt.

Du bist in der Touristeninformation in Greenwich und hilfst einer deutschen Touristin, die kein Englisch spricht.

Touristin: Kannst du ihn bitte fragen, was es in Greenwich zu sehen gibt?
Du: What can she see in Greenwich?
Angestellter: Well, there's the Cutty Sark and the Royal Observatory.
Du: Es gibt …
Touristin: Was ist die Cutty Sark?
Du: What …
Angestellter: It's a very beautiful old ship.
Du: Es ist …
Touristin: Das klingt gut. Könntest du ihn bitte auch fragen, wie viel der Eintritt kostet?
Du: How much …
Angestellter: Er yes, let me see … that's twelve pounds.
Du: Das kostet …
Touristin: Uff, London ist aber teuer! Na ja. Bedanke dich bitte für mich. Und dir natürlich auch vielen Dank für deine Hilfe. Auf Wiedersehen!
Du: Thank … Kein Problem. Auf Wiedersehen!

MEDIATION SKILLS

Wenn du zwischen zwei Personen vermittelst, musst du nicht jedes Wort übersetzen.
Sage nur das, was die Touristin wissen will.

Ich kann touristische Informationen über Greenwich weitergeben. 

Out and about in Greenwich

In dieser „Filmecke" triffst du wieder die zwei Freunde Jinsoo und Marley.

VIEWING SKILLS

Bevor du dir einen Film ansiehst, überlege: Was weißt du schon über das Thema?

1 Talk about Greenwich.

What do you know about Greenwich? (Was weißt du schon über Greenwich?)

CULTURE

Die Briefkästen in England sind rot. Die Busse in London sind auch meistens rot.

2 (VIEWING) Watch the film.

10
5/1–2 a) Put the pictures in the right order.

A

B

10

C

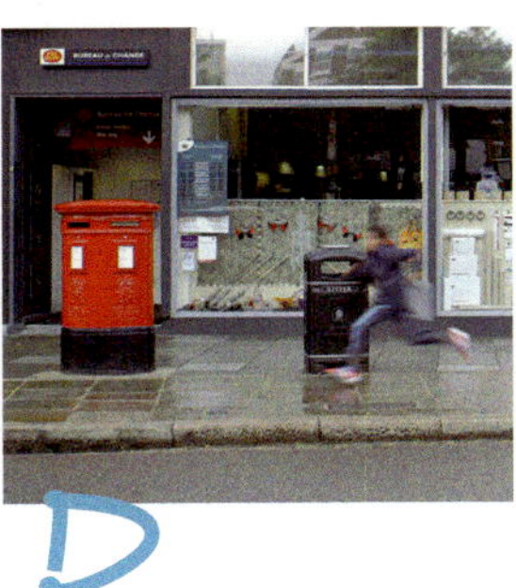
D

b) Finish the sentences.

1. In the film you can see ....
2. Jinsoo and Marley buy popcorn at ....
3. The book in the shop is ....
4. They go to the post office to send ....

- Greenwich Park
- Greenwich Market
- £7.50
- a present
- the Cutty Sark
- at a café
- £8.50
- an invitation

3 (SPEAKING) Make a dialogue.

75/3

A: Excuse me. How much is this book?
B: Let's see ... It's £3.00.
A: Can I come back for it later?
B: Yes, that's OK. See you!

pen	T-shirt	...
£4.00	£5.00	 ...

Ich kann einen Film zum Thema „Einkaufen" verstehen.

Checklist

Ich kann meinen Wohnort vorstellen. 

I live in .... • My house / flat is in .... • There is .... / There are .... • My favourite place is ....

76

Ich kann über mein Wochenende sprechen. 

On Saturday / Sunday I was / we were .... • Yesterday I went .... • At the weekend I played .... • In the afternoon I watched .... • Then I listened to ....

76

Ich kann mich über einen Tagesausflug unterhalten. 

Where did you ... ? I went to ... • When did you ... ? On Sunday / In the afternoon .... • What did you ... ? We played .... • Did you like it?

76

Ich kann Auszüge aus einem Tagebuch verstehen. 

77

Ich kann touristische Informationen über Greenwich weitergeben. 

77

Ich kann einen Film zum Thema „Einkaufen“ verstehen. 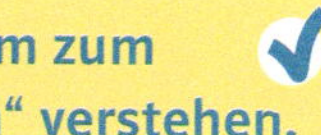

(TASK) A mystery quiz

Step 1

Read the newspaper report and take notes.

daily news

Mystery at Greenwich School: Laptop missing

GREENWICH: On Friday afternoon somebody broke into the school in Baker Street and stole a laptop from the computer room. Greenwich police are investigating. "Nothing else is missing," they say. "Why did they steal a laptop?"

Did you see anything unusual in Baker Street on Friday afternoon? Then please tell the police.

laptop missing – Laptop verschwunden
somebody – jemand
break into, broke into – einbrechen
steal, stole – stehlen
nothing else is missing – nichts anderes fehlt
are investigating – ermitteln
anything unusual – etwas Ungewöhnliches

Diese Wörter habe ich für dich schon nachgeschlagen.

STUDY SKILLS

Um herauszufinden, was passiert ist, finde Antworten auf diese Fragen:
What?
When?
Where?
Who?
Schreibe Stichwörter auf.

Step 2

Look at the pictures and listen.

a) Look at the pictures. Guess who stole the laptop. Talk in groups of four.

Mr Welch (school caretaker)

Mrs Miller (lives in Baker Street)

2, 21 b) Listen to the police interviews (Verhöre) and take notes.

c) In groups of four, talk about your notes. Who stole the laptop?

Achte besonders auf die Uhrzeiten in den beiden Interviews. Vergleiche sie mit den Bildern.

Step 3

Write a newspaper report.

Complete the newspaper report about the thief.

found – *fand*; thief – *Dieb/-in*; gave back – *gab zurück*

daily news **Laptop back at Greenwich school**

The police found the laptop thief yesterday. It was .... broke into ... on ... and stole .... The police gave the laptop back to the school.

Step 4

Find the best report and give feedback. → M Gallery walk, p. 180

Put a smiley on your favourite report. You can also write a comment.

Good job! What an interesting ending!

Well done! I like your report!

Extra practice

○ 1 (WRITING) Match the words. (nach 91/2)

a) Match the words. Write the words.

old ✓ | Cutty | Brook | centre | Lane | pool
shopping | swimming | favourite | town ✓ | place | Sark

1. old town
2. Cutty —

b) Put in the words.

1. Greenwich is an — — .
   Greenwich is an old town.
2. The — — is a famous ship.
3. There are lots of shops in the — — .
4. Dave and Luke often go to the — — .
5. Holly's flat is in — — .
6. Luke's — — is the park.

Verwende die Wortpaare aus Aufgabe a)!

○ 2 What did they do? (nach 95/10)

played | saw | went
did ✓ | watched | played

Put in the words.

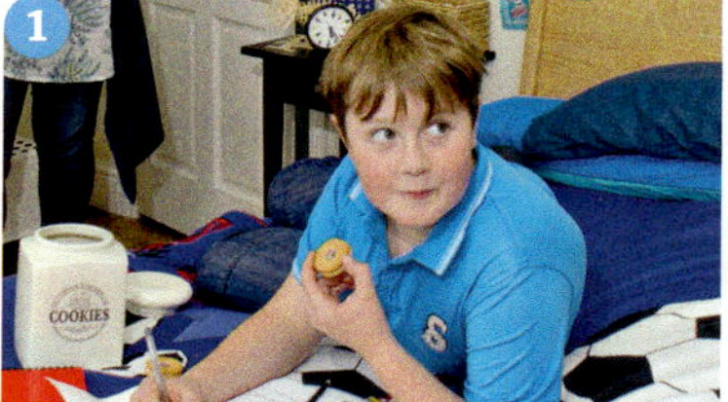

Dave — his homework yesterday.

Olivia — with her sister last night.

Dave — TV with his family on Sunday.

Olivia — computer games at the weekend.

Dave — to the cinema yesterday.

Olivia — her mum on Saturday.

1. Dave did his homework yesterday.

○ 3 How do they go there? (nach 97/4)

Find the words.

Olivia: I often go —— .

Luke: Let's go —— !

Jay: We can go to town —— .

Holly: I go to school —— .

Holly: We went to Margate —— .

by train | on foot | by car | by bus | by bike ✓

1. Olivia: I often go by bike.

○ 4 Match the questions with the answers. (nach 99/11)

1. Where did you go, Holly?
2. When did you go?
3. How did you go?
4. Did you have fish and chips?
5. Did you go shopping?
6. Did you like Margate?

A Dad had fish and chips. I had chips.
B Yes. It's a nice town.
C We went on Sunday.
D Yes, I bought postcards.
E We went by car.
F I went to Margate with my dad.

○ 5 (WRITING) Put the words into two groups. (nach 101/4)

places in town	I can go by …
café	ship

ship ✓ | café ✓ | shop | bus | car | beach | train | park | bike

Hier geht es um das Sprechen.

Asking the way

2, 22 Luke and Dave are at the swimming pool. A tourist talks to them.

Man: Excuse me, can you tell me the way to the Tourist Information Centre, please?

Luke: The Tourist Information Centre? Yes, that's easy. Go along this road.

Man: OK.

Luke: Go straight on, then turn right into King William Walk.

Man: King William Walk. OK.

Luke: Go along the road. Then you can see the Cutty Sark on the left. The Tourist Information Centre is on the right, opposite the Cutty Sark.

Man: Great, thank you.

Dave and Luke: You're welcome.

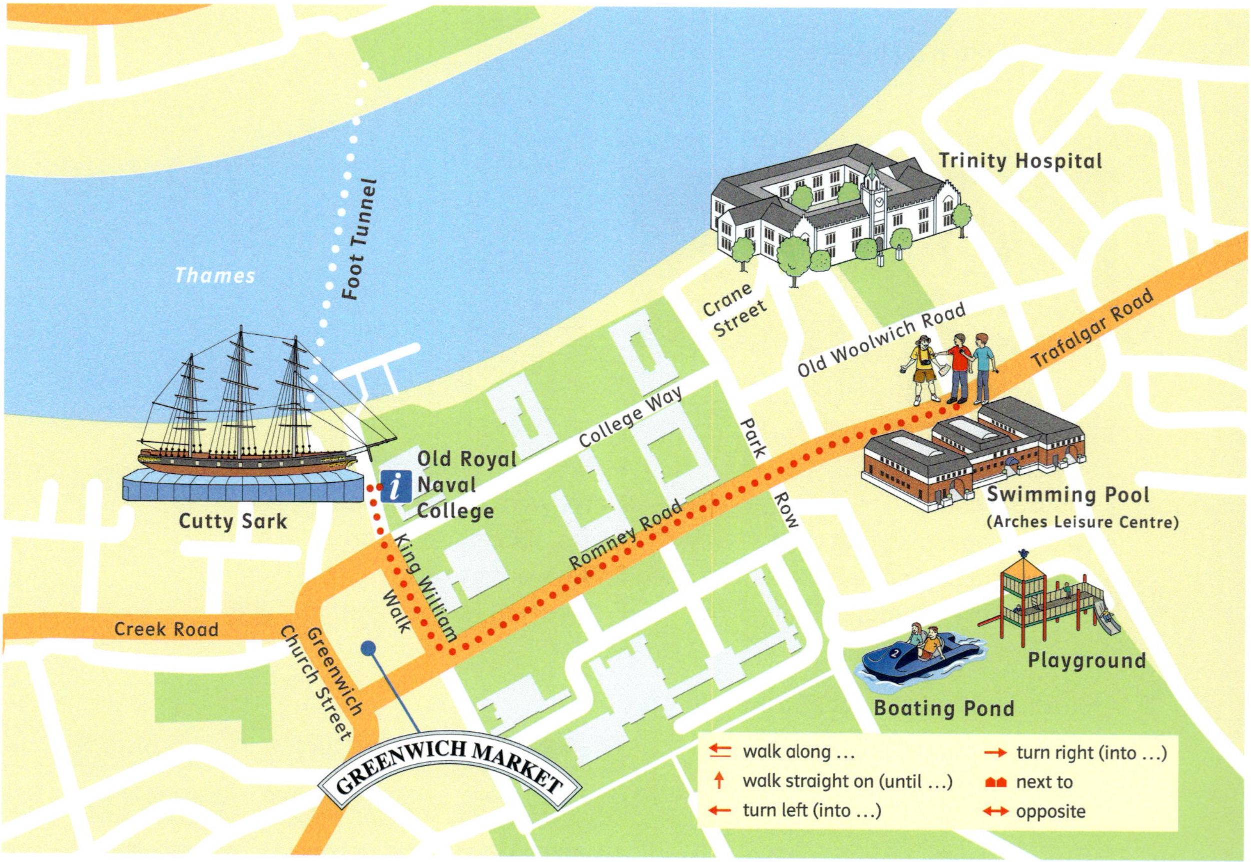

Thames
Foot Tunnel
Trinity Hospital
Crane Street
Old Woolwich Road
Trafalgar Road
College Way
Park Row
Old Royal Naval College
Cutty Sark
Swimming Pool (Arches Leisure Centre)
Romney Road
King William Walk
Creek Road
Greenwich Church Street
Playground
Boating Pond
GREENWICH MARKET

- walk along …
- walk straight on (until …)
- turn left (into …)
- turn right (into …)
- next to
- opposite

1 Listen to the dialogue. Then read it with a partner.

Es ist wichtig, dass ihr deutlich sprecht und einzelne Wörter betont. Hört euch das Muster mehrmals an und sprecht die Sätze genauso nach.

2 Make a dialogue.

You are at the hospital. Your partner asks the way to Greenwich Market. Look at the map. Make the dialogue.

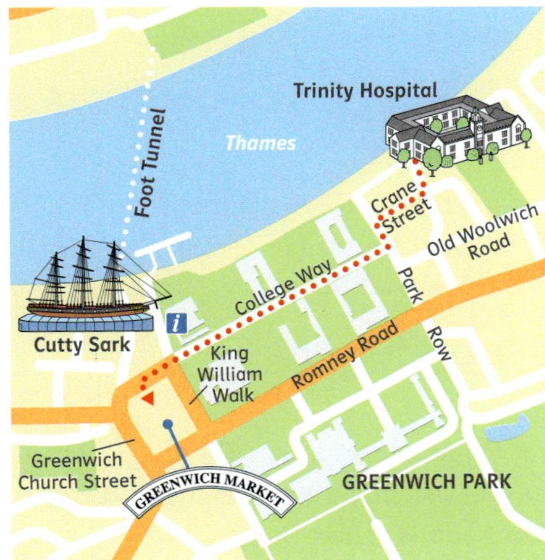

Orientiert euch am Muster links. Dort findet ihr schon viele Informationen, die ihr für euren Dialog nutzen könnt. Wenn du deine Partnerin oder deinen Partner nicht verstehst, sagst du: „Sorry, can you say that again?"

3 Practise your dialogue.

Übt euren Dialog mehrfach. Denkt an die Aussprache. Macht euch als Hilfe eine Skizze mit der Wegbeschreibung.

4 Act it in class.

-81/2

Um euren Dialog vorzutragen, lernt ihn auswendig oder nehmt die Skizze als Hilfestellung. Beim Üben könnt ihr euch durch Bewegungen unterstützen und z. B. die Richtungen anzeigen.

Find more online: fe76m3

Am Ende dieser Unit kann ich …
- sagen, ob mir ein Ausflugsziel gefällt.
- ein Telefongespräch führen.
- eine Postkarte schreiben.
- eine Geschichte über eine Klassenfahrt verstehen, Informationen von Schildern auf dem Land weitergeben und einen Film zum Thema „Geocaching“ verstehen.

11 2, 23

Unit 6
A trip to the country

<1> About us <2> The Animals <3> The Farm <4> Activities <5> Food

Welcome!

<1>

Highfield Farm is great for a trip to the country.
Come and meet us. We're the farmers, Frank and Mary Turner.
And this is our daughter, Rachel.

<2>

There are a lot of animals on Highfield Farm.
There are horses and sheep. You can feed the chickens.
And everyone loves our farm dog, Barry.

1 Find out about the farm.

82/1

a) Match the words with the pictures.

food | activities | animals | the farmers | a modern farm

b) Make sentences.

You can	meet	good food.
	feed	the farmers.
	eat	rock climbing.
	go	the chickens.

c) What else can you see in the pictures?

2 (LISTENING) Choose the right answers.

2, 24

1. Last year a boy fed …
   the chickens. • the horses.
2. A teacher was at the farm …
   in June. • in July.
3. A girl liked …
   the farm dog. • the food.
4. Rock climbing was …
   easy. • scary.

<1> About us <2> The Animals <3> The Farm <4> Activities <5> Food

New!

<3>

Highfield Farm is a modern farm. Our sheep have GPS collars. Frank loves his new tractor.

<4>

There are a lot of interesting activities near the farm. You can go rock climbing and canoeing!

Hundreds of teachers and students came to Highfield Farm last year. What did they say? Click here to listen.

<5>

Food is great on the farm! Everyone loves our breakfasts. You're a vegetarian? You needn't worry – we have good food for you too!

3 (YOUR TURN) Highfield Farm → V In the country, p. 233

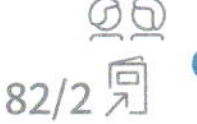
82/2

a) Would you like to go to Highfield Farm with your tutor group? Why?

b) Talk with a partner.

A: Would you like to go to Highfield Farm?
B: I'd like to go there.
I think animals are nice.
Rock climbing is fun.
And you?
A: …

CULTURE

In England gibt es manchmal ein warmes Frühstück. Es besteht unter anderem aus Ei, Toast, Würstchen, Speck und Bohnen in Tomatensoße. Würdest du gern so ein Frühstück essen?

I wouldn't like to

tractors | farms | …

scary | easy | awful | …

canoeing

Ich kann sagen, ob mir ein Ausflugsziel gefällt. 

Hier lerne ich, ein Telefongespräch zu führen.

A phone call to Olivia

1 (READING) Read about a day at Highfield Farm.

2, 25

Holly phoned Olivia yesterday. Luke, Dave and Jay were with her.

Olivia: Hello?

Holly: Hi, is that you, Olivia? It's me, Holly! How are you? Are you OK now?

Olivia: Yes, I'm OK, thanks.

Holly: I'm at the farm. Luke, Dave and Jay are here.

Luke, Dave and Jay: Hi Olivia!

Olivia: Hi! How was your day? What did you do?

Holly: Oh, it was great. I went horse riding! And we had a picnic. That was fun. The boys weren't in my group. Dave and Luke were with Mr Swindon. They went canoeing, and Jay went rock climbing.

Olivia: Rock climbing? Wow!

Jay: It was great. But it wasn't easy. We wore helmets.

Holly: Sorry, Olivia – I must stop now. It's time for the night walk. I must wear warm clothes for that. See you soon!

Olivia: OK! Bye!

2 What did they do?

Was ist mit Olivia? Sie hat sich den Arm gebrochen und musste leider zu Hause bleiben!

a) Are the pictures right or wrong? → ○ p. 146

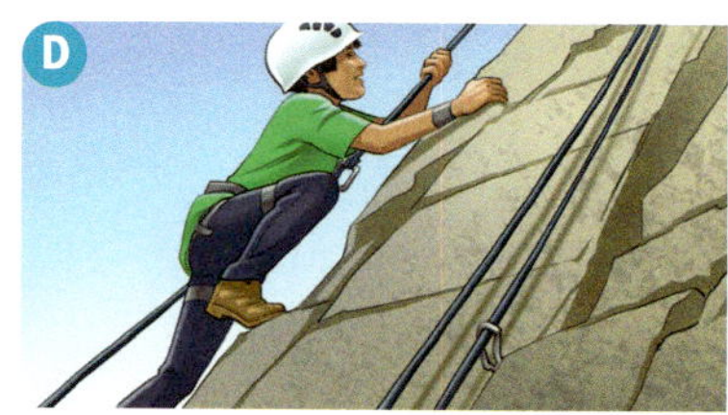

Picture A is right/wrong.

b) Make a sentence for each right picture.

Picture A: Holly went horse riding.

3 (LISTENING) What do they need for the night walk? → V Clothes, p. 228

83/1–2 a) Before you listen, collect words for clothes.

2, 26 b) Look at the pictures and listen to Mr Swindon.
What must the students have for the night walk?

trainers

skirt

socks

coat

trousers

sweatshirt

Language tip → G15, p. 174

They **must** wear warm clothes.
They **needn't** have food.

4 (WRITING) Make a chart. → M Bus stop, p. 181

83/3 Make two lists: one with nouns (like 'coat'), one with adjectives (like 'funny').

cool • coat • sweatshirt • nice • interesting • skirt
T-shirt • funny • trousers • great • socks • trainers

NOUNS	ADJECTIVES
coat	funny
...	...

5 (SPEAKING) Make a clothes dialogue.

a) Make dialogues with the words from exercise 4. → ○ p. 147

A: Hey, I like your T-shirt! It's cool. • Hey, I like your socks! They're great!
B: Oh. Thank you!
A: You're welcome!

b) Make more dialogues. → V Clothes, p. 228

shorts · cap · blouse · top · colourful · chic · pretty

6 (WRITING) Make a poem.

1. Choose a 'clothes' word.
2. Add two adjectives to describe it.
3. Add three more lines with three, four and three words.
4. Add two adjectives.
5. Find an interesting last word.

SWEATSHIRT
RED, BIG
ALWAYS VERY WARM
GOOD ON NIGHT WALKS
PRESENT FROM DAD
COOL, NICE
GREAT!

Language detectives → G16, p. 175

Jay: Hi Mum. I was in the rock climbing group yesterday. It was great. Luke and Dave? They were in Mr Swindon's group.

Dave: Hi Dad. We were in Mr Swindon's group. Holly? She was in the horse riding group.

Schau dir die Sätze an. Wann nimmst du was? Wann nimmst du were?
Schau dir an, um welche Person es geht.

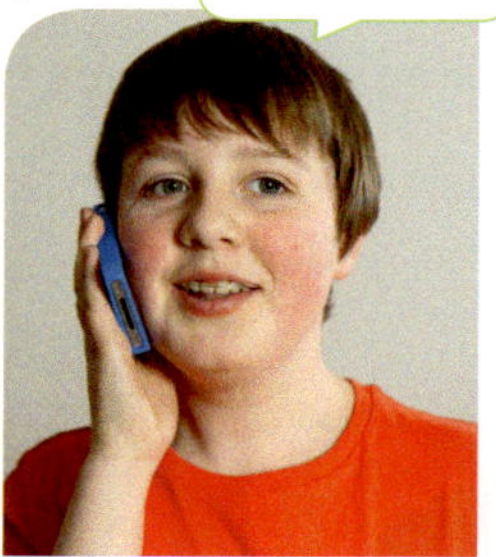

7 Choose the right words.

84/4–5

1. Luke was in Dave's group yesterday.
2. It —— exciting.
3. Holly —— in the horse riding group.
4. Jay and Dave: We —— in the garden this morning, with Barry.
5. The farmers —— nice yesterday.
6. Rachel: I —— in the house and helped my mum.

was
were

8 Complete the sentences. → M Bus stop, p. 181

a) Match the sentence parts. → ○ p. 147

1. Holly	wasn't easy!
2. Horse riding	weren't in the rock climbing group.
3. Luke and Dave	was fun. The sandwiches were cool!
4. Jay: Rock climbing	wasn't in the canoeing group.
5. Mr Swindon	wasn't in the horse riding group.
6. Holly: The picnic	was great. Holly liked her horse.

GRAMMAR → G16, p. 175

was + not = wasn't
were + not = weren't

b) Put in the right word: was or were, wasn't or weren't.

84/6

The students from 7 RS (1) weren't at school last week.
And they (2) at home. Where were they?
They (3) on Highfield Farm. But Olivia (4) at the farm with Holly.
She (5) at home. That (6) very interesting!

35/7–8

9 What did Holly's mum ask?

a) Put the words in the right order. → p. 148

1. the horse riding trip • was • yesterday • how • ?
   How was the horse riding trip yesterday?
2. in your group • Luke and Dave • were • ?
3. nice • your horse • was • ?
4. was • the picnic • where • ?
5. good • was • the food • ?
6. you • when • at the farm • were • ?

GRAMMAR → G16, p. 175

Were you at school yesterday?
How **was** your day?

b) Match Holly's answers with the questions from a).

No, they went canoeing. • Yes, very nice. Her name was Rosie. • We were back at five o'clock. • It was near the river. • It was fun. Horse riding is cool! • Yes. It was great! The sandwiches were brilliant.

10 (YOUR TURN) A phone call → V How was it?, p. 232

79–86/2

Make a phone call. A is at Highfield Farm. B is at home.

A: Hi! Is that you, Olivia? It's me, Holly.
B: Hi Holly! How are you?
A: I'm OK! I went rock climbing today.
B: Wow! How was it?
A: It was great. I wore my new trainers. …
Oh, I must stop now. It's time for lunch.
B: OK. See you soon! Bye!
A: Bye!

horse riding | canoeing | …

It was brilliant. | It was OK. | It was awful. | …

I wore my new coat. | I wore my new T-shirt. | …

for bed | for the night walk | …

Ich kann ein Telefongespräch führen. ✓

Dear Olivia …

1 (READING) **Read Holly's postcard to Olivia.**

2, 27
87/1

18th May

Dear Olivia,
Hi from Highfield Farm!
It's great here. Last night
we went on a night walk!
It was scary. We didn't
have torches so it was very
dark. Guess what!
We saw some bats
and we heard funny noises…
Then it rained. Luke and
Jay got wet because they
didn't wear their coats.
See you soon,
Holly Luke
Jay Dave

EXETER
19. 5. 14
DEVON
50P
Olivia Fraser
52 Begbie Road
Greenwich
London SE3 8DA

2 Finish the sentences.

a) What are the words? → p. 148

1. Holly sent Olivia a postcard from Highfield Farm.
2. Last night they went on a night —— .
3. They didn't have torches so it was very —— .
4. They saw some —— and heard funny —— .
5. Then it —— .
6. Luke and Jay got —— .

b) Answer the questions.

1. Why was the night walk scary?
2. Why did Luke and Jay get wet?
3. What were the funny noises? Any idea?

CULTURE

Englische Adressen sehen anders aus als deutsche. Welche Unterschiede fallen dir auf?

What's the weather like today?

3 (LISTENING) What's the weather like?

87/2

a) Before you listen: What's the weather like today?

2, 28

b) Listen and point.

0°C
25°C

1. sunny 2. wet 3. cold 4. windy 5. hot 6. cloudy

4 (SPEAKING) Talk about the weather.

87/3

a) Make dialogues. → ○ p. 149

A: It's sunny today. Let's have a picnic.
B: That's a good idea! Let's do that.

Or:

A: It's wet today. We can't have a picnic.
B: OK. Let's watch TV.

sunny | wet | cold | … | have a picnic | play football | watch TV

b) Make more dialogues. → V Weather, p. 229

cool | dry | mild | foggy

5 (SOUNDS) Listen, read and say.

2, 29
87/4

[w]: We went for a walk. The weather was windy and wet.
[v]: Dave is in the living room this evening.
[v] and [w]: On Wednesday evening we watched TV.

[w] and [v]

6 (SONG) Living in the countryside

2, 30

Singt das Lied und klatscht dazu.

Here on our farm there's a lot to do,
Out in the field, and in the garden too,
From early in the morning until the sun
goes down again.

(Chorus): Come on let's get something done,
There's a lot to do for everyone,
Here on our farm, here on our farm.

Living in the countryside,
living in the countryside,
There's a lot to see, there's a lot to see,
for you and me.

The tractor is ready to plough the field,
We can feed the chickens and climb a tree.
There's food from the garden and an apple
pie for me!

(Chorus)

Language detectives → G17, p. 176

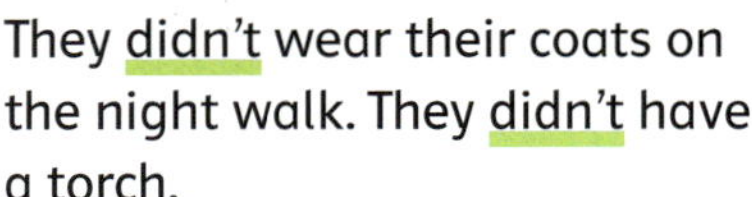

They didn't wear their coats on the night walk. They didn't have a torch.

She didn't get wet last night.

Was drückt das didn't aus? Wo muss es stehen?

7 Match the pictures with the sentences.

1. Mr Swindon didn't see the bats. That's picture C.
2. Holly didn't get wet last night.
3. Jay didn't listen to Mr Turner.
4. Dave and Luke didn't go rock climbing.
5. Jay didn't like the chickens.

8 Complete the sentences.

a) Find the words. → ○ p. 149

88/5 

1. The students didn't have torches on the night walk.
2. Luke and Jay — coats.
3. Holly — sandwiches with meat in them.
4. Jay — football with Dave and Luke.
5. Dave — a postcard to his mum and dad.
6. Olivia — to Highfield Farm.

didn't send | didn't play | didn't eat | didn't have ✓ | didn't go | didn't wear

b) What didn't you do yesterday?

88/6

wear | watch | play | ...

9/7–8

9 What did Luke write?

a) Put in the verbs. (Ein Verb bleibt übrig!) → p. 149

didn't get | talked ✓ | went | had | played | looked at | didn't have

Dear Mum and Dad,
Highfield Farm is great!
On the first day we (1) talked to the farmer. We (2) his tractor.
I (3) canoeing, but I (4) wet.
Yesterday the weather was awful.
We (5) a picnic; we (6) our sandwiches in the house.
Say hi to Jamie and Irina.
See you soon!
Luke

b) What did Luke's dad say about the postcard?

Start like this:
There's a postcard from Luke from Highfield Farm.
He likes the farm. (1) On the first day they .... (2) They ....

10 (YOUR TURN) A postcard → V In the country, p. 233

89/9

Write a postcard to a friend or to your family.

Dear Jonas,
Hi from Highfield Farm! It's great here.
Sorry I didn't phone you.
This morning I played with Barry, the farm dog.
The weather is sunny.
See you next week.
Noah

brilliant | awful | ...
answer your text message
went rock climbing | had a picnic | ...
wet | windy | cold | hot | ...

WRITING SKILLS

Schreibe die Postkarte zuerst auf einem Blatt Papier vor. Zeige sie einem Partner. Kann sie oder er alles verstehen? Hat sie oder er noch Tipps für dich? Korrigiere deinen Text und schreibe ihn auf eine richtige Postkarte.

Ich kann eine Postkarte schreiben. ✓

Stuck in the mud

1 **Think before you read.** → M Think – pair – share, p. 178

Why do the sheep on the farm have GPS collars?

2 (READING) **Read the story.**

2, 31

On their third day at the farm Dave and Jay met Rachel in her wheelchair.
"There's a problem with one of our sheep!" Rachel said. "Can you help me?"
"Yes, what can we do?" asked Dave.
"All the sheep have GPS collars," said Rachel. "You can see the sheep on the computer. This sheep is next to the river. That's not good."
"Where's your dad?" asked Jay.
"I don't know. He didn't answer his mobile," said Rachel.
"We can look for the sheep," said Dave.
"OK. Thanks!" said Rachel.

Dave and Jay went to the river.

"I can see the sheep!" said Dave. "It's stuck in the mud next to the river."

Dave went to where the sheep was. "Come on, Jay!" he said.

"That mud is awful!" said Jay. "I don't want dirty jeans!"

"We must help that sheep, Jay!" said Dave. "Go behind the sheep and push it. I can pull it!"

Jay went behind the sheep and pushed. There was mud on his jeans.

"Well, my sweatshirt isn't dirty," he said.

Dave pulled and Jay pushed. The sheep's feet came out of the mud and Jay fell on his face.

"Baa!" said the sheep. It went to the other sheep.

Jay got up. Now his sweatshirt was dirty too!

3 Which sentence is right?

)/1–2

1. Rachel doesn't know where one of the sheep is.
2. One of the sheep is stuck in the mud near the river.

4 Match the sentence parts.

90/3

1. Rachel saw the sheep	next to the river.
2. The boys helped	and the sheep came out of the mud.
3. The sheep was stuck in the mud	and his sweatshirt was dirty too.
4. Jay pushed, Dave pulled	because Mr Turner didn't answer his mobile.
5. Jay fell on his face	on her computer.

5 Do one of the tasks.

a) Do you like the story? Talk to a partner.

I like/don't like the story because …

- Dave and Jay help Rachel
- boring
- nice pictures
- exciting
- I don't like/like sheep …
- funny

OR

b) Write Jay's postcard to his brother.

Dear Shahid,
This morning Dave and I helped • sheep was stuck in the mud • pushed • fell in the mud • clothes were dirty • Oh no! • See you soon …

Ich kann eine Geschichte über eine Klassenfahrt verstehen.

Signs in the country

1 Was steht auf den Schildern?

Du bist mit deiner Familie im Urlaub in Großbritannien.
Deine kleine Schwester fragt dich, was diese Schilder bedeuten.

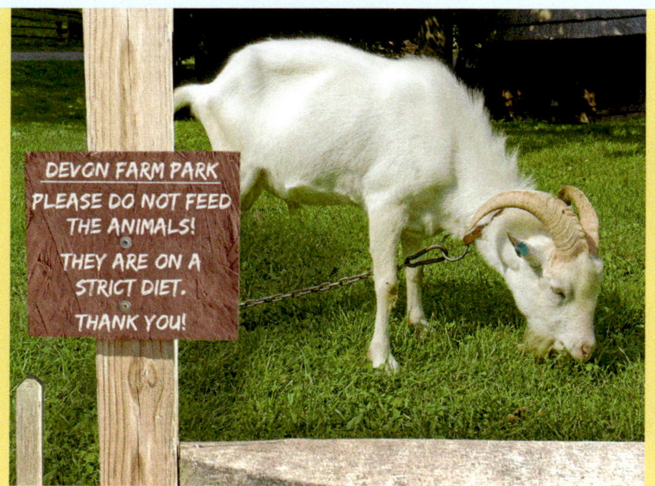

DEVON FARM PARK
PLEASE DO NOT FEED THE ANIMALS!
THEY ARE ON A STRICT DIET.
THANK YOU!

1. Darf man die Ziegen füttern?

← CAR PARK 200m
Okehampton Castle
1,000 years old! The biggest castle in Devon – Now in ruins!
Open every day in summer, closed in winter
Adults: £3.80 Children (5 – 15): £2.30

2. Was gibt es hier zu sehen?
Was kostet der Eintritt für Erwachsene und Kinder?

TOMATOES
FARM FRESH
POTATOES
BEANS
The Taylors' farm shop
Fresh fruit for sale!
Cheese, marmalade, eggs
For a great weekend: cakes and puddings
Come in and have a look!
OPEN

3. Was kann man in diesem Laden kaufen?

Welcome to Uplands Outdoor Centre
Day visitors
Full day: 9:15 a.m. – 4:45 p.m.
Morning: 9:15 a.m. – 12:15 p.m.
Afternoon: 1:30 p.m. – 4:45 p.m.
Families: full day: £100, half day: £50
Choose any or all of these activities:
abseiling, mountain biking, canoeing,
rock climbing, horse riding

4. Was kann man hier unternehmen?
Was kostet der Eintritt?

Ich kann Informationen von Schildern auf dem Land weitergeben. ✓

A trip to the country

In dieser „Filmecke“ triffst du wieder die drei Freunde Laura, Marley und Jinsoo.

1 Talk about the country.

What can you do in the country? What do you like to do in the country?
(Was kannst du auf dem Land machen? Was machst du gerne auf dem Land?)

2 (VIEWING) Watch the film.

12 /1-3

a) Put the pictures in the right order.

A

B

C

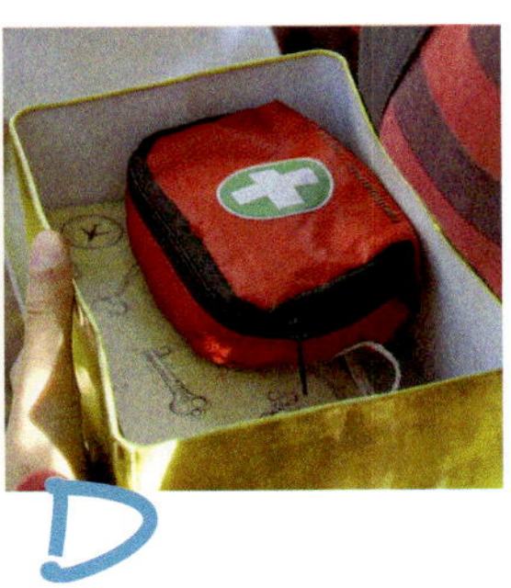

D

b) Answer the questions.

1. What colour is the first cache box?
2. What is Laura's geocaching name?
3. What animals do they find?
4. How many caches do they find?

VIEWING SKILLS

Versuche zuerst die Fragen aus dem Gedächtnis zu beantworten. Dann sieh dir den Film noch einmal an und überprüfe deine Antworten.

3 (SPEAKING) Make a dialogue.

A: Did you like the film about geocaching?
B: Yes, I liked it. It was funny.
A: I didn't like it. It wasn't very good.

Greenwich | party | ...
great | cool | ...

Ich kann einen Film zum Thema „Geocaching“ verstehen.

Checklist

Ich kann sagen, ob mir ein Ausflugsziel gefällt.

I'd like to go to .... • I wouldn't like to go to ....

92

Ich kann ein Telefongespräch führen.

Is that you? • It's me, ... • I must stop now. Bye!

92

Ich kann eine Postkarte schreiben.

Dear Olivia, • Hi from .... • See you soon!

92

Ich kann eine Geschichte über eine Klassenfahrt verstehen.

93

Ich kann Informationen von Schildern auf dem Land weitergeben.

93

Ich kann einen Film zum Thema „Geocaching“ verstehen.

(TASK) A report about a trip

Step 1

Collect ideas.

a) Choose a trip for your report: a school trip, day trip or other special day.

b) Collect ideas and make a mind map.

- **Where** did you go?
- **Who** went with you?
- **When** did you go?
- **How** did you go there?
- **What** did you do?

Herr Faber
bus
Blankenburg
we went canoeing

Step 2

Add notes about your feelings (Gefühle).

→ V How was it?, p. 232

- What did you like/what didn't you like?
- What was interesting/exciting/funny/crazy/boring/... ?
- What was your favourite activity?

Step 3

Ask the other students about your trip.

Choose an interviewer. He or she walks around and asks the other students the questions from Step 2. Take notes. You can add them to your text later.

We want to write about our trip to Blankenburg. What did you like?

I liked rock climbing. It wasn't easy, but it was fun.

Step 4

Find pictures or photos.

a) Choose two or three pictures or photos for your report.

b) Write sentences for your pictures: “We played football in this playground.”

Erinnerst du dich an die Tipps auf Seite 89?

Step 5

Write your report.

a) Write a draft (Entwurf).

- Think of an interesting title.
- Where can the pictures go?
- Add what the other students said.
- Check your draft.

b) Write your report, add your pictures and check it again.

Adventure in Blankenburg

On Wednesday, 25th May tutor group 5E went to Blankenburg. We went by bus and arrived in Blankenburg in the afternoon. On the second day we went canoeing. That was fun. In the evening we went on a night walk. We saw bats. Lukas loved rock climbing: “It wasn't easy, but it was fun.”

VIEWING SKILLS

Wenn du einen Erlebnisbericht schreibst, schreibst du über Tatsachen und über Gefühle. Du schreibst in der Vergangenheit. Überprüfe deinen Bericht: Ist er vollständig, verständlich, interessant und korrekt? Sind die Bilder gut ausgewählt?

Step 6

Show your report. → M Writers' conference, p. 181

a) Make new groups. The new group has one student from each report group.

b) Read your report to your new group and ask for feedback.

c) Do you want to put a report on the school website? Why (not)?

> The tense is right, it's the simple past.

> This report makes sense, it has all the facts.

> The photos are nice.

Extra practice

○ **1** (WRITING) **Make two mind maps.** (nach 111/3)

farm dog

animals

activities

rock climbing | sheep | horses | canoeing | horse riding | chickens | farm dog ✓

○ **2** **Match the pictures with the words.** (nach 113/3)

skirt | trousers | coat | sweatshirt ✓ | trainers | socks

1. sweatshirt
2. —

○ **3** **Put in was or were.** (nach 114/7)

1. Rachel: The students from Greenwich were at Highfield Farm.
2. Olivia: I — at home.
3. Holly: The vegetarian breakfasts — great!
4. Dave: Rock climbing — scary.
5. Jay and Holly: Mr Turner's tractor — cool.
6. Mr Windsor: The farmers — nice.
7. Mr and Mrs Turner: The students — nice too!

Wenn es sich um mehrere Personen oder Dinge handelt, brauchst du „were".

○ 4 What's the weather like? (nach 117/3)

Find the words.

Holly: Wow! It's so hot!

Mr Turner: It's — today.

Luke: It's — .

Rachel: It's — today.

Mrs Turner: It's very — .

Mr Swindon: Brrr! It's — !

windy · cold · hot ✓ · sunny · cloudy · wet

○ 5 Put the words in the right order. (nach 118/8)

1. didn't eat • an English breakfast. • Jay
   Jay didn't eat an English breakfast.
2. the chickens. • didn't like • He
3. didn't have • Holly • trainers.
4. football. • didn't play • She
5. The students • torches. • didn't have
6. the bats. • Mr Swindon • didn't see

Der Teil mit „didn't" steht hier immer als Zweites im Satz.

○ 6 Match the words. (nach 120/4)

mud
it's stuck
he pushed
dirty
river
he pulled

dreckig
er schob
Fluss
er zog
Matsch
es steckt fest

1. mud – Matsch

Diff corner

Unit 1, p.15

○ 5 (WRITING) What are the words?

Write the words.

1. sis — er → **sister**
2. mot — er
3. bro — — er
4. fa — — er
5. fami — —
6. fr — — nd

Schreib die Wörter in dein Heft ab. Welche Buchstaben fehlen hier?

mother | sister ✓ | father | friend | brother | family

Unit 1, p.16

○ 9 What can Olivia say?

1. I **am** / **is** Olivia Fraser.
2. Lucy and I **is** / **are** sisters.
3. Lucy **am** / **is** five.
4. Desmond **am** / **is** my dad.
5. Janet and Desmond **is** / **are** my mum and dad.
6. Claire **am** / **is** my dad's friend.

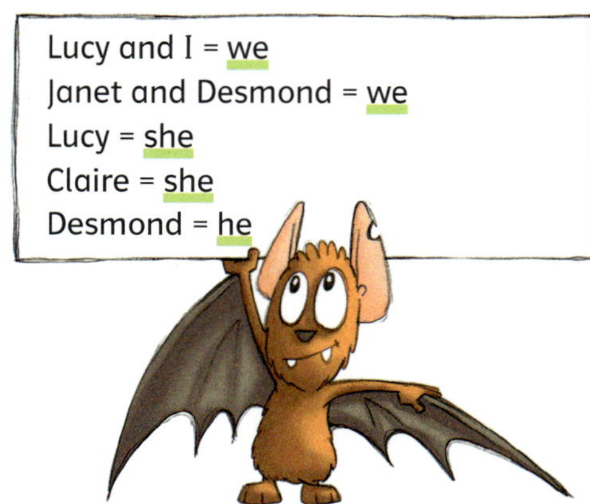

Lucy and I = we
Janet and Desmond = we
Lucy = she
Claire = she
Desmond = he

Unit 1, p.17

○ 10 What can Lucy say?

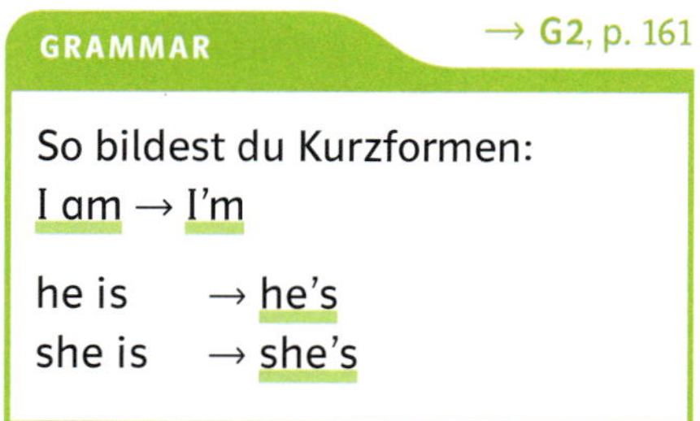

GRAMMAR → G2, p. 161

So bildest du Kurzformen:
I am → I'm

he is → he's
she is → she's

1. This is my family.
   This is my mum. **He's** / **She's** nice.
2. This is my dad. **He's** / **She's** cool.
3. This is my sister, Olivia. **He's** / **She's** eleven.
4. Janet is Olivia's mum. **She's** / **I'm** nice too.
5. This is me. **He's** / **I'm** five!

Unit 1, p.19

○ 5 Who or what is in the room?

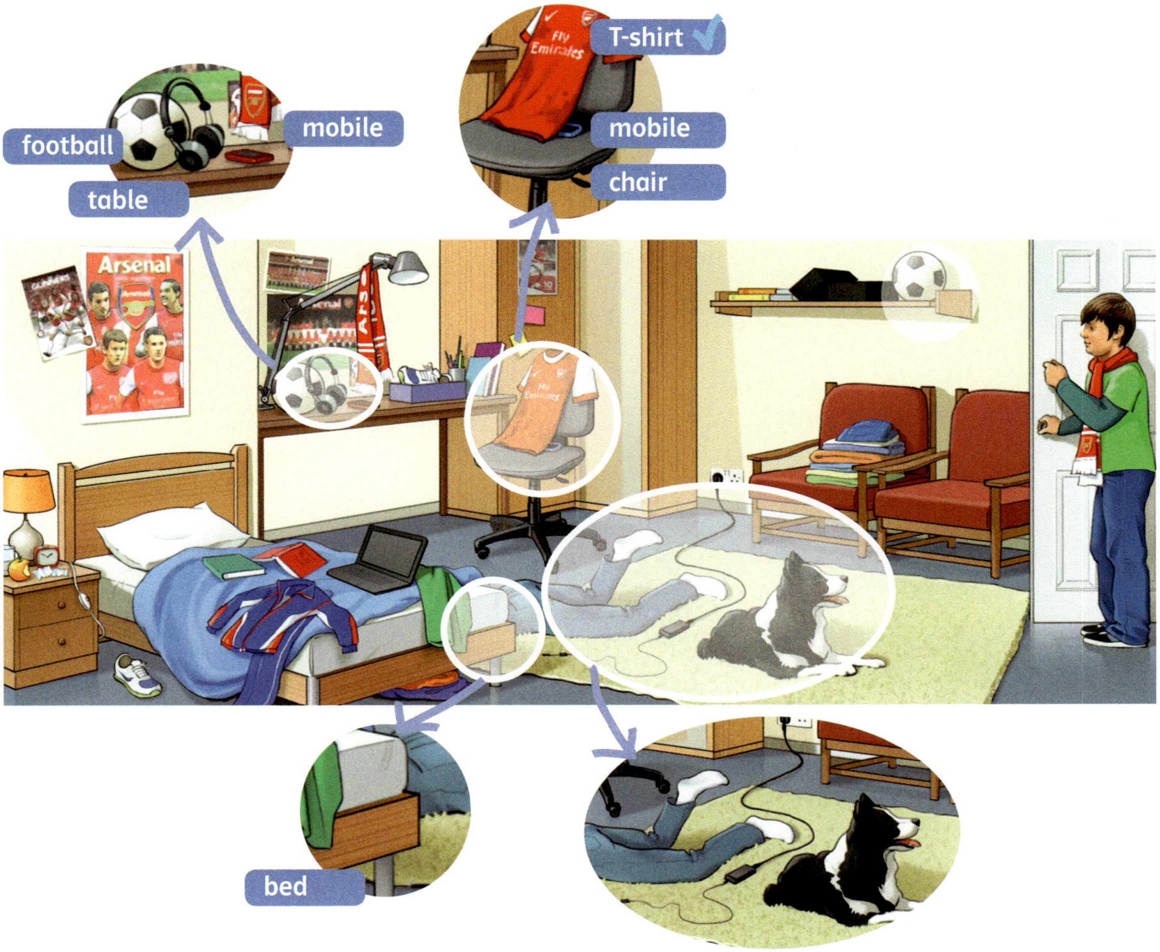

football
mobile
table
T-shirt ✓
mobile
chair
bed

1. It's red and white. It's on the chair.
   It's a T-shirt.
2. It's red and it's on the table.
   It's ___ .
3. It's under the T-shirt. It's blue.
4. He's black and white. He's next to Luke.
5. It's black and white. It's on the table.
6. He's under the bed.

○ 6 Look at the room again.

Make sentences.

There is	one table • one T-shirt • one dog • one bed
There are	two footballs • two mobiles • three chairs • five posters • six books

Unit 1, p. 20

○ 9 Who, what or where?

Make questions about Luke.

1. Where is Luke? – He's **under the bed.**
2. —— is under the T-Shirt? – **Luke's new mobile.**
3. —— is Dave? – He's **Luke's friend.**
4. —— is on the table? – **Luke's red mobile.**
5. —— is Sid? – He's **Dave's cat.**
6. —— is Sherlock? – He's **next to the bed.**

Schau dir die fett gedruckten Wörter in den Antworten an.
Ort = Where
Ding = What
Person = Who

Unit 1, p. 21

○ 10 What are the words?

Look at the picture.

a)
1. **What / Where** is Luke? – He's on the bed.
2. **What/ Where** is that on the table? – It's a red mobile.
3. **Where / Who** is next to the bed? – It's Sherlock, Luke's dog.
4. **Who / Where** is Luke's T-Shirt? – It's on the bed.
5. **Is / Are** Dave in the room? – No, Luke is with Sherlock.
6. **Is / Are** there posters in the room? – Yes, there are football posters.
7. **Is / Are** the room a mess? – No, it's OK.

b) Erkläre deinem Partner, warum du welches Wort genommen hast.
Seid ihr euch einig?

Unit 2, p. 34

3 Right or wrong?

Hello 7RS! This is Jahangir Azad, a new student. OK, you can sit here. Don't talk, please! Can you close the window, Holly?

1 It's Wednesday.

Are you a football fan, Jahangir? I can play football.
2
Really?
Call me Jay. I'm a music fan. I'm a good singer.

This new boy is crazy.

Jay is a good singer.

3 She's the girl … the girl … for me!

Sit down, please, Jay. Don't sing now. There's a talent show next week. Take out your pens and open your exercise books, please.
4
OK, look at the board now! Who can do number one? Put your hands up, please!

Are the sentences right or wrong?

1. It's Saturday. (Photo 1)
   That's wrong.
2. Jay is a new student. (Photo 1)
   That's …
3. Luke can play football. (Poto 2)
4. Jay is a football fan. (Photo 2)
5. Jay can't sing. (Photo 3)
6. "Close your exercise books, please." (Photo 4)

Unit 2, p. 35

5 (SPEAKING) Make dialogues.

A: Can I have your pen, please?
B: Yes, here you are.
A: Thank you.

A: Can I have your —— please?
B: Yes, here you are.
A: Thank you.

A: Can I have your —— , please?
B: Yes, here you are.
A: Thank you.

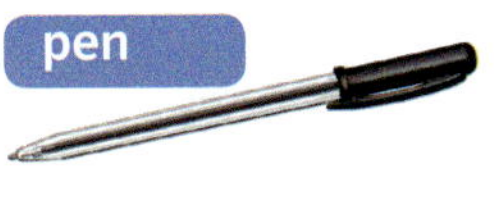

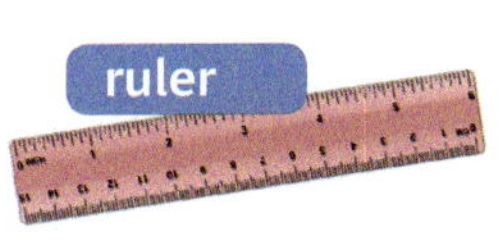

Unit 2, p. 36

○ 8 (WRITING) Write Mr Swindon's sentences.

Don't muss jedes Mal am Satzanfang stehen!

Find the right sentence.

1. Talk, please.
   Don't talk, please.
2. Open your exercise book.
   Don't —.
3. Write on the board, please.
4. Look at your books.
5. Play with your mobile.
6. Sing that song, please.

Don't look at your books. • Don't sing that song, please. • Don't open your exercise book. • Don't play with your mobile. • Don't write on the board, please. • Don't talk, please. ✓

Write the sentences.

Unit 2, p. 37

○ 10 Look at the pictures.

Complete the sentences.

1. D— with my mobile.
   Don't play with my mobile.
2. L— at the board.

Look | Don't play ✓

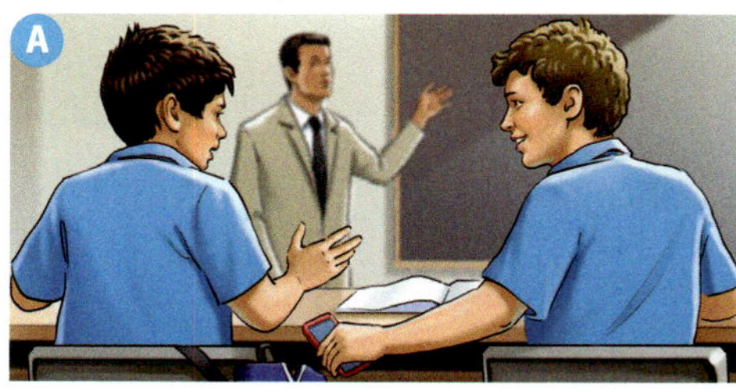

3. L— at this photo.
4. D— the window.

Don't open | Look

5. G— to the playground.
6. L— to this song. It's cool.

Listen | Go

Unit 2, p. 39

6 (SPEAKING) Make a dialogue.

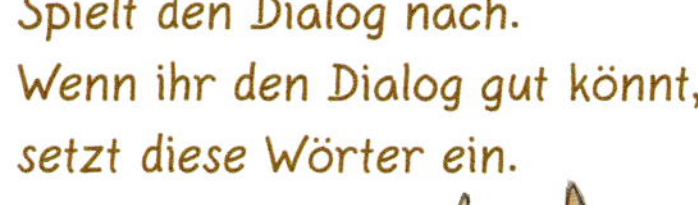

Spielt den Dialog nach.
Wenn ihr den Dialog gut könnt,
setzt diese Wörter ein.

A: What's your favourite subject?
B: My favourite subject is Maths.
It's interesting.
A: What's your favourite subject?
B: My favourite subject is English.
It's cool.

Unit 2, p. 40

9 (SPEAKING) Talk about yourself.

Tell a partner about yourself.

I'm — .
I'm not — .

ten | in tutor group 7RS | at ... school
English | German | good at football | good at spelling

And you?

Unit 2, p. 41

10 Look at the pictures and the sentences.

Complete the sentences.

1. Dave isn't eleven.

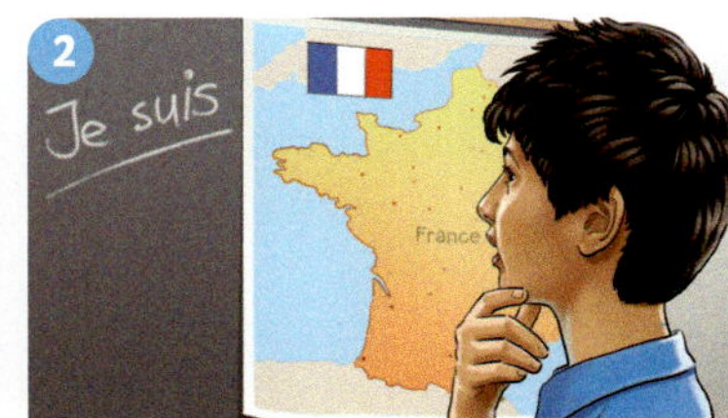

2. French isn't — .

3. They aren't — .

4. Luke isn't — .

5. Dave: I'm not — .

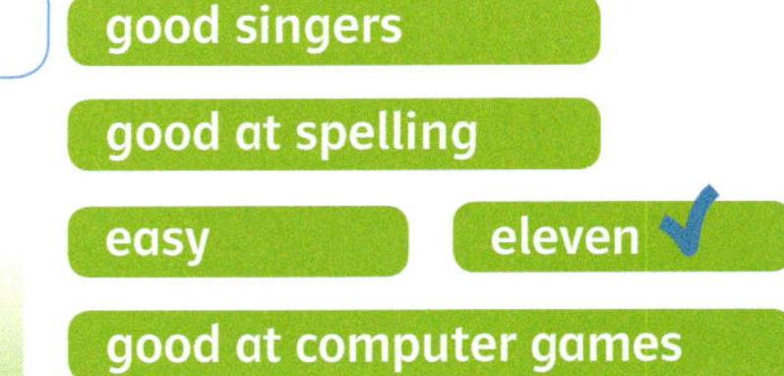

Unit 3, p. 54

3 (WRITING) Make animal words.

Make words.

Unit 3, p. 55

4 Find the right animals.

Which box is about the tiger, the snake or the elephant?

Box 1	Box 2	Box 3
15 kilograms 40 kilometres an hour	5 months	4 hours a day 3 metres high

Box 1 is the …

Unit 3, p. 56

11 Complete the sentences. → M Peer correction, p. 178

Choose the right verbs.

1. Edgar **come** / **comes** from India.
2. Lizzy **eat** / **eats** mice.
3. Tom **sleep** / **sleeps** 18 hours a day.
4. Elephants **eat** / **eats** fruit.
5. Snakes **sleep** / **sleeps** in winter.
6. Tigers **run** / **runs** 40 kilometres an hour.
7. They **eat** / **eats** seven kilograms of meat a day.

Unit 3, p. 57

○ 12 Make sentences about the animals.

Choose the right word.

I come from Africa. I eat bananas. I don't like fish. I play with my friends.

We don't eat fruit, we eat meat!
We sleep eighteen hours a day and run 40 kilometres an hour.
We come from India.

Mary, the monkey

1. Mary comes from Africa.
2. She — bananas.
3. She — fish.
4. She — with the penguins.

Tom and Tim, the tigers

5. Tom and Tim — meat.
6. They — four hours a day.
7. They — 40 kilometres an hour.
8. They — from Germany.

doesn't like
run
eats
don't come
doesn't play
eat
don't sleep
comes

Unit 3, p. 58

○ 2 Find out about Fred.

Holly interviews the zookeeper Fred for the Thomas Tallis school magazine.

Holly: When do you get up on Saturdays?
Fred: I get up at six o'clock. Then I have breakfast. I go to the zoo at seven o'clock.
Holly: Wow! What do you do first at the zoo?
Fred: First I feed Edgar, the elephant.
Holly: Does he eat a lot?
Fred: Yes! Then I feed the giraffes, the monkeys and the penguins. After that I work on the computer. In the afternoon I clean the cages.
Holly: Do you like your work?
Fred: Yes, I love my work. Do you like the zoo?
Holly: Yes! I love animals.

Choose the right answers.

1. Fred gets up at … — six o'clock. • 6:30.
2. At seven o'clock Fred … — has breakfast. • goes to the zoo.
3. First Fred feeds … — the penguins. • Edgar.
4. In the afternoon Fred cleans … — the cages. • the animals.

Unit 3, p. 59

○ 5 (SPEAKING) Say the times.

Match the times with the pictures.

1. Number 1 is eight thirty.

seven thirty • four twenty-eight • two fifteen • eight thirty ✓ • eleven forty-five • six fifty

○ 6 What does Holly do?

Match the sentences with the pictures.

1. Holly gets up at seven thirty.

She goes to school at eight thirty. • She plays on the computer at five fifteen • Holly gets up at seven thirty. ✓ • She has breakfast at eight o'clock. • She feed her pets at five o'clock. • She cleans the cage at four forty-five.

Unit 3, p. 60

○ 8 What are the questions? → M Walking sentences, p. 179

Put the words in the right order.

1. get up • Do you • at six o'clock?
   Do you get up at six o'clock?
2. Do you • science fiction movies? • watch
3. computer games • Do you • play?
4. Does • your friend • watch TV?
5. Do you • animals? • like
6. like football? • your friend • Does
7. Do you • netball • play?

Unit 3, p. 61

○ 10 What do they do in their free time?

Match the pictures with the sentences.

Do you sing at home? • What do you do after school? • Does your dog like the park? • Do you play football? ✓ • When do you go to the zoo? On Saturdays? • Where do your pets sleep?

1. Do you play football?

Unit 4, p. 73

○ 4 (LISTENING) When are their birthdays?

2, 4

What's right?

Olivia's birthday is on **28th February**.

Holly's birthday is on ....

Dave's birthday is on ....

Jay's birthday is on ....

Unit 4, p. 73

5 (WRITING) Match the numbers. → M Peer correction, p. 178

13th
23rd

twenty-third | thirteenth ✓

31st
7th

thirty-first | seventh

5th
12th

fifth | twelfth

Ordne jeder Zahl das richtige Wort zu und schreibe sie dann ab.

Unit 4, p. 74

8 (WRITING) Write sentences. → M Bus stop, p. 181

Put the words in the right order.

1. a party. • Olivia • always has
   Olivia always has a party.
2. her friends. • Olivia • often invites
3. Olivia • the birthday cake. • never makes
4. always gets • nice presents. • Olivia
5. her friends' birthdays. • never forgets • Olivia
6. always writes • birthday cards. • Olivia

Unit 4, p. 75

9 What can you do on a birthday?

Make sentences about Jay's birthday.

1 always has

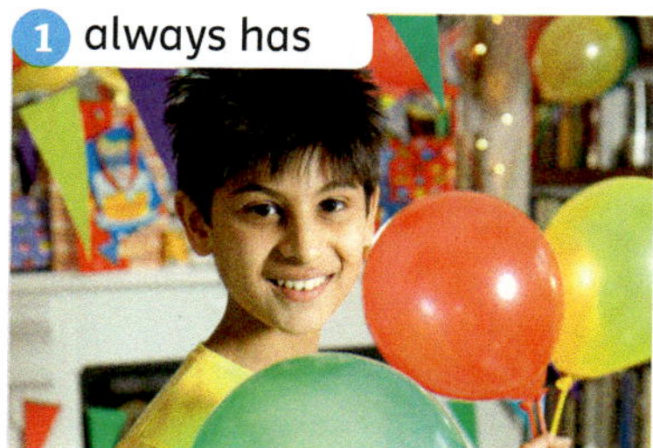

Jay — a party
Jay always has a party.

2 always makes

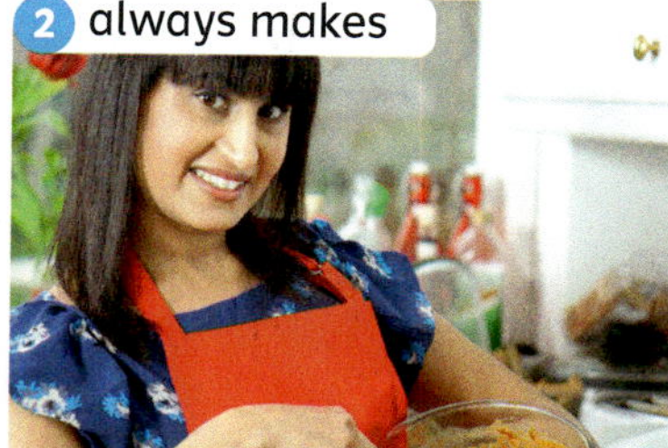

Jay's mum — a cake

3 always gets

Jay — presents from his friends

4 never dances

Jay's dad —

5 often sings

Jay — for his friends

6 often sleep

Jay and his friends — in the living room

Unit 4, p.76

○ 3 Check the sentences.

Let's see … We have crisps, a bar of chocolate and candles.
We don't have coke or balloons, Mum.
You're right. Can you go to the corner shop, please?

Mr Safi: Hello Jay. How can I help you?
Jay: Hi. Can I have a bottle of coke, please?
Mr Safi: Here you are. Anything else?
Jay: Do you have a packet of balloons?
Mr Safi: Yes, here you are.
Jay: Thanks. How much is it?
Mr Safi: The coke is 99p, and the balloons are £1.50.
So that's £2.49, please.
Jay *(gives Mr Safi £5)*: Here you are. Thanks.
Mr Safi: You're welcome. Here's your change.
Jay: Thank you. Bye!

Right or wrong?

1. Jay and his mum don't have chocolate.
   That's wrong.
2. Jay goes to the corner shop.
3. The corner shop doesn't have balloons.
4. The coke is 99p.
5. The balloons are £1.59.
6. Jay gives Mr Safi £3.49.
7. Jay gets his change.

Unit 4, p.77

○ 5 How much is it?

Complete the sentences.

1. A bottle of coke is 99p.
2. A packet of balloons is — .
3. A packet of crisps is — .
4. A packet of candles is — .
5. A bar of chocolate is — .

Unit 4, p. 78

9 (SPEAKING) Make dialogues. → G10, p. 169

Your partner is Mr Safi and gives the right answer.

1. bananas A
2. fish
3. pencils B
4. balloons C
5. oranges
6. sandwiches D
7. chocolate E
8. footballs
9. CDs F
10. DVDs G

MR SAFI'S CORNER SHOP

1. A: Hi! Do you have bananas?
   B: Yes, they're here.
2. A: Hi! Do you have fish?
   B: No, sorry! We don't have fish.

Suche die Sachen im Bild. Wenn sie nicht im Angebot sind, sagst du "No, sorry!" Vielleicht kannst du dem Kunden etwas Anderes anbieten?

Unit 4, p. 79

○ 10 Make a dialogue about Jay's present.

What does Jay do?
Look at the pictures and make questions and answers.

1. play computer games?

2. read books?

3. have a pet?

4. go to the cinema? 

5. like football?

6. listen to music? 

1. Olivia: Does Jay play computer games?
   Holly: Yes, he plays games.
2. Olivia: Does he read books?
   Holly: No, he doesn't read ….
3. Olivia: Does he …?
   Holly: No, he doesn't have a ….
4. Olivia: Does he … ?
   Holly: Yes, he goes to the ….
5. Olivia: Does he … ?
   Holly: No, he doesn't like ….
6. Olivia: Does he … ?
   Holly: Yes, he listens to ….

Unit 5, p. 92

○ 3 (LISTENING) Listen to Dave and Jay.

2, 14

Choose the right answers.

1. On Saturday evening Dave
   played football. • watched TV.
2. In the afternoon he
   helped his dad. • went to the shopping centre.
3. On Sunday he
   watched a DVD. • played a computer game.

Höre gut zu und schreibe die Antwort als Stichwort. Bei Nummer 1 reicht es, „football" oder „TV" zu schreiben.

Unit 5, p. 93

○ 5 (WRITING) What can you do in your town at the weekend?

Write sentences. Choose the best answers.

I can	go swimming	at the shopping centre. at the swimming pool.
I can	play games	in the park. at the cinema.
I can	buy clothes	at the shopping centre. at the cinema.
I can	watch movies	at the cinema. at the swimming pool.

Unit 5, p. 94

○ 8 What did they do at the weekend?

Make sentences.

played netball • Olivia • on Sunday
Olivia played netball on Sunday.

Luke • on Saturday • watched a movie

played computer games • Dave • on Sunday

Dave's mum • on Saturday • worked

listened to Ray-B's songs • on Saturday • Jay

talked to her mum • Olivia • on Saturday

Unit 5, p. 95

○ 10 Complete the sentences.

Choose the right words.

1. Olivia: I — (saw / had) a pizza with my mum in the afternoon.
   I had a pizza with my mum in the afternoon.
2. Olivia: I — (did / bought) my homework last night.
3. Jay: My brother — (was / bought) Ray-B's new CD.
4. Luke: I — (went / was) to the cinema on Saturday evening.
5. Luke: The movie — (had / was) brilliant.

Unit 5, p. 96

○ 2 Check the sentences.

Jay: What did you do at the weekend, Holly?
Holly: I went to Margate with my dad on Sunday.
Jay: Margate? Where's that?
Holly: It's at the seaside.
Jay: How did you go there? By train?
Holly: No, we went by car.
Jay: What did you do there?
Holly: We walked on the beach and played frisbee. It was nice.
Jay: Cool! Did you have fish and chips?
Holly: Dad had fish. I'm a vegetarian. I had chips. They were great! We went to the shops after that and I bought postcards.
Jay: Did you send me a postcard?
Holly: No, Jay! I don't know where you live!

Are the sentences right or wrong?

1. Holly went to Margate with her dad on Saturday.
   That's wrong!
2. They went by train.
3. They played frisbee on the beach.
4. Holly had fish and her dad had chips.
5. She bought some posters.
6. She doesn't know where Jay lives.

Schau dir die Sätze an, die im Text farbig markiert sind. Sie können dir helfen.

Unit 5, p. 97

○ 6 (WRITING) How do they go to school?

Write about your chart.

Six students go to school by bike.
Eight students go to school —— .
No students go —— .

by bus | by bike
on foot | by car
Five | Ten | ...

Unit 5, p. 98

○ 8 Ask questions about last weekend.

Put the words in the right order.

Suche zuerst das Wort „did". Das steht bei diesen Fragen immer als Erstes.

1. Jay • Did • go to Margate • ?
   Did Jay go to Margate?
2. go with her mum • Holly • Did • ?
3. Holly and her dad • go to the shops • Did • ?
4. have fish and chips • Did • Holly's dad • ?
5. Did • go by bus • they • ?
6. Holly • like Margate • Did • ?

Unit 5, p. 99

○ 11 What did Dave and Jay do yesterday?

Look at the picture. Match the questions with the answers.

1. Where did Jay go yesterday?
2. What did Jay and Dave do?
3. Where did they play computer games?
4. When did they play computer games?
5. What did they have for lunch?
6. Did they have fun?

A They had fun.
B They played in Dave's room.
C They played computer games.
D He went to Dave's house.
E They had two pizzas for lunch.
F They played in the afternoon.

Unit 6, p.112

○ 2 What did they do?

Olivia: Hello?

Holly: Hi, is that you, Olivia? It's me, Holly! How are you? Is your arm better?

Olivia: Yes, I'm OK, thanks.

Holly: We're at the farm. Luke, Dave and Jay are here.

Luke, Dave and Jay: Hi Olivia!

Olivia: Hi! How was your day? What did you do?

Holly: Oh, it was great. I went horse riding! And we had a picnic. That was fun. The boys weren't in my group. Dave and Luke were with Mr Swindon. They went canoeing, and Jay went rock climbing.

Olivia: Rock climbing? Wow!

Jay: It was great. But it wasn't easy. We wore helmets.

Holly: Sorry, Olivia – I must stop now. It's time for the night walk. I must wear warm clothes for that. See you soon!

Olivia: Yes! Bye!

Are the pictures right or wrong?

Holly • horse riding?

Luke • rock climbing?

Dave and Mr Swindon • canoeing?

Jay • rock climbing?

Ich gebe dir einen Tipp! Drei Bilder sind richtig, ein Bild ist falsch.

Picture A is right.

D

Unit 6, p.113

5 (SPEAKING) Make a clothes dialogue.

Make dialogues with the words.

A: Hey, I like your — !

T-shirt | coat | sweatshirt | skirt

It's — .

socks | trainers | trousers

They're — .

cool | nice | interesting | great | funny | ...

B: Oh. Thank you!
A: You're welcome!

Unit 6, p.114

8 Complete the sentences. → M Bus stop, p.181

What's right?

1. Holly **wasn't / weren't** in the canoeing group.
2. Horse riding **was / were** great. Holly liked her horse.
3. Luke and Dave **wasn't / weren't** in the rock climbing group.
4. Jay: Rock climbing **wasn't / weren't** easy!
5. Mr Swindon **wasn't / weren't** in the horse riding group.
6. Holly: The picnic **was / were** fun. The sandwiches were cool!

GRAMMAR → G16, p.175

was + not = wasn't
were + not = weren't

Unit 6, p. 115

9 What did Holly's mum ask?

Put the words in the right order.

1. the horse riding trip • was • yesterday • how • ?
   How was the horse riding trip yesterday?
2. in your group • Luke and Dave • were • ?
3. nice • your horse • was • ?
4. was • the picnic • where • ?
5. good • was • the food • ?
6. you • when • back at the farm • were • ?

GRAMMAR → G16, p. 175

Were you at school yesterday?
How was your day?

Unit 6, p. 116

2 Finish the sentences.

What are the words?

1. Holly sent Olivia a postcard from Highfield Farm.
2. Last night they went on a night —— .
3. They didn't have torches so it was very —— .
4. They saw some —— and heard funny —— .
5. Then it —— .
6. Luke and Jay got —— .

dark | wet | bats | walk | rained | Farm ✓ | noises

18th May

Dear Olivia,
Hi from Highfield Farm!
It's great here. Last night
we went on a night walk!
It was scary. We didn't
have torches so it was very
dark. Guess what!
We saw some bats
and we heard funny noises...
Then it rained. Luke and
Jay got wet because they
didn't wear their coats.
See you soon,
Holly Luke
Jay Dave

EXETER 19. 5. 14 DEVON 50P

Olivia Fraser
52 Begbie Road
Greenwich
London SE3 8DA

Unit 6, p.117

4 (SPEAKING) Talk about the weather.

Make dialogues.

A: It's sunny today. Let's have a picnic.

B: That's a good idea! Let's do that.

Or:

A: It's wet today. We can't have a picnic.

B: OK. Let's watch TV.

A:
- It's sunny today. Let's have a picnic.
- It's wet today. We can't have a picnic.
- It's cold today. We can't go canoeing.
- It's windy today. Let's play computer games.
- It's hot today. Let's play football in the farmyard.

B:
- That's a good idea! Let's do that!
- OK. Let's watch TV.
- OK. Let's play computer games.

Unit 6, p.118

8 Complete the sentences.

Match the sentence parts.

1. The students didn't have	sandwiches with meat in them.
2. Luke and Jay didn't wear	to Highfield Farm.
3. Holly didn't eat	torches on the night walk.
4. Jay didn't play	coats.
5. Dave didn't send	football with Dave and Luke.
6. Olivia didn't go	a postcard to his mum and dad.

Unit 6, p.119

9 What did Luke write?

Put in the verbs.

didn't get | talked ✓ | had | looked at | didn't have | went

Dear Mum and Dad,
Highfield Farm is great! On the first day we (1) talked to the farmer. We (2) his tractor.
I (3) canoeing, but I (4) wet. Yesterday the weather was awful. We (5) a picnic; we (6) our sandwiches in the house.
Say hi to Jamie and Irina.
See you soon!
Luke

Extra

Poems[1]

2, 32 A letter[2] poem: S

I am an S-
Born on a Saturday
In September.
I don't like Sharks
But I love Swimming.
I eat Strawberries.
I Sing and Sleep on Sundays.
I am an S.

2, 33 A diamond[4] poem

My
Dog, Fluffy
I really like him
He always runs and plays with me
in the garden or the park
I really like him
Fluffy, my
Dog

2, 34 I'm ...

JANIS
And my friends are
Naomi and Becky
I watch cool DVDs and go
Shopping with them!

SPEAKING SKILLS

Wie man ein Gedicht vorträgt:
- Weißt du, was die Wörter alle bedeuten? Weißt du, wie man sie ausspricht? Wenn du unsicher bist, frage deine Lehrerin oder deinen Lehrer.
- Lerne das Gedicht Zeile für Zeile.
- Sage das Gedicht nicht zu schnell auf.

1 Write a poem.

a) Write a poem like 'Janis' with your own name, or a diamond poem.

b) Learn your poem or a poem from this page by heart[5]. Say the poem to a partner or your tutor group.

1 poem ['pəʊɪm] – *Gedicht*; 2 letter ['letə] – *Buchstabe*; 3 born [bɔːn] – *geboren*; 4 diamond ['daɪəmənd] – *Diamant*; 5 by heart [baɪ 'hɑːt] – *auswendig*

2, 35

Who stole it?

Milford Ripple has a great stamp collection[1]. One special stamp in his collection is the famous and very valuable[2] 'Pink Magdalena'.

One Thursday afternoon, after tea, Milford goes to his study[3]. He wants to look at his favourite stamp. But he gets a big shock[4]: Where's the star of his collection, his beautiful Magdalena?
"It's gone[5]!" he says and he calls Ridley Long.
The detective comes to his house.
"Three people were here this morning," says Milford Ripple. "Billy, Chuck Hostle and Trixie Dustly. But I was in my garden then. One of them stole my valuable stamp!"

Later Detective Long listens to what the three people say.

Billy the boiler[6] man says: Mr Ripple's boiler had a leak[7]. The boiler is in the bathroom. So that's where I was this morning. Of course[8] I wasn't in any other room!
With his cigar[9] in his mouth[10] Chuck Hostle says: I'm Mr Ripple's insurance agent[11]. He wanted some information from me. So I came to the house in the late[12] morning and put[13] it on the kitchen table. Then I went to town for lunch.
Trixie Dustly says in surprise: The study? No, I never go in there! I clean Mr Ripple's house every Thursday morning. But Mr Ripple says I mustn't[14] clean that room. So I don't.

Detective Long goes to Ripple's study and looks around. Then he finds a small[15] clue. One of the three people lied[16] and now he knows who!

2 What do you think?

What and where is the clue in the study? Who stole the Pink Magdalena?

1 stamp collection ['stæmp kəˌlekʃn] – *Briefmarkensammlung;* 2 valuable ['væljuəbl] – *wertvoll;* 3 study ['stʌdi] – *Arbeitszimmer;* 4 shock [ʃɒk] – *Schreck;* 5 gone [gɒn] – *verschwunden;* 6 boiler ['bɔɪlə] – *Boiler;* 7 leak [li:k] – *undichte Stelle;* 8 of course [əv 'kɔ:s] – *selbstverständlich;* 9 cigar [sɪ'gɑ:] – *Zigarre;* 10 mouth [maʊθ] – *Mund;* 11 insurance agent [ɪn'ʃʊərns ˌeɪdʒnt] – *Versicherungsvertreter/-in;* 12 late [leɪt] – *spät;* 13 put [pʊt] – *legen;* 14 mustn't ['mʌsnt] – *nicht dürfen;* 15 small [smɔ:l] – *klein;* 16 lie [laɪ] – *lügen*

2.36 Sherlock's story

1 Before you read

What do you already know about Luke and his dog, Sherlock?
(Was weißt du über Luke und seinen Hund, Sherlock?)

Hello. I'm Sherlock. I'm a dog. My people are the Elliots – Jack, Anna, Irina, Luke and Jamie.

Luke is my pet. Every morning I get up and wash[1] his face. Then he gets up and washes his face again. After that he makes my breakfast. Then he has his breakfast. I love breakfast!

Jack goes to work early[2]. Then Luke, Irina and Jamie go to school. I always help Luke with his school bag. Then Anna goes to work.

In the mornings I look after[3] the house. I often see cats in my garden. I always bark[4]. Then the cats run away[5].

1 wash [wɒʃ] – *waschen*; 2 early ['ɜ:li] – *früh*; 3 look after [ˌlʊk‿'ɑ:ftə] – *aufpassen auf*; 4 bark [bɑ:k]– *bellen*; 5 run away [ˌrʌn‿ə'weɪ] – *weglaufen*

We often have a picnic in the park. I like picnics because there is no table and I can sit[1] in the middle[2].

In the evening we play a game. I watch TV with my people, and they throw[3] shoes[4] at me. I take[5] the shoes to my room. I like shoes.

At nine o'clock I take Luke to our room. He's a good pet, so he can always sleep in my bed.

2 Talk about the story.

Do you like the story?
What is special about it?
(Was ist das Besondere an der Geschichte?)

I like it ...	nice
It's funny	because ...
I don't like it ...	...

1 sit [sɪt] – *sich hinsetzen*; 2 in the middle [ɪn ðə 'mɪdl] – *in der Mitte*; 3 throw [θrəʊ] – *werfen*; 4 shoes [ʃuːz] – *Schuhe*; 5 take [teɪk] – *nehmen, bringen*

Bats – not birds[1], not mice

Bats fly[2], but they aren't birds.
They look[3] like[4] mice with wings[5].
But no, they aren't mice.
Bats are often in vampire[6] movies.
But what do you really know about these creatures[7] of the night?

1 Right or wrong? What do you think?

1. Bats can't see.
2. Be careful: Bats can fly into[8] your hair.
3. Bats can't be mammals[9] because they fly.
4. The smallest[10] bat is the size[11] of a bumblebee[12].

Now read about bats.

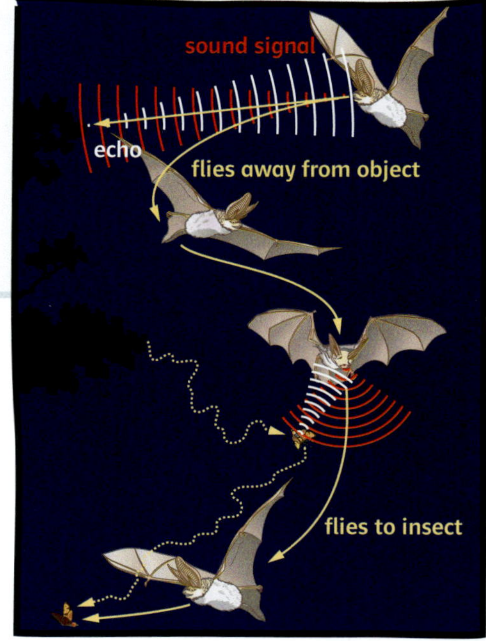

It's a bat's life!

Bats sleep in the daytime[13]. At night they look for insects[14] and other food. Bats' eyes[15] aren't very good but they can see in the daytime.
At night they don't use their eyes.
They use their big ears[16]!
The bat makes very high sounds.
The sounds hit[17] things around[18] the bat and it hears an echo[19].
That's how bats can find very small insects.
And it's also why they don't fly into houses – or into your hair at night!

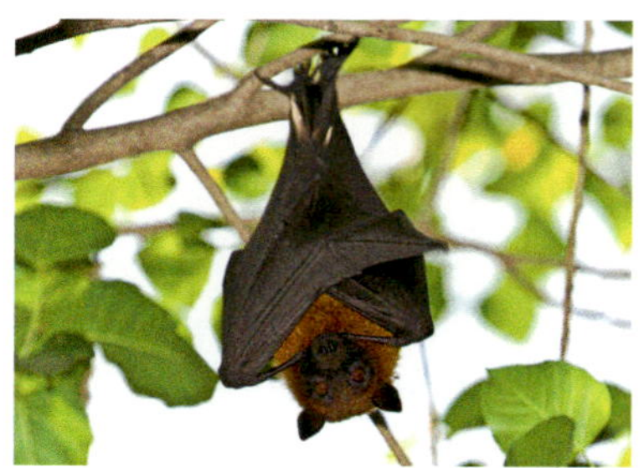

1 bird [bɜːd] – *Vogel;* 2 fly [flaɪ] – *fliegen;* 3 look [lʊk] – *aussehen;* 4 like [laɪk] – *(so) wie;* 5 wing [wɪŋ] – *Flügel;* 6 vampire ['væmpaiə] – *Vampir;* 7 creature ['kriːtʃə] – *Lebewesen;* 8 into ['ɪntu] – *in … (hinein);* 9 mammal ['mæml] – *Säugetier;* 10 small, the smallest ['smɔːl, 'smɔːləst] – *klein, die kleinste;* 11 size [saɪz] – *Größe;* 12 bumblebee ['bʌmblˌbiː] – *Hummel;* 13 daytime ['deɪtaɪm] – *am Tag;* 14 insect ['ɪnsekt] – *Insekt;* 15 eye [aɪ] – *Auge;* 16 ear [ɪə] – *Ohr;* 17 hit [hɪt] – *auftreffen;* 18 around [ə'raʊnd] – *um … (herum);* 19 echo ['ekəʊ] – *Echo*

Did you know?

- People often find bats scary.
  But many[1] Chinese[2] people think bats bring luck[3]. 'Fu' is Chinese for 'bat' and for 'happy'!
- Bats are mammals. No other mammal can fly.
- Bats fly with their hands! They have long arms and long, thin[4] fingers[5] in their wings.
- The smallest bat in the world[6] is the bumblebee bat.
  It is the size of a bumblebee and weighs[7] under 1.7g[8] (one cent weighs 2g)!

Bat care tips[9]

- Never disturb[10] a sleeping[11] bat.
- Make a 'bat box' and put[12] it in a tree for bats to live in.
- If[13] you find a bat in the daytime, call the hotline of a bat or animal club in your town. They can help you.

2 Now check your answers from exercise 1.

1 many ['meni] – *viele;* 2 Chinese [tʃaɪ'ni:z] – *chinesisch;* 3 bring luck [ˌbrɪŋ 'lʌk] – *Glück bringen;* 4 thin [θɪn] – *dünn;* 5 finger ['fɪŋgə] – *Finger;* 6 in the world [ɪn ðə 'wɜ:ld] – *auf der Welt;* 7 weigh [weɪ] – *wiegen;* 8 1.7g [wʌn pɔɪnt ˌsevn 'græmz] – *1,7 Gramm;* 9 care tips ['keə tɪps] – *Pflegehinweise;* 10 disturb [dɪ'stɜ:b] – *stören;* 11 sleeping ['sli:pɪŋ] – *schlafend;* 12 put [pʊt] – *anbringen;* 13 if [ɪf] – *wenn*

What time is it?

When[1] a friend asks "Hey, what time is it?", you can look at your mobile or watch[2] and give an answer. But how did people know the time when there were no watches and mobiles?

Sundials[3]

In old times people had clocks[4] but they were very simple[5] and used sunlight[6]. A good example[7] is the sundial. Even[8] today you can find sundials on some old buildings[9]. But they don't work[10] at night or when it is cloudy. The shadow[11] is like[12] the hand[13] of a modern clock.

Hourglasses[14]

Hourglasses use sand[15] and they're very exact[16]. They can be big or small[17]. But they only[18] work for a few[19] minutes or an hour.

A sundial

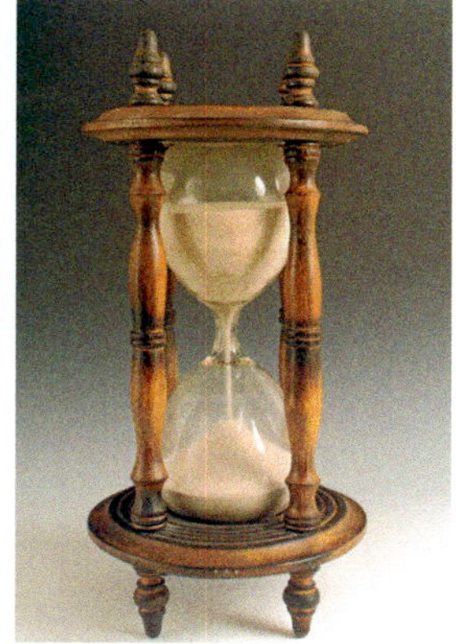

An hourglass

1 What do you think?

1. Why don't sundials work when it's cloudy?
2. Where do people still[20] use small hourglasses today?

1 when [wen] – *wann immer;* 2 watch [wɒtʃ] – *Armbanduhr;* 3 sundial ['sʌndeɪl] – *Sonnenuhr;* 4 clock [klɒk] – *Uhr;* 5 simple ['sɪmpl] – *einfach;* 6 sunlight ['sʌnlaɪt] – *Sonnenlicht;* 7 example [ɪg'zɑ:mpl] – *Beispiel;* 8 even ['i:vn] – *sogar;* 9 building ['bɪldɪŋ] – *Gebäude;* 10 work [wɜ:k] – *funktionieren;* 11 shadow ['ʃædəʊw] – *Schatten;* 12 like [laɪk] – *(so) wie;* 13 hand [hænd] – *Uhrzeiger;* 14 hourglass ['aʊəglɑ:s] – *Sanduhr;* 15 sand [sænd] – *Sand;* 16 exact [ig'zækt] – *genau;* 17 small [smɔ:l] – *klein;* 18 only ['əʊnli] – *nur;* 19 a few [ə 'fju:] – *wenige;* 20 still [stɪl] – *noch*

2 (PROJECT) A special hourglass – an egg timer[1]

How long do you boil[2] your egg[3] so it's right for you?

Make your own[4] egg timer for the perfect[5] egg!

You need:
- 2 small bottles
- sticky tape[6]
- 2–3 mm hand drill[7]
- fine sand (or salt[8])

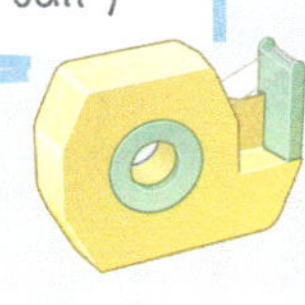

3

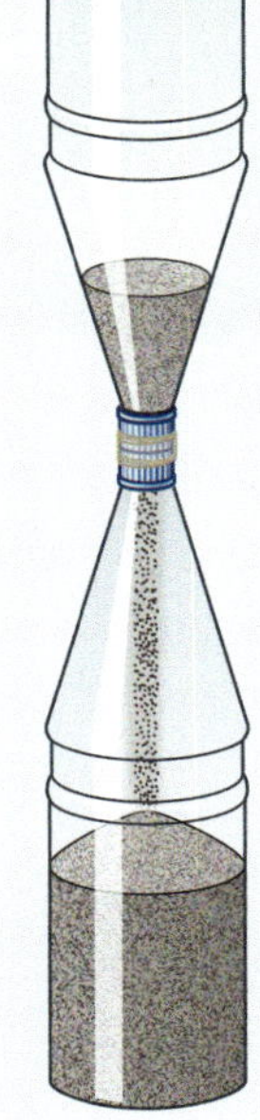

How much sand do you need?

Here's an example: If you like a five-minute egg, let the sand flow through[9] for five minutes and then throw away[10] the rest[11]. Now you have the perfect egg timer!

Exact time

Do all the clocks, mobiles and watches in your house show[12] the same time[13]?
Probably[14] not!
So how do we know the exact time?
Well, the best clock for this – the atomic[15] clock – doesn't look like a clock! And did you know your radio[16] clock gets its time from an atomic clock too?

An atomic clock

3 (YOUR TURN) Be on time[17]!

Think of three situations when it's very important to be on time.

Does your partner have the same or different[18] ideas?

1 egg timer ['eg ˌtaɪmə] – *Sanduhr/Eieruhr;* 2 boil [bɔɪl] – *kochen (lassen);* 3 egg [eg] – *Ei;* 4 own [əʊn] – *eigene;*
5 perfect ['pɜːfɪkt] – *perfekt;* 6 sticky tape ['stɪki ˌteɪp] – *Klebeband;* 7 drill [drɪl] – *Bohrer;* 8 salt [sɔːlt] – *Salz;*
9 let flow through [let ˌfləʊ 'θruː] – *durchfließen lassen;* 10 throw away [θrəʊ ə'weɪ] – *wegwerfen;* 11 the rest [rest] – *der Rest;*
12 show [ʃəʊ] – *zeigen;* 13 the same time [seɪm 'taɪm] – *dieselbe Zeit;* 14 probably ['prɒbəbli] – *wahrscheinlich;*
15 atomic [ə'tɒmɪk] – *Atom-;* 16 radio ['reɪdiəʊ] – *Radio;* 17 be on time [ˌbiː ɒn 'taɪm] – *pünktlich sein;*
18 different ['dɪfrənt] – *verschieden*

Grammar

G2

Mit G sind die Grammatikkapitel gekennzeichnet und der Reihe nach durchnummeriert. Eine Übersicht über alle Themen in diesem Band findest du auf der nächsten Seite.

Language tip G3

Die Seiten kennzeichnen zusätzliche Grammatikkapitel. Du kannst dir die neuen Formen dort wie neue Vokabeln merken oder – wenn du es genau wissen willst – ein paar Regeln dazu lernen.

Hier stehen Besonderheiten und Tipps.

(TEST YOURSELF)

Hier kannst du üben. Die Lösungen findest du auf Seite 177.

(FÜR PROFIS)

Hier findest du knifflige Extras zum Thema.

Unit 1 Unit 2 Unit 3 Unit 4 Unit 5 Unit 6

G

Unit 1

Language tip

G1 Besitzangaben mit 's

The possessive form with 's

Psst. This is Olivia's bike.

Psst. Das ist Olivias Fahrrad.

Wenn du sagen willst, zu wem etwas gehört, hängst du **'s an die Person.**

Lucy's sister	Lucys Schwester
Dave's cat	Daves Katze
Kate's mum	Kates Mama
Rob's brother	Robs Bruder
my **mother's** father	der Vater meiner Mutter
my **friend's** football	der Fußball meines Freundes

my mother's father =

der Vater meiner Mutter

Achtung, wenn mehreren Personen etwas gehört und bereits ein **s am Wortende** steht. Vergleiche:

my **brother's** room	das Zimmer meines Bruders (ein Bruder)
Aber: my **brothers'** room	das Zimmer meiner Brüder (mehrere Brüder)

Im Deutschen kannst du Besitzangaben unterschiedlich ausdrücken. Vergleiche:

Sherlock is **Luke's** dog.	Sherlock ist Lukes Hund. Sherlock ist der Hund von Luke.

Im Deutschen gibt es kein Häkchen (Apostroph) vor dem s.

(TEST YOURSELF) **Put in the right form.**

1. — bike is cool. (Olivia)
2. — dog is crazy. (Luke)
3. Sid is — cat. (Dave)
4. Fluff and Honey are — pets. (Holly)
5. Olivia is — sister. (Lucy)
6. Janet is — mother. (Olivia)

G2 Das Verb be (Aussagen)

The verb be (statements)

Hello. I'm Ben. I'm a bat.
This is Sherlock.
He's my friend.
We're from Greenwich.

Hello. I am Ben. I am a bat.
This is Sherlock.
He is my friend.
We are from Greenwich.

Hallo. Ich bin Ben. Ich bin eine Fledermaus.
Das ist Sherlock. Er ist mein Freund.
Wir sind aus Greenwich.

Das Verb **be** (sein) hat verschiedene Formen: **am**, **are** und **is**.
Es gibt Langformen und Kurzformen.

I **am**	**I'm**	ich bin
you **are**	**you're**	du bist / Sie sind
he **is**	**he's**	er ist
she **is**	**she's**	sie ist
it **is**	**it's**	es ist
we **are**	**we're**	wir sind
you **are**	**you're**	ihr seid / Sie sind
they **are**	**they're**	sie sind

Beim Schreiben verwendest du meistens Langformen und beim Sprechen Kurzformen.

(TEST YOURSELF) Put in the right form of be.

1. I —— Luke.
2. You —— my friend.
3. Lucy and Olivia —— my friends too.
4. Claire —— nice.
5. Desmond —— here too.
6. We —— in the garden.

(FÜR PROFIS)

Diese Formen darf man nicht verwechseln. Vergleiche:

You're at home. — Du bist zu Hause.
Your room is nice. — Dein Zimmer ist schön.

Language tip

G3 Der Plural

The plural

Hey, look, three balls and two boxes!

Hey, schau mal, drei Bälle und zwei Schachteln!

Möchtest du von Dingen oder Personen in der **Mehrzahl** (Plural) sprechen, hängst du in den meisten Fällen einfach ein -s an.

one book, seven **books**	ein Buch, sieben Bücher
one CD, five **CDs**	eine CD, fünf CDs
one mobile, two **mobiles**	ein Handy, zwei Handys

Bei Nomen, die auf einen **Zischlaut** enden, zum Beispiel **box**, hängst du in der Mehrzahl ein **-es** an.

There are three **boxes** on the table.	Drei Schachteln sind auf dem Tisch.

Die meisten Nomen, die auf **-y** enden, sehen im Plural so aus:

one family, two families	eine Familie, zwei Familien
Aber: one boy, two boys	ein Junge, zwei Jungen

Manche Nomen haben unregelmäßige Pluralformen.

one shelf, two **shelves**	ein Regal, zwei Regale

(TEST YOURSELF) Put in the plural form.

1. There are eight — (boy) in the park.
2. I can see three — (book) on the table.
3. The — (T-shirt) are red.
4. I can't find my — (CD).
5. There are four — (box) on the bed.
6. There are two — (family) in this photo.

G4 Fragen mit be

Questions with be

Fluff and Honey! Are you there?
Where are you?

Fluff und Honey! Seid ihr da?
Wo seid ihr?

Fragen, auf die man mit Ja oder Nein antworten kann, bildest du so:

Am I late?	Bin ich zu spät?
Is Holly from Greenwich?	Ist Holly aus Greenwich?
Are you at home?	Bist du zu Hause? Seid ihr zu Hause?
Are Sherlock and Sid guinea pigs?	Sind Sherlock und Sid Meerschweinchen?

Bei Fragen mit Fragewörtern steht das Fragewort immer am Satzanfang.

Who is Holly?	Wer ist Holly?
Where are Fluff and Honey?	Wo sind Fluff und Honey?
What is under the bed?	Was ist unter dem Bett?

Who? = Wer?
Where? = Wo?

(TEST YOURSELF) Put in Who, Is, Are, Where, What or How.

1. —— is Dave? He's in the garden.
2. —— your mobile blue? No, it's red.
3. —— old are you? I'm eleven.
4. —— is the girl's name? Laura.
5. —— the boys from London? No, they're from Berlin.
6. —— is it? It's Ben.

(FÜR PROFIS)

Manchmal benutzt man im Englischen andere Verben als im Deutschen. Vergleiche:

What colour **is** your mobile?	Welche Farbe **hat** dein Handy?

Unit 2

Language tip

G5 Der Artikel: a, an und the

The article: a, an and the

What's in Olivia's bag? A ruler, an exercise book and … a sandwich.

Was ist in Olivias Tasche? Ein Lineal, ein Heft und … ein Sandwich.

Der **unbestimmte Artikel** (ein, eine) heißt im Englischen **a** oder **an**.
Beginnt das folgende Wort mit einem **Konsonanten**, sagt man a.

a [ə] **bag**	eine Tasche

Beginnt das folgende Wort mit einem **Vokal**, sagt man **an**.

an [ən] **exercise book**	ein Heft

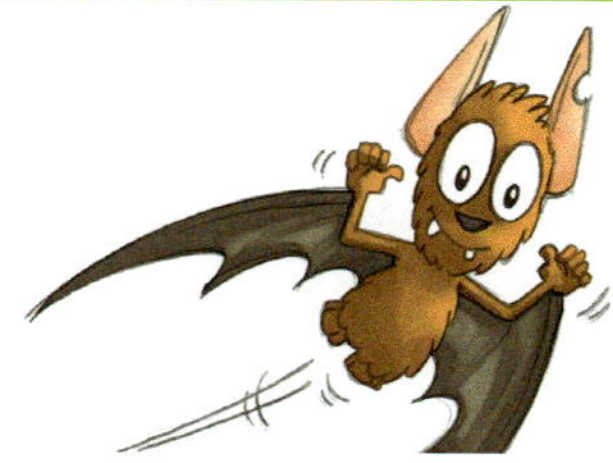

Vokale sind a, e, i, o, u. Alle anderen Buchstaben sind Konsonanten.

Der **bestimmte Artikel** (der, die, das) heißt im Englischen immer **the**.
Beginnt das folgende Wort mit einem Konsonanten, sagt man **[ðə]**.
Beginnt das folgende Wort mit einem Vokal, sagt man **[ði]**.

the [ðə] bag	die Tasche
the [ði] exercise book	das Heft

Auch wenn **u** ein Vokal ist, steht vor Wörtern wie **uniform** ein **a**. Achte auf die Aussprache.

a uniform [ə ˈjuːnɪfɔːm]	eine Uniform

(TEST YOURSELF) Put in a, an or the.

1. My favourite place at school is —— cafeteria.
2. Ms Kapoor is —— English teacher.
3. There is —— mobile in my bag.
4. —— ruler in my bag is white.
5. My sister is —— good singer.
6. In my room there is —— old table.

G6 Der Imperativ

The imperative

Don't run away, Sherlock.
Play with me, please!

Renn' nicht weg, Sherlock.
Spiel' mit mir, bitte!

Der Imperativ ist die **Befehlsform**. So forderst du jemanden auf, etwas zu tun:

Open the window, please.	Öffne das Fenster, bitte.
Look at the board.	Schau an die Tafel.
Be quiet.	Sei still.

So forderst du jemanden auf, etwas **nicht** zu tun:

Don't talk now.	Rede jetzt nicht.
Don't look in your books.	Schaut nicht in eure Bücher.
Don't be late, please.	Sei bitte nicht zu spät.

(TEST YOURSELF) Put in the right imperative form.

1. — (close) the door, please.
2. — (not play) football.
3. — (not open) your books.
4. — (look) at the board.
5. — (not sing) now.
6. — (go) to the board, please.

(FÜR PROFIS)

Die Befehlsform gilt für eine oder mehrere Personen. Vergleiche:

	(eine Person)	(mehrere Personen)
Come in.	Komm herein.	Kommt herein.
	Kommen Sie herein.	Kommen Sie herein.
Don't sit down.	Setz dich nicht hin.	Setzt euch nicht hin.
	Setzen Sie sich nicht hin.	Setzen Sie sich nicht hin.

G7 Die Verneinung von be

The negative of be

This isn't my sandwich.
This is NOT my sandwich.

Das ist nicht mein Sandwich.
Das ist NICHT mein Sandwich.

So bildest du die **Verneinung** mit **be**. Es gibt Langformen und Kurzformen.

I **am not**	I'**m not**	ich bin nicht
you **are not**	you **aren't**	du bist nicht / Sie sind nicht
he **is not**	he **isn't**	er ist nicht
she **is not**	she **isn't**	sie ist nicht
it **is not**	it **isn't**	es ist nicht
we **are not**	we **aren't**	wir sind nicht
you **are not**	you **aren't**	ihr seid nicht / Sie sind nicht
they **are not**	they **aren't**	sie sind nicht

Beim Schreiben verwendest du meistens Langformen und beim Sprechen Kurzformen.

(TEST YOURSELF) Write negative sentences.

1. Maths is my best subject.
2. I'm very good at English.
3. Holly is a new student.
4. You are a good singer.
5. Mr Swindon is my tutor.
6. Luke and Dave are football stars.

(FÜR PROFIS)

Du kannst **is not** und **are not** unterschiedlich verkürzen.

Vergleiche: it **is not** → it **isn't** oder **it's not**
you **are not** → you **aren't** oder **you're not**

Unit 3

G8 Die einfache Gegenwart: Aussagen

The simple present: statements

I like Edgar, the elephant.
He eats fruit.

Ich mag Edgar, den Elefanten.
Er frisst Obst.

Wenn du über **Gewohnheiten** oder Dinge sprichst, die **allgemein gültig** sind, verwendest du die einfache Gegenwart.

Signalwörter	
on Mondays	montags
every day	jeden Tag
always	immer

I	**play**	ich spiele
you	**play**	du spielst / Sie spielen
he	**plays**	er spielt
she	**plays**	sie spielt
it	**plays**	es spielt
we	**play**	wir spielen
you	**play**	ihr spielt / Sie spielen
they	**play**	sie spielen

Bei Verben mit Zischlaut wie **watch**, **finish**, **guess**, hängst du bei **he**, **she**, **it** ein **-es** an.

Luke **watches** [ɪz] TV every Saturday.	Luke sieht jeden Samstag fern.

Manche Verben haben unregelmäßige Formen bei **he**, **she**, **it**.

I **have** → he **has**   I **go** → she **goes** [gəʊz]   I **do** → he **does** [dʌz]

(TEST YOURSELF) **Put in the right verb form.**

1. Luke —— (have) a nice dog, Sherlock.
2. He —— (like) long walks in the park.
3. They —— (go) out every day.
4. Sherlock —— (eat) a lot.
5. He —— (play) with a ball every day.
6. Luke —— (like) his dog.

G9 Die einfache Gegenwart: Verneinung

The simple present: negatives

I don't sleep at night.

Ich schlafe nachts nicht.

Mit **don't** (= do not) oder **doesn't** (= does not) vor einem Verb kannst du sagen, was man **nicht** macht. So bildest du die Verneinung:

I	**don't**	play	ich spiele nicht
you	**don't**	play	du spielst nicht / Sie spielen nicht
he	**doesn't**	play	er spielt nicht
she	**doesn't**	play	sie spielt nicht
it	**doesn't**	play	es spielt nicht
we	**don't**	play	wir spielen nicht
you	**don't**	play	ihr spielt nicht / Sie spielen nicht
they	**don't**	play	sie spielen nicht

Die Verneinung von **be** kennst du schon (→ G7). Vergleiche:

We **aren't** from Greenwich. Aber: We **don't come** from Greenwich.

(TEST YOURSELF) Put in don't or doesn't.

1. An elephant — eat meat.
2. Ben — sleep much.
3. Penguins — like bananas.
4. Snakes — eat fruit.
5. A tiger — go to school.
6. Animals — work at the zoo.

(FÜR PROFIS)

Im Deutschen haben wir manchmal zwei Möglichkeiten, verneinte Sätze zu sagen. Vergleiche:

I **don't listen** to music. Ich **höre nicht** Musik. / Ich **höre keine** Musik.

G10 Die einfache Gegenwart: Fragen

The simple present: questions

Do you have a pet?
Where does your pet sleep?

Hast du ein Haustier?
Wo schläft dein Haustier?

Bei **Fragen mit Vollverben**, auf die man mit Ja oder Nein antworten kann, steht immer **do** oder **does** am Satzanfang.

Do	I	**have** ...?	Habe ich ...?
Do	you	**have** ...?	Hast du ...?/Haben Sie ...?
Does	he	**have** ...?	Hat er ...?
Does	she	**have** ...?	Hat sie ...?
Does	it	**have** ...?	Hat es ...?
Do	we	**have** ...?	Haben wir ...?
Do	you	**have** ...?	Habt ihr ...?/Haben Sie ...?
Do	they	**have** ...?	Haben sie ...?

Bei Fragen mit Fragewörtern steht das Fragewort immer am Satzanfang.

What do you **do** on Mondays?	Was machst du montags?
Where do they **meet**?	Wo treffen sie sich?
When does Holly **have** breakfast?	Wann frühstückt Holly?
Why does Fred **work** at the zoo?	Warum arbeitet Fred im Zoo?

(TEST YOURSELF) Make questions.

1. you • do • like the zoo • ?
2. monkeys • do • eat bananas • why • ?
3. Fred • does • clean the cages • when • ?
4. the zookeeper • does • love his work • ?
5. the animals • do • eat meat or fruit • ?
6. does • Fred • do next • what • ?

Unit 4

Language tip

G11 Personalpronomen und Possessivbegleiter

Personal pronouns and possessive determiners

Look at me. I'm a good singer and my costume is so cool.

Schaut mich an! Ich bin ein guter Sänger und mein Kostüm ist so cool.

Pronomen stehen **für** ein anderes Nomen, z. B. **the boy** → **he**, **the girl** → **she**, usw.
Personalpronomen haben eine Subjektform und eine Objektform.
Possessivbegleiter drücken aus, wem oder zu wem etwas gehört.

Personalpronomen Subjektform		Objektform		**Possessivbegleiter** (Besitzform)	
I	ich	me	mir / mich	my	mein(e)
you	du / Sie	you	dir / dich / Ihnen / Sie	your	dein(e) / Ihr(e)
he	er	him	ihm / ihn	his	sein(e)
she	sie	her	ihr / sie	her	ihr(e)
it	es	it	ihm / es	its	sein(e)
we	wir	us	uns	our	unser(e)
you	ihr / Sie	you	euch / Ihnen / Sie	your	euer(e) / Ihr(e)
they	sie	them	ihnen / sie	their	ihr(e)

It steht im Englischen für alle Dinge. Im Deutschen ist das nicht so. Vergleiche:

the pen → **It** is blue.	der Stift → **Er** ist blau.
the bag → **It** is nice. I like **it**.	die Tasche → **Sie** ist schön. Ich mag **sie**.
the house → **It** is old.	das Haus → **Es** ist alt.

(TEST YOURSELF) **Complete the sentences.**

1. I never forget —— birthday. (he / his)
2. She goes shopping with —— mum. (her / its)
3. How old is your sister? —— is ten. (He / She)
4. This is —— invitation. (my / me)
5. When is —— birthday? (you / your)
6. I have a great present for —— . (he / him)

G12 Die Wortstellung im Satz

Word order

I like football. I always win.

Ich mag Fußball. Ich gewinne immer.

Die wichtigste Wortstellungsregel in englischen Aussagesätzen lautet: **Subjekt – Verb – Objekt**.

Subjekt	Verb	Objekt	
I	like	parties.	Ich mag Partys.
Olivia	has	a cool costume.	Olivia hat ein cooles Kostüm.
Honey and Fluff	eat	grass.	Honey und Fluff essen Gras.

Wenn du sagen möchtest, wie oft etwas passiert, kannst du **Häufigkeitsadverbien** (adverbs of frequency) benutzen. Sie stehen im Englischen **vor dem Verb**. Vergleiche:

Mum	**always**	**makes** a cake for us.	Mama macht immer einen Kuchen für uns.
Jay	**often**	**has** a party.	Jay macht oft eine Party.
My friends	**never**	**forget** my birthday.	Meine Freunde vergessen nie meinen Geburtstag.

In Sätzen mit **be** steht das Adverb **dahinter**.

Mr Swindon **is never** late.	Mr Swindon kommt nie zu spät.

(TEST YOURSELF) Put the words in the right place. Write the sentences.

1. My mum and dad forget my birthday. (never)
2. I invite friends to my party. (often)
3. We have parties in our garden. (often)
4. I watch TV in the evening. (always)
5. My sister is at home. (often)
6. We eat pizza on Fridays. (always)

Unit 5

G13 Die einfache Vergangenheit: Aussagen

The simple past: statements

Hi Sherlock, I had a great weekend. I watched a lot of films.

Hallo Sherlock, ich hatte ein tolles Wochenende. Ich habe mir viele Filme angeschaut.

Um über Dinge zu sprechen, die in der **Vergangenheit** passiert und **vorbei** sind, verwendest du im Englischen die einfache Vergangenheit (simple past).

Signalwörter	
yesterday	gestern
last week	letzte Woche

Bei den meisten Verben hängst du für das **simple past** die Endung **-ed** an das Verb. Sie ist für alle Personen gleich. Im Deutschen gibt es zwei Möglichkeiten, Vergangenes auszudrücken.

I **played** netball.	Ich spielte Netzball. / Ich habe Netzball gespielt.
You **watched** TV yesterday.	Du sahst gestern fern.
He **walked** on the beach.	Er lief am Strand. / Er ist am Strand gelaufen.
She **worked** last weekend.	Sie arbeitete letztes Wochenende.
We **talked** to Ray-B last week.	Wir sprachen letzte Woche mit Ray-B.
They **wanted** to buy things.	Sie wollten Sachen kaufen.

Achtung Aussprache: want**ed** [ˈwɒntɪd]

Achtung Schreibweise: stop → sto**pped** [stɒpt]

Einige Verben haben unregelmäßige Formen.

go → **went**	see → **saw**
buy → **bought**	have → **had**
do → **did**	win → **won**

Eine Liste der unregelmäßigen Verben findest du auf Seite 235.

(TEST YOURSELF) Put in the verbs in the simple past.

1. I —— (clean) my bike on Monday.
2. Yesterday my father —— (work) at home.
3. We —— (listen) to cool music last Friday.
4. They —— (play) netball in the park last week.
5. I —— (help) my mother last weekend.
6. Kim —— (want) to watch a DVD yesterday.

G14 Die einfache Vergangenheit: Fragen

The simple past: questions

Ben, did you eat our food?

Ben, hast du unser Essen gegessen?

Du kennst bereits Fragen mit **do** und **does**. Für **Fragen in der Vergangenheit**, auf die man mit ja oder nein antworten kann, steht immer **did** am Satzanfang.

Did	I	**have** …?	Hatte ich …?
Did	you	**have** …?	Hattest du …?/Hatten Sie …?
Did	he	**have** …?	Hatte er …?
Did	she	**have** …?	Hatte sie …?
Did	it	**have** …?	Hatte es …?
Did	we	**have** …?	Hatten wir …?
Did	you	**have** …?	Hattet ihr …?/Hatten Sie …?
Did	they	**have** …?	Hatten sie …?

Bei Fragen mit Fragewörtern steht das Fragewort immer am Satzanfang.

What (was)	**did**	you	**do**?
Where (wo)	**did**	he	**go**?
When (wann)	**did**	she	**eat**?
Why (warum)	**did**	we	**walk**?
How (wie)	**did**	they	**go** there?

(TEST YOURSELF) Put in How did, Did, Where did, Did, What did, Did.

1. —— Holly send Jay a postcard? (no)
2. —— Holly go with her mum? (no)
3. —— Holly go on Sunday? (to Margate)
4. —— they go to the seaside? (by car)
5. —— Holly eat a pizza? (yes)
6. —— Holly buy at the shops? (postcards)

Unit 6

Language tip

G15 Modale Hilfsverben: can / can't, must und needn't

Modal auxiliaries: can / can't, must and needn't

I must help Sherlock. He can't eat the cake alone.

Ich muss Sherlock helfen.
Er kann den Kuchen nicht alleine essen.

Modale Hilfsverben sind z. B. **can**, **can't**, **must** und **needn't**.
Sie kommen immer zusammen mit einem anderen Verb vor.

I	**must**	**stop** now.	Ich muss jetzt aufhören.
He	**can't**	**go** now.	Er kann jetzt nicht gehen.
She	**needn't**	**do** it.	Sie muss es nicht machen.
We	**can**	**help** you.	Wir können dir helfen.
They	**needn't**	**be** sad.	Sie müssen nicht traurig sein.

Fragen mit **can** oder **must** bildest du so:

Can you **help** me, please?	Kannst du mir bitte helfen?
Must I **go** now?	Muss ich jetzt gehen?
What can we **do**?	Was können wir tun?

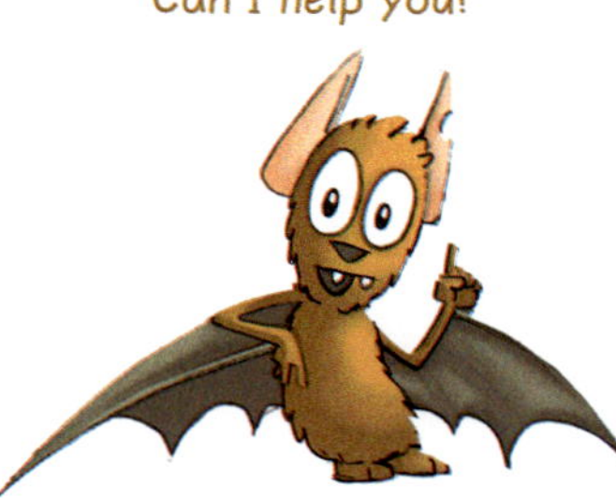

(TEST YOURSELF) **Choose the right word.**

1. I'm not hungry. We — eat now. (needn't / can't)
2. It's cold outside. We — wear warm clothes. (can't / must)
3. Dad, — you help me, please? (needn't / can)
4. Sorry, I — speak English. (can't / can)
5. It's late. I — go home now. (must / needn't)
6. You — worry – we have great food here. (must / needn't)

G16 Die einfache Vergangenheit von be

The simple past of be

I was at Highfield Farm last weekend.

Ich war letzte Woche auf der Highfield Farm.

Das Verb **be** hat in der Vergangenheit zwei verschiedene Formen: **was** und **were**. Für die **Verneinung** setzt du einfach **not** dahinter. Es gibt dabei Langformen und Kurzformen.

I **was**	ich war	I **was not**	I **wasn't**	ich war nicht
you **were**	du warst / Sie waren	you **were not**	you **weren't**	du warst nicht
he **was**	er war	he **was not**	he **wasn't**	er war nicht
she **was**	sie war	she **was not**	she **wasn't**	sie war nicht
it **was**	es war	it **was not**	it **wasn't**	es war nicht
we **were**	wir waren	we **were not**	we **weren't**	wir waren nicht
you **were**	ihr wart / Sie waren	you **were not**	you **weren't**	ihr wart nicht
they **were**	sie waren	they **were not**	they **weren't**	sie waren nicht

Bei **Fragen**, die man mit Ja oder Nein beantworten kann, steht **was** oder **were** am Satzanfang.

Was Sid at home?	War Sid zu Hause?
Were they at Highfield Farm?	Waren sie auf der Highfield Farm?

Bei Fragen mit Fragewörtern steht das Fragewort am Satzanfang. Darauf folgt **was** oder **were**.

Where was Sid at the weekend?	**When were** they at Highfield Farm?

(TEST YOURSELF) **Put in was or were, wasn't or weren't.**

1. The children — in the country.
2. Their weekend — great.
3. Olivia — with them.
4. The boys — in Holly's group.
5. Rock climbing — easy.
6. Highfield Farm — interesting.

G17 Die einfache Vergangenheit: Verneinung

The simple past: negatives

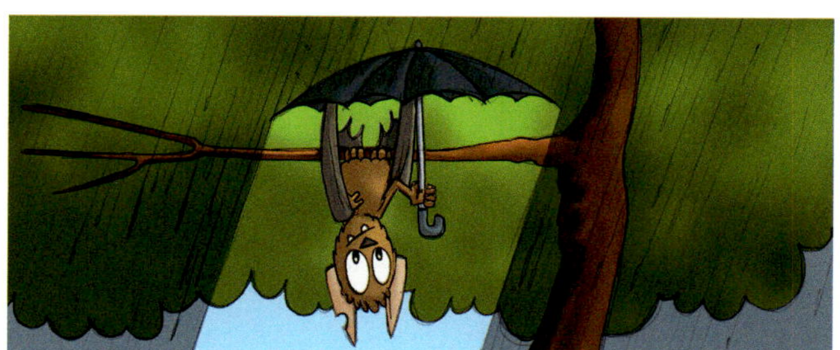

I didn't forget my umbrella.

Ich habe meinen Schirm nicht vergessen.

Du kennst schon die Verneinung für die Gegenwart mit **don't** und **doesn't**. Um zu sagen, was in der Vergangenheit nicht passiert ist, setzt du **didn't** vor das Verb.

Signalwörter	
last Monday	letzten Montag
last week	letzte Woche
yesterday	gestern

I	**didn't go**	ich ging nicht
you	**didn't go**	du gingst nicht / Sie gingen nicht
he	**didn't go**	er ging nicht
she	**didn't go**	sie ging nicht
it	**didn't go**	es ging nicht
we	**didn't go**	wir gingen nicht
you	**didn't go**	ihr gingt nicht / Sie gingen nicht
they	**didn't go**	sie gingen nicht

Das Verb nach **didn't** steht immer in der **Grundform.** Vergleiche:

We **went** to the farm last weekend.	Wir **fuhren** letztes Wochenende auf die Farm.
Aber: We **didn't go** to the farm last weekend.	Wir **fuhren** letztes Wochenende **nicht** auf die Farm.

(TEST YOURSELF) **Write sentences with didn't.**

1. Holly — wet. (not get)
2. Luke — football. (not play)
3. We — canoeing. (not go)
4. I — the chickens. (not like)
5. They — a picnic in the garden. (not have)
6. She — the sheep in the morning. (not feed)

Lösungen

TEST YOURSELF

G1 1. Olivia's 2. Luke's 3. Dave's 4. Holly's 5. Lucy's 6. Olivia's

G2 1. am/'m 2. are/'re 3. are 4. is 5. is 6. are/'re

G3 1. boys 2. books 3. T-shirts 4. CDs 5. boxes 6. families

G4 1. Where 2. Is 3. How 4. What 5. Are 6. Who

G5 1. the 2. an 3. a 4. The 5. a 6. an

G6 1. Close 2. Don't play 3. Don't open 4. Look 5. Don't sing 6. Go

G7
1. Maths is not/isn't my best subject.
2. I am not/'m not very good at English.
3. Holly is not/isn't a new student.
4. You are not/aren't a good singer.
5. Mr Swindon is not/isn't my tutor.
6. Luke and Dave are not/aren't football stars.

G8 1. has 2. likes 3. go 4. eats 5. plays 6. likes

G9 1. doesn't 2. doesn't 3. don't 4. don't 5. doesn't 6. don't

G10
1. Do you like the zoo?
2. Why do monkeys eat bananas?
3. When does Fred clean the cages?
4. Does the zookeeper love his work?
5. Do the animals eat meat or fruit?
6. What does Fred do next?

G11 1. his 2. her 3. She 4. my 5. your 6. him

G12
1. My mum and dad never forget my birthday.
2. I often invite friends to my party.
3. We often have parties in our garden.
4. I always watch TV in the evening.
5. My sister is often at home.
6. We always eat pizza on Fridays.

G13 1. cleaned 2. worked 3. listened 4. played 5. helped 6. wanted

G14 1. Did 2. Did 3. Where did 4. How did 5. Did 6. What did

G15 1. needn't 2. must 3. can 4. can't 5. must 6. needn't

G16 1. were 2. was 3. wasn't 4. weren't 5. wasn't 6. was

G17 1. didn't get 2. didn't play 3. didn't go, 4. didn't like 5. didn't have 6. didn't feed

Methods

Double circle

(Kugellager)

Step 1

Teilt euch in zwei Gruppen A und B.
Gruppe A bildet den inneren Kreis. Gruppe B bildet den äußeren Kreis. Steht dabei so, dass ihr euch anseht.

Step 2

Wenn ein Signal ertönt, sprecht ihr mit der Person, die euch gegenübersteht.

Step 3

Beim nächsten Signal rückt der mittlere Kreis zwei Plätze weiter nach links. Wiederholt den Vorgang.

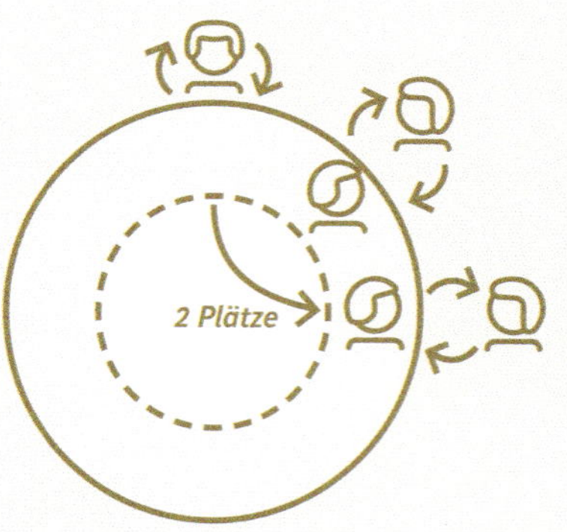

Think – pair – share

Step 1

Schreibe deine Ideen, Gedanken oder Lösungen zur Aufgabe auf.

Step 2

Tauscht eure Notizen zu zweit aus und besprecht sie.

Step 3

Präsentiert euer Ergebnis anderen Paaren oder der gesamten Klasse.

Peer correction

(Partnerkontrolle)

Step 1

Bearbeite die Aufgabe zunächst selbstständig.

Step 2

Tausche deine Lösungen mit einem Partner/einer Partnerin. Kontrolliere seine oder ihre Lösungen.

Step 3

Tauscht euch danach zu der Aufgabe aus und korrigiert den Text.

Milling around
(Marktplatz)

Step 1
Bearbeite die Aufgabe zunächst allein.
Auf ein Zeichen vom Lehrer oder der Lehrerin steht ihr auf und geht durch den Raum.
Vergesst nicht, die Aufgabe und einen Stift mitzunehmen.

Step 2
Wenn ein Signal ertönt, bleibt ihr stehen.
Besprecht mit der Person die Aufgabe, die euch am nächsten steht.

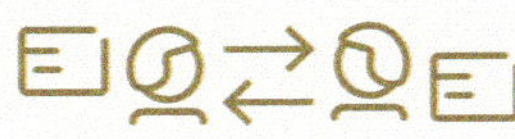

Step 3
Beim nächsten Signal trennt ihr euch und geht weiter durch den Raum. Wiederholt den Vorgang.

Walking sentences

Step 1
Nehmt eine Karte. Ihr findet darauf ein Wort und/oder ein Satzzeichen.

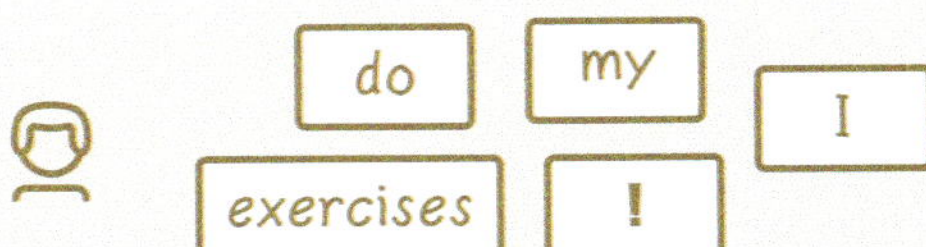

Step 2
Wenn ein Signal ertönt, geht durch die Klasse und bildet vollständige Sätze.
Stellt euch dazu in der richtigen Reihenfolge auf. Haltet eure Karten vor euch, so dass alle sie lesen können.

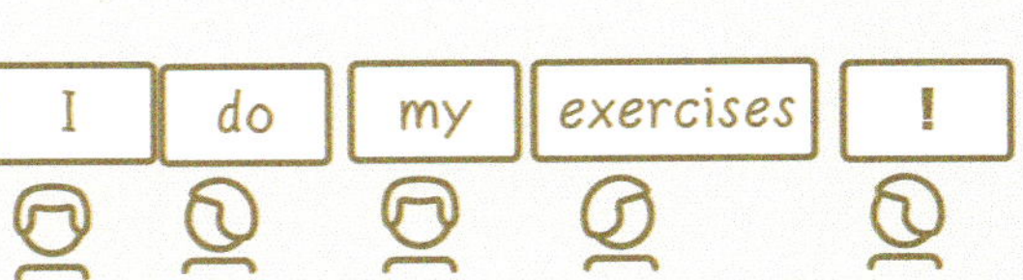

Step 3
Lest euren Satz vor und schreibt ihn auf.

Freeze frame

(Standbild)

Step 1

Entscheidet euch in der Gruppe, welche Szene oder Personen ihr darstellen wollt. Verteilt die Rollen.

Step 2

Probiert verschiedene Standbilder aus und entscheidet euch dann für eines. Denkt daran, ihr müsst euer Standbild eine Minute lang durchhalten. Keiner darf sich bewegen oder etwas sagen.

Step 3

Präsentiert der Klasse euer Standbild. Die anderen beschreiben, was sie sehen.

Gallery walk

Step 1

Hängt nach eurer Gruppenarbeit euer Produkt gut sichtbar im Klassenzimmer auf.

Step 2

Seht euch die Produkte der anderen an und bewertet sie.

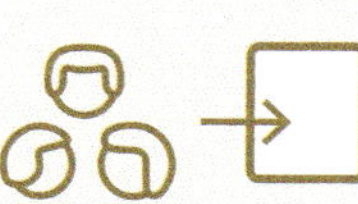

Step 3

Wertet im Anschluss eure Ergebnisse in der Klasse aus.

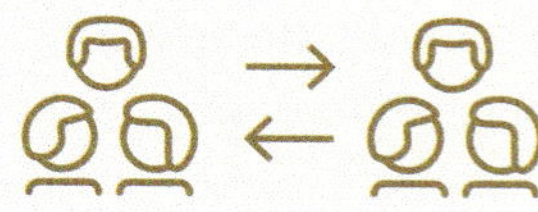

Bus stop
(Lerntempoduett)

Step 1
Bearbeite die Aufgabe zunächst allein. Schreibe deine Lösungen auf.

Step 2
Wenn du fertig bist, gehe zum „bus stop“. Warte dort auf die nächste Person bzw. triff die Person, die dort schon wartet. Vergleicht und korrigiert eure Ergebnisse.

Step 3
Gehe danach wieder zu deinem Platz zurück. Bearbeite die nächste Aufgabe.

Writers' conference
(Schreibwerkstatt)

Step 1
Bildet Vierergruppen.

Step 2
Lest euch eure Sätze/Texte gegenseitig vor.

Step 3
Die anderen sagen, was ihnen gefallen hat.

Step 4
Die Zuhörer können Verbesserungsvorschläge machen.

Step 5
Jede Gruppe wählt den besten Text aus und liest ihn der Klasse vor.

Hier geht es darum, wie du Vokabeln lernen kannst. Jeder Mensch lernt anders. Finde heraus, welche Lernstrategie für dich am besten geeignet ist.

Vocabulary

Vocabulary tips

Lernen ganz klassisch: Das Vokabelheft
Dein Vokabelheft sollte drei Spalten haben: In die erste Spalte schreibst du das englische Wort, in die zweite die deutsche Übersetzung. In die dritte Spalte kannst du einen Beispielsatz schreiben oder hilfreiche Merkbilder aus deinem Buch dazu malen. Natürlich kannst du dir auch selber Bilder ausdenken.

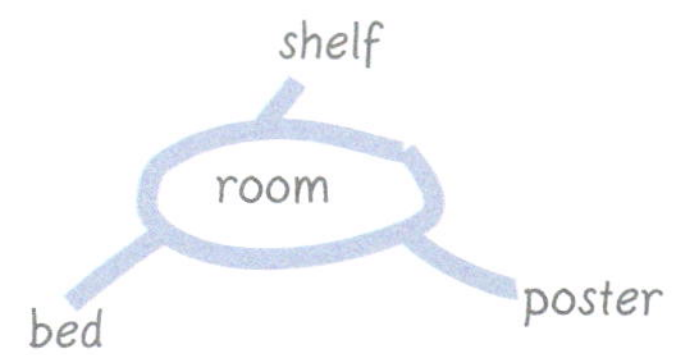

Vernetztes Lernen: Die Vokabel-Mind-Map
Du kannst zu einem bestimmten Thema neue Wörter in Wortfeldern ordnen und sie mit bekannten Wörtern verbinden.

Lernen durch Zuhören: Vokabeln aufnehmen
Kannst du mit dem Mikrofon auf deinem Computer oder mit deinem Handy Wörter aufnehmen? Dann nimm ein deutsches Wort oder einen deutschen Satz auf. Mach dann eine kurze Pause. Sprich nach der Pause das englische Wort oder den englischen Satz. Am besten wählst du eine andere Reihenfolge als im Buch. So kannst du dir deine Vokabeln immer wieder anhören und prüfen, ob du alle Wörter weißt.

Ich bin eine Fledermaus. – I'm a bat.

Sounds

Dir sind bestimmt schon die Zeichen aufgefallen, die hinter jedem Wort in deiner Wortliste stehen. Diese „Geheimschrift“ (Lautschrift) hilft dir, wenn du nicht weißt, wie du das Wort aussprichst oder auch gerade niemand da ist, der dir helfen kann.

Die meisten Zeichen sprichst du genauso aus wie sie dastehen.

Beispiele: [pet] – ‚pet‘ oder [maɪ] – ‚my‘

Hier sind ein paar einfache Wörter. Sprich sie laut aus.

1. [gri:n] 2.  [naɪt] 3. [blu:] 4. [pɑ:k] 5. [haɪ] 6. [bed]

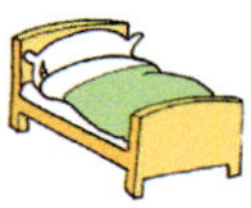

Einige Laute haben besondere Zeichen. Erkennst du trotzdem, welche Wörter hier dargestellt sind? Tipp: Diese Wörter hast du alle schon gelernt.

1. [kæt] 2.  [kəm'pju:tə] 3. [faɪv] 4. ['sʌni] 5. [fɪʃ] 6. [θɪŋk]

Versuche doch jetzt zum Schluss einmal folgende zwei Sätze zu lesen.
Tipp: Sie stammen aus einem Lied deines Schulbuchs.

[ðɪs] [ɪz] [aʊə] ['klɑ:srʊm]
[hɪə] [wi:] [ɔ:l] [lɜ:n] ['ɪŋlɪʃ].

Achtung: Die Lautschrift zeigt dir nur die Aussprache, aber nie die Schreibweise an.

Instructions

Arbeitsanweisungen mit Operatoren

Act the dialogue with a partner.	**Spielt** den Dialog zu zweit.
Add notes.	**Füge** Notizen **hinzu**.
Answer the questions.	**Beantworte** die Fragen.
Ask a partner.	**Frage** eine Partnerin/einen Partner.
Ask for feedback.	**Bitte** um Rückmeldung.
Check the sentences.	**Überprüfe** die Sätze.
Choose one of the tasks • the right question word.	**Wähle** eine der Aufgaben • das richtige Fragewort **aus**.
Collect ideas.	**Sammle** Ideen.
Compare with your partner.	**Vergleicht** zu zweit.
Complete the sentences • the dialogue.	**Vervollständige** die Sätze • den Dialog.
Correct the wrong sentences.	**Verbessere** die falschen Sätze.
Draw a picture • your family tree.	**Zeichne** ein Bild • deinen Familienstammbaum.
Find the words • the right answers.	**Finde** die Wörter • die richtigen Antworten.
Finish the sentences.	**Vervollständige** die Sätze.
Give feedback.	**Gib Rückmeldung.**
Guess.	**Überlege.**
Listen and **point**.	**Höre zu** und **zeige darauf**.
Listen, **read** and **say**.	**Höre zu**, **lies mit** und **sprich nach**.
Look at the photos • pictures (again).	**Schau** dir die Fotos • Bilder (noch einmal) **an**.
Make a card.	**Bastle** eine Karte.
Make a list • a chart • a mind map.	**Erstelle** eine Liste • eine Tabelle • ein Wörternetz.
Match the sentences with the pictures.	**Ordne** den Bildern die richtigen Sätze **zu**.
Match the words • the sentence parts.	**Ordne** die Wörter • die Satzteile **zu**.
Present your profile to your tutor group.	**Stelle** dein Profil deiner Klasse **vor**.
Put in the right verbs.	**Setze** die richtigen Verben **ein**.
Put the words **in the right order**.	**Bringe** die Wörter **in die richtige Reihenfolge**.
Read your sentences to a partner.	**Lest** euch gegenseitig eure Sätze **vor**.
Read the story **again**.	**Lies** die Geschichte **noch einmal**.
Right or wrong?	**Richtig oder falsch**?
Say the names.	**Nenne** die Namen.
Show your leaflet.	**Zeige** (den anderen) deine Broschüre.
Take notes.	**Mache** dir Notizen.
Talk with a partner.	**Sprich mit** deiner Partnerin oder deinem Partner.
Tell a partner **about** your family.	**Erzählt** euch gegenseitig **von** euren Familien.
Use the words from exercise 4.	**Benutze** die Wörter aus Übung 4.
Watch the film.	**Schau** den Film **an**.
What are the words?	**Wie** heißen die Wörter?
What else can you see?	**Was** kannst du **noch** sehen?
Where are the things?	**Wo** sind die Dinge?
Who says it?	**Wer** sagt das?
Why (not)?	**Warum** (nicht)?
Write sentences • the questions.	**Schreibe** Sätze • die Fragen.

Classroom phrases

Before or after the lesson

Good morning, Mr/Mrs/Miss …	Guten Morgen, Herr/Frau …
I'm sorry I'm late.	Tut mir leid, dass ich mich verspätet habe.
I'm sorry I don't have my exercise book/ my homework with me.	Tut mir leid, ich habe mein Heft/ meine Hausaufgaben nicht dabei.
What's for homework?	Was haben wir als Hausaufgabe auf?

Asking for help

Can you help me, please?	Können Sie/Kannst du mir bitte helfen?
Can you say that again, please?	Können Sie/Kannst du das bitte wiederholen?
Can I go to the toilet, please?	Kann ich bitte auf Toilette gehen?
Mr/Mrs … I don't feel well.	Herr/Frau …, mir geht es nicht gut.
Can you write that on the board?	Können Sie das an die Tafel schreiben?

Asking for information

What page is it, please?	Auf welcher Seite ist das?
What's for homework?	Was ist die Hausaufgabe?
What's the German/English word for …?	Was ist das deutsche/englische Wort für …?
How do you spell …?	Wie schreibt man …?
What does that mean?	Was heißt/bedeutet das?
Sorry, I don't understand.	Tut mir leid, ich verstehe das nicht.
Sorry, I don't know.	Tut mir leid, ich weiß es nicht.

Working together

Can we work in pairs/groups?	Können wir zu zweit/in Gruppen arbeiten?
Do you want to work with me/us?	Willst du/Wollt ihr mit mir/uns arbeiten?
Let's make a/draw a …	Lass(t) uns ein … machen/zeichnen.
Whose turn is it?	Wer ist dran?
It's my/your turn.	Ich bin dran./Du bist dran.

Your teacher can say …

Open your books at page …	Öffnet eure Bücher auf Seite …
Turn to page …	Schlagt Seite … auf.
Take out your pens.	Holt eure Stifte raus.
Look at the board.	Schaut an die Tafel.
Who can do number …?	Wer kann Nummer … machen?
Put your hands up, please!	Meldet euch, bitte!
Try again!	Versuche es noch einmal.
Sit down, please, and be quiet.	Setz dich bitte und sei ruhig./Setzt euch bitte und seid ruhig.

Vocabulary

Das Vocabulary enthält alle neuen Wörter und Wendungen. Sie stehen in der Reihenfolge, wie sie im Buch vorkommen.

Die Wortliste ist in drei Spalten aufgeteilt:

Links findest du das englische Wort mit der Lautschrift in Klammern. (Die Lautschrift wird auf S. 183 und ganz unten auf jeder Seite im *Dictionary* erklärt.)

In der mittleren Spalte steht die deutsche Übersetzung.

Rechts findest du Beispielsätze, Hinweise und Tipps, die dir beim Lernen helfen.

Die **fett** gedruckten Wörter musst du lernen.
Die blau gedruckten Wörter kannst du lernen, musst du aber nicht.
Die Wörter aus den Liedern und Checkpoints musst du nicht lernen.

Symbole und Abkürzungen:

👄	Achte auf die Aussprache!	=	entspricht
✎	Achte auf die Schreibung!	*(sg)*	Einzahl (Singular)
↔	ist das Gegenteil von	*(pl)*	Mehrzahl (Plural)
→	ist verwandt mit	R	ähnlich wie im Russischen
		T	ähnlich wie im Türkischen

Die *Word bank*-Seiten helfen dir, die *Your turn*-Aufgaben in den *Units* zu bearbeiten. Du findest dort nützlichen individuellen Wortschatz zum Thema der *Unit*, der dir hilft, über deine eigene Situation zu sprechen oder zu schreiben. Diese Wörter findest du auch im *Dictionary*.

Wenn du ein Wort nicht weißt und im Wörterbuch nachschlagen willst, schau auf den *Dictionary*-Seiten ab S. 236 nach. Oder bei den *Instructions* auf S. 184.

Welcome – Hello!

p. 8	**welcome (to)** ['welkəm tʊ]	willkommen (bei/in)	
	Hello. [hə'ləʊ]	Hallo.	**Hello** Ben!
	I'm (= I am) [aɪm]	ich bin	✎ I schreibst du immer groß.
	the [ðə]	der; die *(auch Pl.)*; das	☺ Im Englischen gibt es nur einen Artikel.
	bat [bæt]	Fledermaus	
	Nice to meet you. [ˌnaɪs tə 'mi:t ju:]	Nett, dich kennen zu lernen.	Ganze Sätze am besten als Einheit lernen.
	What's your name? [ˌwɒts jə 'neɪm]	Wie heißt du?	

I like [aɪ 'laɪk]	ich mag; gefällt mir	I **like** bats.
English ['ɪŋglɪʃ]	Englisch	Achtung Schreibweise! Engli**sh**
Hi. [haɪ]	Hi.; Hallo.	Wird auch im Deutschen so verwendet.
My name is ... [maɪ 'neɪm‿ɪz]	Ich heiße ...	What's your name? – **My name is** Ben.
music ['mju:zɪk]	Musik	T müsik R музыка
And you? [ənd 'ju:]	Und du?	I like music. **And you?**
sport [spɔ:t]	Sport	Achtung Aussprache!
animal ['ænɪml]	Tier	**Animals:** bat, cat, dog, ...
computer [ˌkəm'pju:tə]	Computer	
It's time to go. [ɪts ˌtaɪm tə 'gəʊ]	Es ist Zeit, zu gehen.	Ganze Sätze am besten als Einheit lernen.
See you! ['si: ju:]	Tschüss!; Bis bald!	
yes [jes]	ja	☺ Dieses Wort kennst du bestimmt schon!
Bye! [baɪ]	Tschüss!	**bye** ↔ hello, hi
Goodbye! [gʊd'baɪ]	Auf Wiedersehen.	

The welcome song

is the colour of your [ɪz ðə 'kʌlər‿əv jɔ:]	ist die Farbe deiner/ deines
shoe [ʃu:]	Schuh
hat [hæt]	Hut; Mütze
shirt [ʃɜ:t]	Hemd; Shirt
dress [dres]	Kleid
come with me ['kʌm wɪð mi:]	komm mit mir
a colour mix [ə 'kʌlə ˌmɪks]	eine Farbmischung
you look so fine [ju: 'lʊk səʊ ˌfaɪn]	du siehst so schön aus
I like you [aɪ 'laɪk ju:]	ich mag dich
England ['ɪŋglənd]	England
Greenwich ['grenɪdʒ]	*Stadtteil im Südosten Londons*
hair [heə]	Haar; Haare
skirt [skɜ:t]	Rock
top [tɒp]	Top
cap [kæp]	Kappe; Mütze

numbers

zero 0 ['zɪərəʊ]	null
one 1 [wʌn]	eins
two 2 [tu:]	zwei
three 3 [θri:]	drei
four 4 [fɔ:]	vier
five 5 [faɪv]	fünf
six 6 [sɪks]	sechs
seven 7 ['sevn]	sieben
eight 8 [eɪt]	acht
nine 9 [naɪn]	neun
ten 10 [ten]	zehn

Zoom in – In a park

p. 10	**in** [ɪn]	in; im	
	a [ə]	ein; eine	In a park.
	park [pɑːk]	Park	
	colour [ˈkʌlə]	Farbe	**Colours**: red, blue, green, …
	activity [ækˈtɪvəti]	Aktivität	Nomen schreibst du im Englischen immer klein.
	number [ˈnʌmbə]	Nummer; Zahl	**Numbers**: zero, one, two, three, four, …
	people *(pl only)* [ˈpiːpl]	Leute; Menschen	
	dog [dɒg]	Hund	
	tennis [ˈtenɪs]	Tennis	
	boy [bɔɪ]	Junge	
p. 11	**I spy with my little eye …** [aɪ spaɪ wɪð ˌmaɪ lɪtl ˈaɪ]	Ich sehe was, was du nicht siehst …	Ganze Sätze am besten als Einheit lernen.
	something [ˈsʌmθɪŋ]	etwas	
	it's (= it is) [ɪts]	es ist	It is black. **It's** a bat.
	here [hɪə]	hier	Achtung Schreibweise! h**ere**
	bus [bʌs]	Bus	Achtung Aussprache!
	I can play football. [aɪ kən pleɪ ˈfʊtbɔːl]	Ich kann Fußball spielen.	
	I can buy … [baɪ]	Ich kann … kaufen.	

colours

red	[red]	rot		**brown**	[braʊn]	braun
green	[griːn]	grün		**white**	[waɪt]	weiß
blue	[bluː]	blau		**orange**	[ˈɒrɪndʒ]	orange
yellow	[ˈjeləʊ]	gelb		**purple**	[ˈpɜːpl]	lila; violett
black	[blæk]	schwarz		**pink**	[pɪŋk]	rosa; pink
grey	[greɪ]	grau				

Unit 1 I'm from Greenwich

Way in

p. 12	**I'm from …** ['aɪm ˌfrɒm]	ich komme aus …	Olivia: **I'm from** Greenwich.
	from [frɒm]	aus; von	
	this [ðɪs]	das; dies	Hello! I'm Luke and **this** is David.
	my [maɪ]	mein	**My** name is Olivia Fraser.
	bike [baɪk]	Fahrrad	
	cool [ku:l]	cool; super	This is my bike. It's **cool**.
	fan [fæn]	Fan	I'm a football **fan**.
	eleven [ɪ'levn]	elf	11
	How old are you? [haʊ‿'əʊld‿ə ˌju:]	Wie alt bist du?	**How old are you?** – I'm eleven.
p. 13	**that's (= that is)** [ðæts]	das ist	**That's** in England.
	England ['ɪŋglənd]	England	Greenwich? That's in **England**.
	Where are you from? [ˌweər‿ə ju 'frɒm]	Woher kommst du?	**Where are you from?** – I'm from Greenwich.
	pet [pet]	Haustier	Sherlock is a **pet**.
	they're (= they are) [ðeə]	sie sind	**They're** my pets. They are cool.
	nice [naɪs]	nett; schön	Holly is **nice**.
	twelve [twelv]	zwölf	12
	cat [kæt]	Katze	
p. 12	**photo** ['fəʊtəʊ]	Foto	Achtung Aussprache und Schreibweise! photo
p. 13	**Germany** ['dʒɜ:məni]	Deutschland	Frankfurt is in **Germany**.

Station 1

family

dad / father [dæd / 'fɑ:ðə]	Papa / Vater	**aunt** [ɑ:nt]	Tante
mum / mother [mʌm / 'mʌðə]	Mama / Mutter	**uncle** ['ʌŋkl]	Onkel
parents *(pl)* ['peərnts]	Eltern	**grandmother** ['grænˌmʌðə]	Großmutter
sister ['sɪstə]	Schwester	**grandfather** ['grænˌfɑ:ðə]	Großvater
brother ['brʌðə]	Bruder		

p. 14	**her** [hɜː]	ihr	Olivia's sister is five. = **Her** sister is five.
	family ['fæmli]	Familie	The Frasers are a **family**.
	with [wɪð]	mit	I'm **with** my family in this photo.
	we're (= we are) [wɪə]	wir sind	**We're** from Germany.
	garden ['gɑːdn]	Garten	
	she's (= she is) [ʃiːz]	sie ist	Lucy? **She's** in the garden.
	I have [aɪ 'hæv]	ich habe; ich besitze	**I have** a sister.
	no brothers [nəʊ 'brʌðəz]	keine Brüder	I have **no brothers**.
	me [miː]	*hier:* ich	That's **me** in the photo.
	our [aʊə]	unser	**Our** father is cool.
	his [hɪz]	sein	
	name [neɪm]	Name	His **name** is Dave.
	he's (= he is) [hiːz]	er ist	Desmond? **He's** cool.
	too [tuː]	auch	Claire is nice. She's here **too**.
	friend [frend]	Freund; Freundin	Olivia is my **friend**.
	a photo of [ə 'fəʊtəʊ‿əv]	ein Foto von	This is **a photo of** my family.

The family song

game [geɪm]	Spiel	on the door [ɒn ðə 'dɔː]	an der Tür
crazy ['kreɪzi]	verrückt	my brother and me [maɪ ˌbrʌðə ænd 'miː]	mein Bruder und ich
kid [kɪd]	Kind	come in [ˌkʌm‿'ɪn]	komm herein
together [tə'geðə]	zusammen	meet my family [miːt maɪ 'fæmli]	lerne meine Familie kennen
everyone ['evriwʌn]	jeder		
we live [wiː 'lɪv]	wir wohnen		

p. 16	to **be** [biː]	sein	
p. 17	**you're (= you are)** [jɔː]	du bist	**You're** my family. You are my mum and dad.

personal pronouns

I [aɪ]	ich	**we** [wi:]	wir
you [ju:]	du; Sie	**you** [ju:]	ihr; Sie
he [hi:]	er	**they** [ðeɪ]	sie *(Pl.)*
she [ʃi:]	sie		
it [ɪt]	es		

Station 2

room things

table ['teɪbl]	Tisch	**shelf** *(sg)* [ʃelf], **shelves** *(pl)* [ʃelvz]	Regal; Regalbrett
chair [tʃeə]	Stuhl	**wardrobe** ['wɔ:drəʊb]	Kleiderschrank
box [bɒks]	Box; Kiste	**trainer** ['treɪnə]	Turnschuh
mobile (phone) ['məʊbaɪl (ˌfəʊn)]	Handy; Mobiltelefon	**carpet** ['kɑ:pɪt]	Teppich
T-shirt ['ti:ʃɜ:t]	T-Shirt	**scarf** *(sg)* [skɑ:f], **scarves** *(pl)* [skɑ:vz]	Schal; Tuch
poster ['pəʊstə]	Poster	**lamp** [læmp]	Lampe
book [bʊk]	Buch; Heft	**alarm clock** [ə'lɑ:m ˌklɒk]	Wecker
bed [bed]	Bett		

p. 18	**bedroom** ['bedrʊm]	Schlafzimmer; Kinderzimmer	My **bedroom** is green and it's nice.
	Saturday ['sætədeɪ]	Samstag	It's **Saturday**. Luke is in his bedroom.
	at home [ət 'həʊm]	zu Hause	Luke is **at home**.
	home [həʊm]	Zuhause; Heim	This is my **home** and my family.
	who [hu:]	wer	who
	It's me! [ɪts 'mi:]	Ich bin es!	Who is it? – **It's me!**
	Are you ready? [ɑ: ju: 'redi]	Bist du bereit?	
	under ['ʌndə]	unter	
	I can't find … [aɪ kɑ:nt 'faɪnd]	ich kann … nicht finden	**I can't find** my T-shirt.
	new [nju:]	neu	new
	there is (= there's) [ðeə‿'ɪz]	da ist; es gibt	**There is** a football under the table.

	on [ɒn]	auf	**on** ↔ under
	where [weə]	wo; wohin; woher	
	there are [ðeər‿'ɑ:]	da sind; es gibt	**There are** two books on the table.
	next to ['nekst tə]	neben	The box is **next to** your bed.
	your [jɔ:]	dein; euer	**Your** books are on the table.
	no [nəʊ]	nein	**no** ↔ yes
	Your room is a mess! [jɔ: ˌru:m ɪz ə 'mes]	Dein Zimmer ist ein Durcheinander!	
	what's (= what is) [wɒts]	was ist	**What's** under the table?
p. 19	**wrong** [rɒŋ]	falsch	
	right [raɪt]	richtig; korrekt	**right** ↔ wrong

Reading corner

p. 22	**tree house** ['tri: ˌhaʊs]	Baumhaus	A house in a tree is a **tree house.**
	house [haʊs]	Haus	
	tree [tri:]	Baum	
	wood [wʊd]	Holz	**Wood** is from trees.
	ladder ['lædə]	Leiter	
	busy ['bɪzi]	beschäftigt	Achtung Aussprache!
	later ['leɪtə]	später	**Later** they're in Olivia's bedroom.
p. 23	**then** [ðen]	dann; danach	**Then** Olivia is in the tree house.
	night [naɪt]	Nacht	
	funny ['fʌni]	merkwürdig; komisch	
	noise [nɔɪz]	Geräusch	There's a funny **noise**. What is it?
	no one ['nəʊ wʌn]	niemand	no people = **no one**
	wind [wɪnd]	Wind	
	or [ɔ:]	oder	Are you eleven **or** twelve? – I'm twelve.

Film corner

rooms

bedroom ['bedrʊm]	Schlafzimmer; Kinderzimmer	**kitchen** ['kɪtʃɪn]	Küche
living room ['lɪvɪŋ ˌrʊm]	Wohnzimmer	**bathroom** ['bɑ:θrʊm]	Bad(ezimmer)

p. 25	**around the house** [əˌraʊnd ðə 'haʊs]	zu Hause	
	hair straightener ['heə ˌstreɪtnə]	Haarglätter	
	Well, look … [wel 'lʊk]	Na ja, schau mal … nach.	Where's my mobile? – **Well, look** in your bedroom.
	Thanks. [θæŋks]	Danke.	Here is your mobile. – **Thanks.**

Checkpoint

presentation [ˌprezn'teɪʃn]	Präsentation; Vortrag	It was very interesting! [ɪt wɒz ˌveri 'ɪntrəstɪŋ]	Sie (die Präsentation) war sehr interessant!
How was my presentation? [ˌhaʊ wɒz maɪ ˌprezn'teɪʃn]	Wie war meine Präsentation?	I'd like to know more about … [aɪd laɪk tə ˌnəʊ 'mɔ:‿ əbaʊt]	Ich würde gerne mehr wissen über …

Listening skills

p. 31	**dining room** ['daɪnɪŋ ˌrʊm]	Esszimmer	rooms: **dining room**, living room, bedroom
	computer game [ˌkəm'pju:tə geɪm]	Computerspiel	

Word bank: **My family**

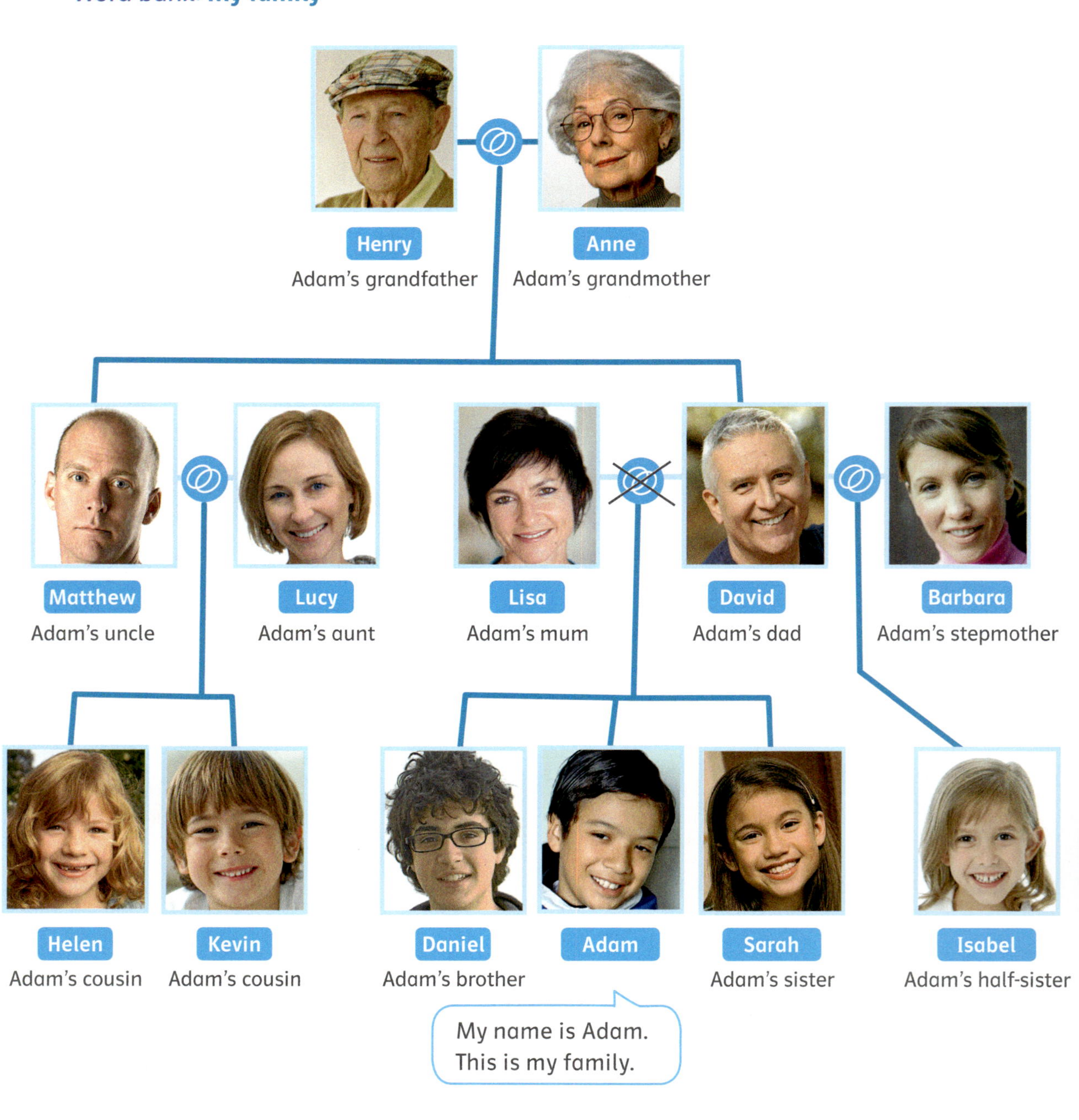

mother = mum
father = dad
parents = mum and dad
no brothers and sisters = only child

stepfather = mum's new partner
stepbrother = stepfather's son
partner = friend
married ↔ divorced

Word bank: **In my room**

1. table
2. chair
3. wardrobe
4. bed
5. floor
6. carpet
7. window
8. door
9. shelf, shelves
10. notice board
11. poster
12. lamp
13. alarm clock
14. mobile
15. book
16. computer
17. ceiling
18. DVD
19. CD

Unit 2 This is my school

Way in

p. 32	**school** [sku:l]	Schule	My **school** is cool.
	to **go** [gəʊ]	gehen	Holly: I **go** to Thomas Tallis School.
	to [tu:]	in; nach; zu	go **to** school = in die Schule gehen
	year [jɪə]	Jahr; Jahrgangsstufe; Klasse	Holly and friends are in **Year** 7. Year 7 (England) = 5. Klasse (Deutschland)
	uniform ['ju:nɪfɔ:m]	Uniform	
	favourite ['feɪvrɪt]	Lieblings-	Green is my **favourite** colour.
	place [pleɪs]	Platz; Stelle; Ort	What's your favourite **place**? – My bedroom.
	at school [ət 'sku:l]	in der Schule	**at school** – in der Schule at home – zu Hause at the weekend – am Wochenende at one o'clock – um 1 Uhr
	playground ['pleɪgraʊnd]	Schulhof; Pausenhof; Spielplatz	
	game [geɪm]	Spiel	We can play **games** in the playground.
	to **talk (to)** [tɔ:k]	sprechen (mit); reden (mit)	We can **talk** in the playground.
p. 33	**cafeteria** [kæfə'tɪəriə]	Cafeteria; Mensa	
	student ['stju:dnt]	Schüler; Schülerin	Achtung Aussprache!
	to **eat** [i:t]	essen	eat
	food [fu:d]	Essen; Lebensmittel	
	Mrs ['mɪsɪz]	Frau *(Anrede)*	**Mrs** Preston is Dave's mother.
	caretaker ['keəˌteɪkə]	Hausmeister; Hausmeisterin	Mrs Warren is the **caretaker** at TTS.
	classroom ['klɑ:srʊm]	Klassenzimmer	There are chairs and tables in the **classroom**.
	tutor group ['tju:tə ˌgru:p]	Klasse *(in einer englischen Schule)*	Holly: I'm in **tutor group** 7RS.
	tutor ['tju:tə]	Klassenlehrer; Klassenlehrerin	
	Mr ['mɪstə]	Herr *(Anrede)*	**Mr** Swindon is Holly's tutor.
	Maths [mæθs]	Mathe	M+A×T-H=S
	teacher ['ti:tʃə]	Lehrer; Lehrerin	Es gibt nur ein Wort für Lehrer/Lehrerin.
p. 32	**I don't like** [aɪ ˌdəʊnt 'laɪk]	ich mag nicht; gefällt mir nicht	I **don't like** school. ↔ I like school.

Station 1

school things

pen [pen]	Füller; Stift	**calculator** ['kælkjəleɪtə]	(Taschen-) Rechner
exercise book ['eksəsaɪz ˌbʊk]	Übungsheft	**pencil case** ['pensl ˌkeɪs]	Federmäppchen
ruler ['ru:lə]	Lineal	**glue** [glu:]	Klebstoff
eraser [ɪ'reɪzə]	Radiergummi	**felt-tip** [ˌfelt'tɪp]	Filzstift
pencil ['pensl]	Bleistift; Buntstift	**pencil sharpener** ['pensl ˌʃɑ:pnə]	Anspitzer
bag [bæg]	Tasche		

p. 34	**Wednesday** ['wenzdeɪ]	Mittwoch	Achtung Schreibweise! We<u>dn</u>esday
	don't talk [ˌdəʊnt 'tɔ:k]	sei still; rede nicht	
	please [pli:z]	bitte	Don't talk, **please**.
	to **close** [kləʊz]	schließen; zumachen	Can you **close** the window?
	window ['wɪndəʊ]	Fenster	
	call me ['kɔ:l ˌmi]	nenne mich	**Call me** Jay.
	good [gʊd]	gut	Sherlock is a **good** dog.
	singer ['sɪŋə]	Sänger; Sängerin	
	Really? ['rɪəli]	Wirklich?	I'm a football fan. – **Really?** I like football too.
	crazy ['kreɪzi]	verrückt	Our new teacher is **crazy**.
	girl [gɜ:l]	Mädchen	Holly is a nice **girl**.
	for [fɔ:]	für	Achtung Schreibweise! f<u>or</u>
	to **sit (down)** [ˌsɪt 'daʊn]	sich (hin)setzen	**Sit down** on the chair, please.
	to **sing** [sɪŋ]	singen	**sing** → singer
	now [naʊ]	jetzt; nun	Please don't sing **now**.
	talent show ['tælənt ˌʃəʊ]	Talentwettbewerb	
	next [nekst]	nächste	Achtung Schreibweise! n<u>ext</u>
	week [wi:k]	Woche	The talent show is next **week**.
	to **take out** [ˌteɪk 'aʊt]	herausnehmen	**Take out** your pens.

	to **open** ['əʊpn]	öffnen; aufmachen	
	to **look at** ['lʊk‿ət]	anschauen	
	board [bɔ:d]	Tafel	
	to **do** [du:]	machen; tun	Who can **do** number one?
	Put your hands up. [pʊt jɔ: ˌhændz‿'ʌp]	Meldet euch.	
p. 35	**an** [ən]	ein; eine	a pen; **an** exercise book
	Here you are. [ˌhɪə ju‿'ɑ:]	Bitte schön.	
	Thank you. ['θæŋk ju]	Danke.	Here you are. – **Thank you.**

This is our classroom

so have a look around [səʊ ˌhæv‿ə ˌlʊk‿ə'raʊnd]	also schau dich um	I know [aɪ 'nəʊ]	ich weiß
tell me what you see [tel mi: ˌwɒt jʊ 'si:]	sage mir, was du siehst	we come here every day [wi: ˌkʌm hɪə ˌevri 'deɪ]	wir kommen jeden Tag hierher
carpet ['kɑ:pɪt]	Teppich	here we all learn ['hɪə wi: ɔ:l ˌlɜ:n]	hier lernen wir alle
for us all [fɔ:r‿ʌs 'ɔ:l]	für uns alle	It's easy, hooray! [ɪts ˌi:zi hʊ'reɪ]	Es ist einfach, hurra!
wall [wɔ:l]	Wand	English is fun [fʌn]	Englisch macht Spaß
door [dɔ:]	Tür	All together now! [ɔ:l tə'geðə ˌnaʊ]	Jetzt alle zusammen!
with curtains we can pull [wɪð ˌkɜ:tnz wi: kən 'pʊl]	mit Vorhängen, die wir zuziehen können	that's what it's all about [ˌðæts wɒt‿ɪts ɔ:l ə'baʊt]	darum geht es
but [bʌt]	aber		

p. 36	to **write** [raɪt]	schreiben	
	to **read** [ri:d]	lesen	
	question ['kwestʃən]	Frage	Read the **question**.
	answer ['ɑ:nsə]	Antwort	**answer** ↔ question
p. 37	**group** [gru:p]	Gruppe	T grup R группа
	to **say** [seɪ]	sagen; sprechen	**Say** your name.

Station 2

days

Monday ['mʌndeɪ] **(Mon)**	Montag	**Friday** ['fraɪdeɪ] **(Fri)**	Freitag
Tuesday ['tju:zdeɪ] **(Tues)**	Dienstag	**Saturday** ['sætədeɪ] **(Sat)**	Samstag
Wednesday ['wenzdeɪ] **(Wed)**	Mittwoch	**Sunday** ['sʌndeɪ] **(Sun)**	Sonntag
Thursday ['θɜ:zdeɪ] **(Thurs)**	Donnerstag		

school subjects

(DT) [ˌdi:'ti:] **Design Technology** [dɪˌzaɪn tek'nɒlədʒi]	Technik	**Music** [mju:zɪk]	Musik
PE [ˌpi:'i:] **(Physical Education)** [ˌfɪzɪkl edʒʊ'keɪʃn]	Sportunterricht	**German** ['dʒɜ:mən]	Deutsch
Maths [mæθs]	Mathe	**RE** [ˌɑ:‿'ri:] **(Religious Education)** [rɪˌlɪdʒəs‿edʒʊ'kəɪʃn]	Religionsunterricht
French [frentʃ]	Französisch	**IT** [ˌaɪ'ti:] **(Information Technology)** [ɪnfəˌmeɪʃn tek'nɒlədʒi]	Informatik; Informationstechnik
Art [ɑ:t]	Kunst	**History** ['hɪstri]	Geschichte
Science [saɪəns]	Wissenschaft; Naturwissenschaft	**Geography** [dʒi'ɒgrəfi]	Geografie; Erdkunde
English ['ɪŋglɪʃ]	Englisch	**Biology** [baɪ'ɒlədʒi]	Biologie

p. 38	**at break** [ət 'breɪk]	in der Pause	**At break** I go to the cafeteria.
	lesson ['lesn]	Schulstunde; Unterricht	Maths is my favourite **lesson**.
	Ms [mɪz]	Frau *(Anrede)*	**Ms** Kapoor is my English teacher.
	subject ['sʌbdʒɪkt]	Schulfach	My favourite **subjects** are Maths and English.
	easy ['i:zi]	einfach; leicht	This question is **easy**.
	You're right. [jɔ:‿'raɪt]	Du hast Recht.	
	to **be good at** [bi 'gʊd‿ət]	gut sein in; gut sein bei	I'**m good at** English.
	not [nɒt]	nicht	I'm **not** good at Music.
	very ['veri]	sehr	I'm **very** good at Maths.
	spelling ['spelɪŋ]	Rechtschreibung	I'm good at **spelling**. And you?
	joke [dʒəʊk]	Witz	

funny ['fʌni]	lustig; witzig	Your jokes are **funny**.
interesting ['ɪntrəstɪŋ]	interessant	I like Art. It's **interesting**.
on Tuesday [ˌɒn 'tju:zdeɪ]	am Dienstag	We have English **on Tuesday**.
day [deɪ]	Tag	
to **spell** [spel]	buchstabieren	Can you **spell** Monday? It's easy.
like that [laɪk 'ðæt]	so	Don't talk **like that**!
timetable ['taɪmˌteɪbl]	Stundenplan	
registration [ˌredʒɪ'streɪʃn]	*Überprüfung der Anwesenheit*	
p. 39 **boring** ['bɔ:rɪŋ]	langweilig	**boring** ↔ interesting
difficult ['dɪfɪklt]	schwierig	**difficult** ↔ easy
fun [fʌn]	Freude; Spaß	Geography is **fun**.
alphabet ['ælfəbet]	Alphabet	

the alphabet

a [eɪ]	**g** [dʒi:]	**m** [em]	**s** [es]	**y** [waɪ]
b [bi:]	**h** [eɪtʃ]	**n** [en]	**t** [ti:]	**z** [zed]
c [si:]	**i** [ai]	**o** [əʊ]	**u** [ju:]	
d [di:]	**j** [dʒeɪ]	**p** [pi:]	**v** [vi:]	
e [i:]	**k** [keɪ]	**q** [kju:]	**w** ['dʌbl ju:]	
f [ef]	**l** [el]	**r** [ɑ:]	**x** [eks]	

The alphabet

Let's all go out and play. [lets ɔ:l 'gəʊ ˌaʊtˌən 'pleɪ]	Lasst uns alle rausgehen und spielen.
Come over here and stand by me. [ˌkʌm əʊvə hɪə ən ˌstænd baɪ 'mi:]	Komm her und stelle dich neben mich.
Can you fly? [kæn ju: 'flaɪ]	Kannst du fliegen?
all alone [ˌɔ:lˌə'ləʊn]	ganz allein
but not [ˌbʌt 'nɒt]	aber nicht
Now you're set to go ahead. [naʊ jɔ: ˌset tʊ gəʊ ə'hed]	Jetzt bist du bereit, um weiterzumachen.

Reading corner

p. 42	**trick** [trɪk]	Trick; Streich	
	saxophone ['sæksəfəʊn]	Saxophon	
	lunch [lʌnʃ]	Mittagessen	We eat **lunch** in the cafeteria.
	let's (= let us) [lets]	lass(t) uns	**Let's** go to the talent show.
	What's your talent? [wɒts jɔ: 'tælənt]	Was ist dein Talent?	Achtung Aussprache!
	to **see** [si:]	sehen	see
	winner ['wɪnə]	Gewinner; Gewinnerin	
p. 43	**Well done!** [ˌwel 'dʌn]	Gut gemacht!	Olivia is the winner. **Well done!**
	star [stɑ:]	Star	Wird auch im Deutschen so verwendet.

Film corner

p. 45	to **make friends** [ˌmeɪk 'frendz]	Freundschaften schließen	
	chewing gum ['tʃu:ɪŋ ˌgʌm]	Kaugummi	No **chewing gum** at school.
	jeans *(pl)* [dʒi:nz]	Jeans	**Jeans** gibt es nur in der Mehrzahl.
	Alicia put it in there. [ə'lɪʃə pʊt‿ɪt ɪn ˌðeə]	Alicia hat es dort hinein getan.	
	film [fɪlm]	Film	T film R фильм

Checkpoint

leaflet ['li:flət]	Broschüre; Prospekt	circus ['sɜ:kəs]	Zirkus
club [klʌb]	Klub; Schul-AG	I don't understand [ˌʌndə'stænd]	ich verstehe nicht

Word bank: **At school**

assembly hall

talk
sit down
listen

playground

play games

recording studio

sing

cafeteria

drink
eat

sports hall

play football
do sport

Science lab

do experiments

Music room

play music

Art room

draw a picture

toilets

go to the toilet

classroom

"Sit down, please!"
"Open your exercise books!"
"Look at the board!"
"Write on the board!"

"Close the window!"
"Open the window!"
"Close the door!"
"Open the door!"

"Put your hands up!"
"Take out your pens!"
"Do exercise two."
"Talk to your partner."

Word bank: **Subjects at our school**

Geography	 DT = Design Technology	 Biology		
	 German	 Science	 French	
	 RE	 IT		
 History	 English	 Physics	 Art	 Chemistry
 Food Technology	 Social Studies	 PE	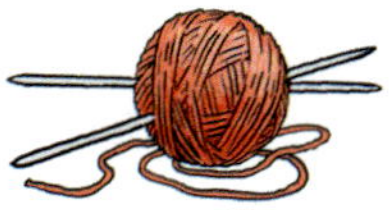 Textiles	Maths

3 x 4 = 12

My favourite subject is ... I like ... I don't like ...	It's / It isn't	interesting. easy. OK. nice.

Unit 3 My free time

Way in

p. 52	**free time** [ˌfriː ˈtaɪm]	Freizeit	I play tennis in my **free time**.
	after [ˈɑːftə]	nach	
	to **listen (to)** [ˈlɪsn (tə)]	hören; anhören; zuhören	After school I **listen** to music.
	to **watch TV** [ˌwɒtʃ tiːˈviː]	fernsehen	
	to **love** [lʌv]	lieben; gern mögen	I **love** animals.
	on Saturdays [ɒn ˈsætədeɪz]	samstags	**on Saturdays** = jeden Samstag
	netball [ˈnetbɔːl]	Korbball	Olivia: On Saturdays I play **netball**.
	to **win** [wɪn]	gewinnen; siegen	
	a lot [əˈlɒt]	viel	We are good. We win **a lot**.
	team [tiːm]	Team; Gruppe	
p. 53	**practice** [ˈpræktɪs]	Training; Übung	netball **practice** = netball training
	lunchtime [ˈlʌnʃtaɪm]	Mittagszeit; Mittagspause	I eat in the cafeteria at **lunchtime**.
	captain [ˈkæptɪn]	Kapitän; Kapitänin	I'm **captain** of the football team.
	to **help** [help]	helfen	I **help** animals.
	animal rescue shelter [ˌænɪml ˈreskjuː ˌʃeltə]	Tierheim	My cat is from the **animal rescue shelter**.
	at the weekend [ət ðə ˌwiːkˈend]	am Wochenende	**at the weekend** = am Wochenende at school/break = in der Schule/Pause at home = zu Hause at 8.50 a.m. = um 8.50 Uhr
	cinema [ˈsɪnəmə]	Kino	T sinema
	science fiction [ˌsaɪəns ˈfɪkʃn]	Science-Fiction	*Star wars* is a **science fiction** movie.
	movie [ˈmuːvi]	Film	**movie** = film

Station 1

animals

monkey ['mʌŋki]	Affe	**fish** *(sg)* [fɪʃ], **fish** *(pl)* [fɪʃ]	Fisch
tiger ['taɪgə]	Tiger	**lion** ['laɪən]	Löwe
elephant ['elɪfənt]	Elefant	**flamingo** [flə'mɪŋgəʊ]	Flamingo
snake [sneɪk]	Schlange	**zebra** ['zebrə]	Zebra
giraffe [dʒɪ'rɑːf]	Giraffe	**crocodile** ['krɒkədaɪl]	Krokodil
penguin ['peŋgwɪn]	Pinguin	**camel** ['kæml]	Kamel
mouse *(sg)* [maʊs], **mice** *(pl)* [maɪs]	Maus		

numbers 11 – 100

eleven 11 [ɪ'levn]	elf	**twenty-one 21** ['twenti,wʌn]	einundzwanzig
twelve 12 [twelv]	zwölf	**twenty-two 22** ['twenti,tuː]	zweiundzwanzig
thirteen 13 [θɜː'tiːn]	dreizehn	**thirty 30** ['θɜːti]	dreißig
fourteen 14 [,fɔː'tiːn]	vierzehn	**forty 40** ['fɔːti]	vierzig
fifteen 15 [,fɪf'tiːn]	fünfzehn	**fifty 50** ['fɪfti]	fünfzig
sixteen 16 [,sɪk'stiːn]	sechzehn	**sixty 60** ['sɪksti]	sechzig
seventeen 17 [,sevn'tiːn]	siebzehn	**seventy 70** ['sevnti]	siebzig
eighteen 18 [,eɪ'tiːn]	achtzehn	**eighty 80** ['eɪti]	achtzig
nineteen 19 [,naɪn'tiːn]	neunzehn	**ninety 90** ['naɪnti]	neunzig
twenty 20 ['twenti]	zwanzig	**a/one hundred 100** ['hʌndrəd]	einhundert

p. 54	**at the zoo** [ət ðə 'zuː]	im Zoo	You can see animals **at the zoo.** Achtung Aussprache!
	to **come** [kʌm]	kommen	I **come** from Greenwich in London.
	India ['ɪndiə]	Indien	Edgar, the elephant, comes from **India.**
	metre ['miːtə]	Meter	Achtung Schreibweise! metre
	high [haɪ]	hoch; groß	high
	fruit [fruːt]	Frucht; Obst	fruit
	to **sleep** [sliːp]	schlafen	sleep
	much [mʌtʃ]	viel	I like fruit but I don't eat **much.**

	four hours a day [ˌfɔːr aʊəz͜ ə ˈdeɪ]	vier Stunden täglich	The elephant sleeps **four hours a day**.
	age [eɪdʒ]	Alter	Luke's **age**? He's eleven.
	meat [miːt]	Fleisch	
	7 kilograms a day [ˌkɪləgræmz ə ˈdeɪ]	sieben Kilogramm täglich	The tiger eats a lot, **7 kilograms a day**.
	centimetre (cm) [ˈsentɪˌmiːtə]	Zentimeter (cm)	Tom, the tiger, is 93 **centimetres** high.
	to **run** [rʌn]	rennen; laufen	I **run** with my dog in the park.
	40 kilometres an hour [kɪˈlɒmiːtəz͜ ən͜ ˈaʊə]	40 Kilometer pro Stunde	The tiger runs **40 kilometres an hour**.
	long [lɒŋ]	lang	long
	for five months [fə ˌfaɪv ˈmʌnθs]	fünf Monate lang	
	winter [ˈwɪntə]	Winter	Lizzy, the snake, sleeps for 5 months in **winter**.
p. 57	**banana** [bəˈnɑːnə]	Banane	
	Africa [ˈæfrɪkə]	Afrika	Monkeys come from **Africa**.

Station 2

daily routines

get up [ˌget͜ˈʌp]	aufstehen	**clean ...** [kliːn]	... sauber machen; ... putzen
eat ... [iːt]	... essen	**have breakfast** [ˌhæv ˈbrekfəst]	frühstücken
go ... [gəʊ]	... gehen	**have lunch** [ˌhaev ˈlʌnʃ]	zu Mittag essen
feed ... [fiːd]	... füttern	**go to bed** [ˌgəʊ tə ˈbed]	ins Bett gehen
play ... [pleɪ]	... spielen	**call** [kɔːl]	rufen; anrufen
sleep [sliːp]	schlafen		

p. 58	**zookeeper** [ˈzuːˌkiːpə]	Tierpfleger; Tierpflegerin	A **zookeeper** loves animals.
	a busy day [ə ˌbɪzi ˈdeɪ]	ein ausgefüllter Tag	
	to **interview** [ˈɪntəvjuː]	interviewen; befragen	Holly **interviews** the zookeeper Fred.
	magazine [ˌmægəˈziːn]	Zeitschrift	
	when [wen]	wann	
	o'clock [əˈklɒk]	Uhr *(Zeitangabe bei vollen Stunden)*	When do you get up? – I get up at seven **o'clock**.

first [fɜ:st]	zuerst; als Erstes	**First** I get up, then I have breakfast.
after that [ˌɑ:ftə 'ðæt]	danach	I get up at six o'clock. **After that** I have breakfast.
to **work** [wɜ:k]	arbeiten	I **work** on the computer.
in the afternoon [ɪn ðiˌɑ:ftə'nu:n]	am Nachmittag	**in the afternoon** = 12.00 – 17.00 Uhr
cage [keɪdʒ]	Käfig	
work [wɜ:k]	Arbeit	**work** → to work
What time is it? [ˌwɒt 'taɪm ɪz ɪt]	Wie spät ist es?; Wie viel Uhr ist es?	**What time is it?** – It's six o'clock.
p. 59 **half past (two)** [ˌhɑ:f 'pɑ:st]	halb (drei)	2:30 = It's **half past** two.
oh [əʊ]	null *(bei Uhrzeiten und Telefonnummern)*	9:05 = It's nine **oh** five.
past [pɑ:st]	nach *(bei Uhrzeitangaben)*	11:10 = It's ten **past** eleven.
quarter past ['kwɔ:tə pɑ:st]	Viertel nach	12:15 = It's **quarter past** twelve.
quarter to ['kwɔ:tə tə]	Viertel vor	7:45 = It's **quarter to** eight.
to [tu:]	vor *(bei Uhrzeitangaben)*	8:50 = It's ten **to** nine.
tea [ti:]	Tee; (frühes) Abendessen	

I'm going to the zoo

I'm going to the zoo [aɪm ˌgəʊɪŋ tə ðə 'zu:]	ich gehe in den Zoo
to want (to) ['wɒnt tə]	wollen
to dance [dɑ:ns]	tanzen
to give a high-five [gɪv ə 'haɪfaɪv]	abklatschen
gang [gæŋ]	Gang; Bande
to go skiing [ˌgəʊ 'ski:ɪŋ]	Skifahren gehen
to climb a tree [ˌklaɪm ə 'tri:]	einen Baum hinaufklettern
panda ['pændə]	Pandabär
to go fishing [ˌgəʊ 'fɪʃɪŋ]	zum Angeln gehen
grizzly bear [ˌgrɪzli 'beə]	Grizzlybär
to play chess [ˌpleɪ 'tʃes]	Schach spielen
gorilla [gə'rɪlə]	Gorilla
to go surfing [ˌgəʊ 'sɜ:fɪŋ]	Surfen gehen
crocodile ['krɒkədaɪl]	Krokodil
to play hide-and-seek [pleɪ ˌhaɪd ən 'si:k]	Verstecken spielen
chameleon [kə'mi:liən]	Chamäleon
ball [bɔ:l]	Ball
seal [si:l]	Seehund; Robbe
to go roller skating [ˌgəʊ 'rəʊlə ˌskeɪtɪŋ]	Rollschuhlaufen gehen

Reading corner

p. 62	**café** ['kæfeɪ]	Café	Let's have tea in a **café** on Saturday.
	mystery ['mɪstri]	Rätsel; Geheimnis	It's a **mystery**. What's the answer?
	story ['stɔ:ri]	Geschichte	**story** *(sg)*, stories *(pl)*
	to **take the dog for a walk** [ˌteɪk ðə dɒg fɔ:r‿ə 'wɔ:k]	den Hund ausführen	
	police officer [pə'li:s‿ɒfɪsə]	Polizeibeamter; Polizeibeamtin	
	the first time [ðə ˌfɜ:st 'taɪm]	das erste Mal	
	every ['evri]	jede	I play football **every** day.
	I don't know! [ˌaɪ dəʊnt 'nəʊ]	Ich weiß (es) nicht!	What's 'Wurst' in English? – **I don't know!**
	how [haʊ]	wie	
	to **get in** ['get‿ɪn]	hereinkommen	How do they **get in** the café?
	to **solve** [sɒlv]	lösen	Let's **solve** the mystery!
	to **look for** ['lʊk ˌfə]	suchen	
	clue [klu:]	Hinweis; Spur	Let's look for **clues**!
	nut [nʌt]	Nuss	
	ceiling ['si:lɪŋ]	Zimmerdecke	There is a noise from the **ceiling**.
	hole [həʊl]	Loch	Look, there's a **hole** in the ceiling!
	raccoon [rə'ku:n]	Waschbär	

Film corner

p. 65	**the fastest** [ðə 'fɑ:stɪst]	der/die/das schnellste	Who is **the fastest**?
	race [reɪs]	Wettrennen	Who's the winner of the **race**?

Checkpoint

survey ['sɜ:veɪ]	Umfrage	number ['nʌmbə]	Anzahl
DVD [ˌdi:vi:'di:]	DVD	That was very clear. [ðæt wɒz veri 'klɪə]	Das war sehr klar.
to see friends [si: 'frendz]	sich mit Freunden treffen		

Word bank: Free-time activities

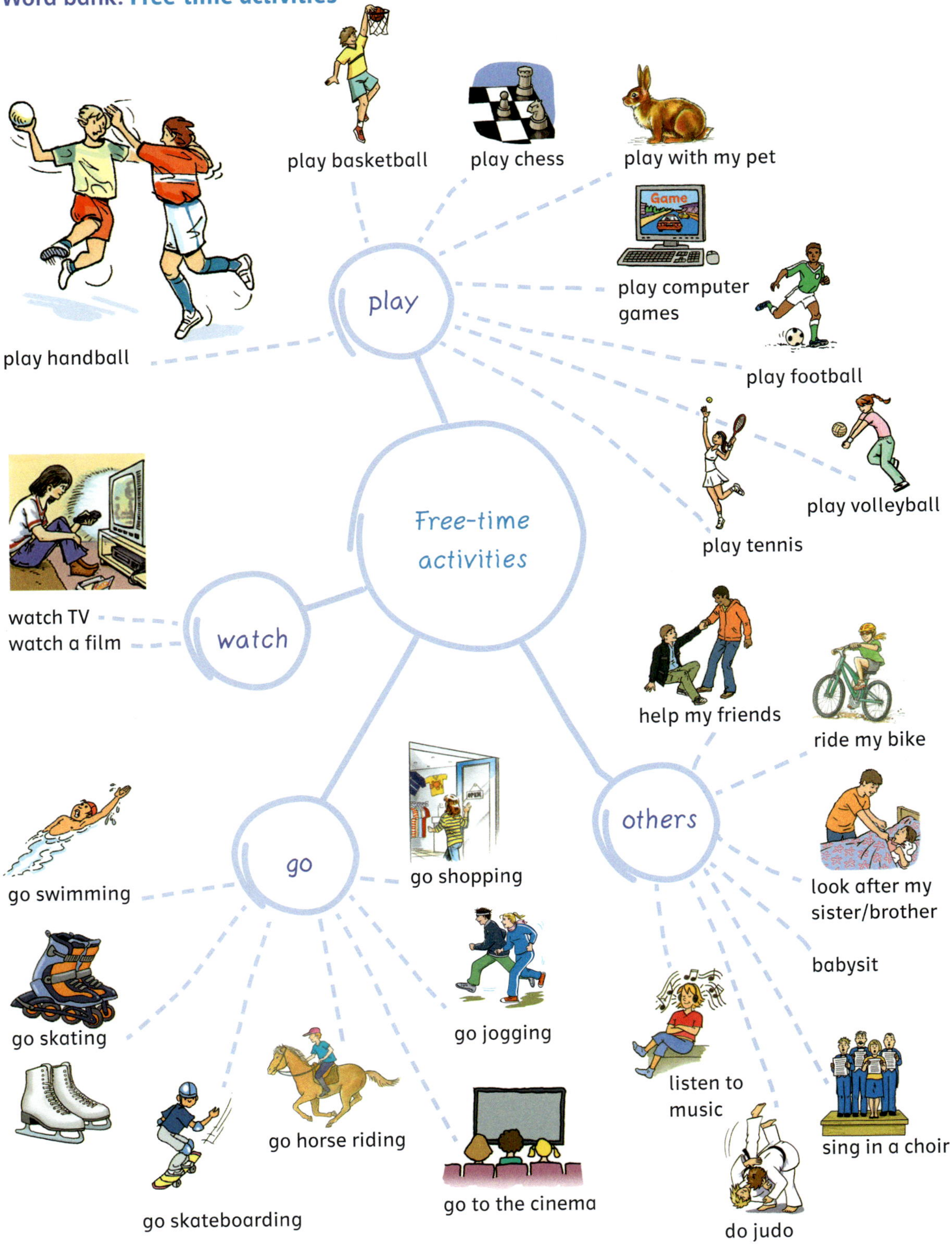

Free-time activities

play
- play basketball
- play chess
- play with my pet
- play computer games
- play football
- play volleyball
- play tennis
- play handball

watch
- watch TV
- watch a film

go
- go swimming
- go skating
- go skateboarding
- go horse riding
- go to the cinema
- go jogging
- go shopping

others
- help my friends
- ride my bike
- look after my sister/brother
- babysit
- sing in a choir
- do judo
- listen to music

Word bank: **Animals**

1. horse	10. parrot	19. lion	28. water
2. mouse, mice	11. monkey	20. zebra	29. leaf, leaves
3. bird	12. fish	21. camel	30. Africa
4. tiger	13. crocodile	22. raccoon	31. North America
5. penguin	14. panda	23. banana	32. South America
6. bear	15. gorilla	24. meat	33. Asia
7. snake	16. chameleon	25. plant	34. Europe
8. elephant	17. seal	26. fruit	35. Antarctica
9. giraffe	18. flamingo	27. grass	36. Australia

Word bank: **What time is it?**

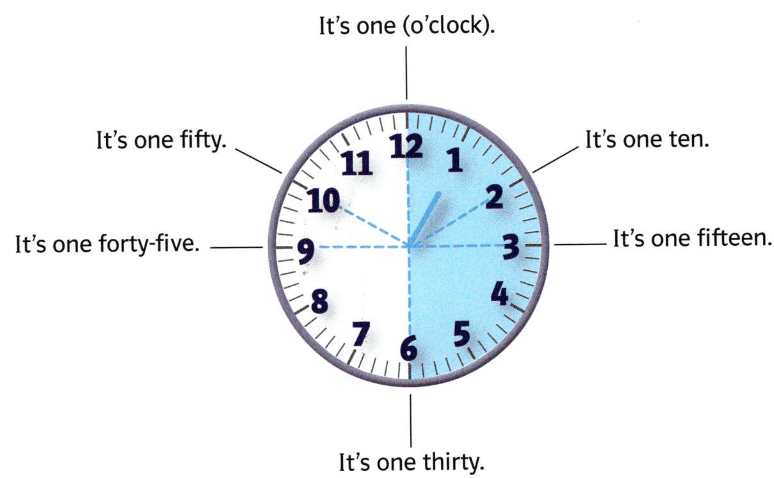

It's one (o'clock).
It's one fifty.
It's one ten.
It's one forty-five.
It's one fifteen.
It's one thirty.

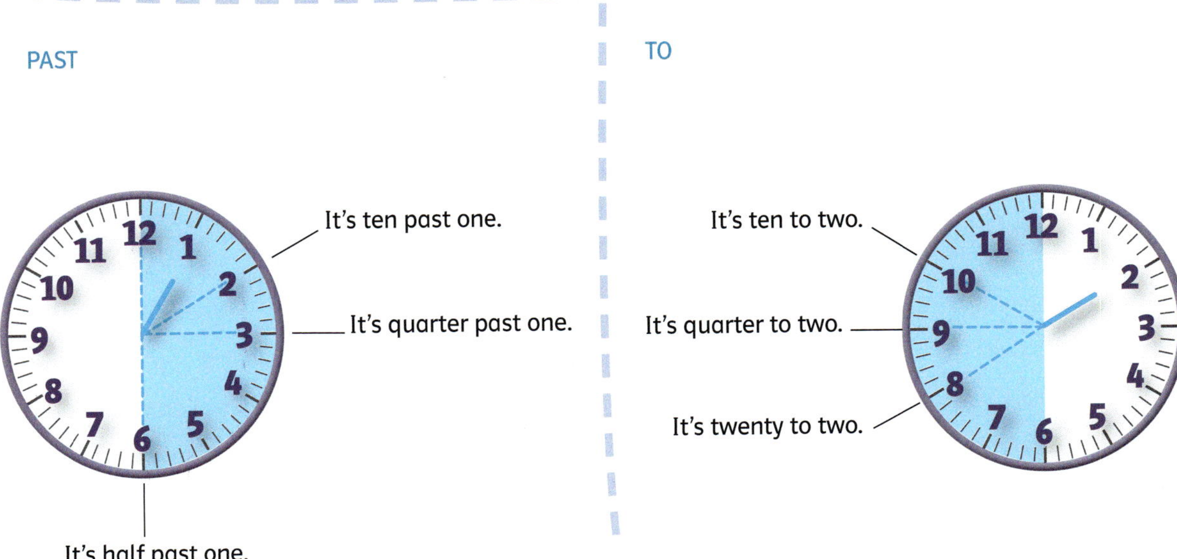

PAST
It's ten past one.
It's quarter past one.
It's half past one.
TO
It's ten to two.
It's quarter to two.
It's twenty to two.

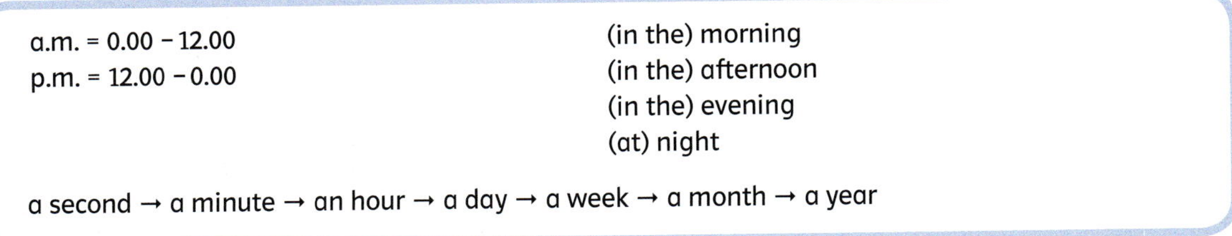

a.m. = 0.00 – 12.00
p.m. = 12.00 – 0.00

(in the) morning
(in the) afternoon
(in the) evening
(at) night

a second → a minute → an hour → a day → a week → a month → a year

Unit 4 Let's celebrate!

Way in

months

January ['dʒænjuri]	Januar	**July** [dʒʊ'laɪ]	Juli
February ['februri]	Februar	**August** ['ɔ:gəst]	August
March [mɑ:tʃ]	März	**September** [sep'tembə]	September
April ['eɪprl]	April	**October** [ɒk'təʊbə]	Oktober
May [meɪ]	Mai	**November** [nə'vembə]	November
June [dʒu:n]	Juni	**December** [dɪ'sembə]	Dezember

p. 70	to **celebrate** ['seləbreɪt]	feiern	I **celebrate** with my family and friends.
p. 71	**Trick or treat!** [ˌtrɪk‿ə 'tri:t]	Süßes, sonst gibt's Saures!	
p. 70	**in August** [in 'ɔ:gəst]	im August	The Notting Hill Carnival is **in August**.
	carnival ['kɑ:nɪvl]	Karneval; Fasching	Achtung Aussprache und Schreibweise! carnival
	to **dance** [dɑ:ns]	tanzen	I can sing and **dance**.
	special ['speʃl]	besonders; speziell	Olivia's **special** day is the Notting Hill Carnival.
	evening ['i:vnɪŋ]	Abend	afternoon – **evening** – night
	to **wear** [weə]	tragen	I **wear** a T-shirt at football practice.
	scary ['skeəri]	gruselig	There are **scary** people at Halloween.
	costume ['kɒstju:m]	Kostüm	People wear **costumes** at Notting Hill Carnival.
	Christmas ['krɪsməs]	Weihnachten	
	together [tə'geðə]	zusammen; gemeinsam	We go to school **together**.
	to **get** [get]	bekommen	We **get** presents at Christmas.
	present ['preznt]	Geschenk	
	nose [nəʊz]	Nase	
	to **collect** [kə'lekt]	sammeln	
	money ['mʌni]	Geld	
	other ['ʌðə]	andere	I eat bananas and **other** fruit.

Eid [i:d]	*muslimisches Fest*	
Muslim ['mʊzlɪm]	Muslim; Muslimin	Eid is a special day for **Muslims**.
clothes *(pl)* [kləʊðz]	Kleider *(Pl.)*; Kleidung	
sweet [swi:t]	Süßigkeit; Bonbon	At Eid we get new clothes and **sweets**.

Station 1

ordinal numbers

first (1st) [fɜ:st]	erste
second (2nd) ['seknd]	zweite
third (3rd) [θɜ:d]	dritte
fourth (4th) [fɔ:θ]	vierte
fifth (5th) [fɪfθ]	fünfte
sixth (6th) [sɪkθ]	sechste
seventh (7th) ['sevnθ]	siebte
eighth (8th) [eɪtθ]	achte
ninth (9th) [naɪnθ]	neunte
tenth (10th) [tenθ]	zehnte
eleventh (11th) [ɪ'levnθ]	elfte
twelfth (12th) [twelfθ]	zwölfte
thirteenth (13th) [ˌθɜ:'ti:nθ]	dreizehnte
fourteenth (14th) [ˌfɔ:'ti:nθ]	vierzehnte
fifteenth (15th) [ˌfɪf'ti:nθ]	fünfzehnte
sixteenth (16th) [ˌsɪk'sti:nθ]	sechzehnte
seventeenth (17th) [ˌsevn'ti:nθ]	siebzehnte
eighteenth (18th) [ˌeɪ'ti:nθ]	achtzehnte
nineteenth (19th) [ˌnaɪn'ti:nθ]	neunzehnte
twentieth (20th) ['twentiəθ]	zwanzigste
21st [ˌtwenti'fɜ:st]	einundzwanzigste
22nd [ˌtwenti'seknd]	zweiundzwanzigste
23rd [ˌtwenti'θɜ:d]	dreiundzwanzigste
24th [ˌtwenti'fɔ:θ]	vierundzwanzigste
25th [ˌtwenti'fɪfθ]	fünfundzwanzigste
26th [ˌtwenti'sɪkθ]	sechsundzwanzigste
27th [ˌtwenti'sevnθ]	siebenundzwanzigste
28th [ˌtwenti'eɪtθ]	achtundzwanzigste
29th [ˌtwenti'naɪnθ]	neunundzwanzigste
thirtieth (30th) ['θɜ:tiəθ]	dreißigste
fortieth (40th) ['fɔ:tiəθ]	vierzigste
fiftieth (50th) ['fɪftiəθ]	fünfzigste
sixtieth (60th) ['sɪkstiəθ]	sechzigste
seventieth (70th) ['sevntiəθ]	siebzigste
eightieth (80th) ['eɪtiəθ]	achtzigste
ninetieth (90th) ['naɪntiəθ]	neunzigste
hundredth (100th) ['hʌndrədθ]	hundertste

birthday activities

to **have a fancy dress party** [ˌfænsi 'dres]	eine Verkleidungsparty machen	to **have a picnic in the park** ['pɪknɪk]	ein Picknick im Park machen
to **have a barbecue party** ['bɑ:bɪkju:]	eine Grillparty machen	to **have a sleepover** ['sli:pˌəʊvə]	eine Übernachtungsparty machen
to **invite my friends** [ɪn'vaɪt]	meine Freunde einladen	to **go to a theme park** ['θi:m ˌpɑ:k]	in einen Freizeitpark gehen
to **go to the cinema** ['sɪnəmə]	ins Kino gehen	to **go to a fast food restaurant** [ˌfɑ:st fu:d 'restrɒnt]	in ein Fastfood-Restaurant gehen
to **watch movies** ['mu:vi:z]	Filme schauen	to **have a favourite meal** ['feɪvrɪt ˌmi:l]	ein Lieblingsessen genießen

p. 72	**birthday** ['bɜ:θdeɪ]	Geburtstag	birthday
	party ['pɑ:ti]	Party; Feier	It's my birthday, let's have a **party**.
	great [greɪt]	großartig; toll	The party is **great**!
	him [hɪm]	ihn; ihm	It's Jay's party. I have a present for **him**.
	big [bɪg]	groß	Elephants are **big** animals.
	surprise [sə'praɪz]	Überraschung	Olivia's costume is a big **surprise**.
	on 7th July [ɒn ðə ˌsevnθ əv 'dʒʊlaɪ]	am 7. Juli	Du schreibst **on 7th July**, aber du sagst „on **the** seventh **of** July".
	always ['ɔ:lweɪz]	immer	I **always** get up at 6:30.
	to **make** [meɪk]	machen; tun	I always **make** a cake for Mum's birthday.
	chocolate ['tʃɒklət]	Schokolade	T çikolata R шоколад
	cake [keɪk]	Kuchen	
	to **forget** [fə'get]	vergessen	Don't **forget** my birthday!
	to **give** [gɪv]	geben	
	me [mi:]	*hier:* mir	My sister always gives **me** a present for my birthday.
	never ['nevə]	nie; niemals	**never** ↔ always
	but [bʌt]	aber	My brother is crazy, **but** he's OK.
	often ['ɒfn]	oft; häufig	I **often** get up late on Saturdays.
p. 73	**date** [deɪt]	Zeitpunkt; Datum	What **date** is Eid this year?
	burger ['bɜ:gə]	Hamburger	My favourite food is **burgers**.
	ice cream [ˌaɪs 'kri:m]	Eis(creme)	
	strawberry ['strɔ:bri]	Erdbeere	strawberry

The birthday song

today [tə'deɪ]	heute	everyone's invited [ˌevrɪwʌnz ɪn'vaɪtɪd]	ihr seid alle eingeladen
we're going to a party [wɪər ˌɡəʊɪŋ tu ə 'pɑ:ti]	wir gehen auf eine Party	Happy birthday! [ˌhæpi 'bɜ:θdeɪ]	Alles Gute zum Geburtstag!
we will [wi: 'wɪl]	wir werden	all [ɔ:l]	alle

Station 2

food

coke [kəʊk]	Cola	**egg** [eɡ]	Ei
crisp [krɪsp]	Kartoffelchip	**peach** [pi:tʃ]	Pfirsich
chocolate ['tʃɒklət]	Schokolade	**butter** ['bʌtə]	Butter
orange ['ɒrɪndʒ]	Orange	**flour** [flaʊə]	Mehl
cheese [tʃi:z]	Käse	**milk** [mɪlk]	Milch
sandwich ['sænwɪdʒ]	Sandwich; belegtes Brot	**lemonade** [ˌlemə'neɪd]	Limonade
		water ['wɔ:tə]	Wasser
cake [keɪk]	Kuchen	**pasta** ['pæstə]	Pasta; Nudeln

p. 76 **shopping** ['ʃɒpɪŋ]	Einkaufen	
a bar of chocolate [bɑ:r‿əv 'tʃɒklət]	eine Tafel Schokolade	
candle ['kændl]	Kerze	
balloon [bə'lu:n]	Luftballon	
corner shop ['kɔ:nə ˌʃɒp]	Tante-Emma-Laden	You can buy balloons at the **corner shop**.
shop [ʃɒp]	Geschäft; Laden	
How can I help you? [ˌhaʊ kæn aɪ 'help‿ju:]	Was kann ich für dich tun?	
a bottle of ['bɒtl]	eine Flasche …	
Anything else? [ˌeniθɪŋ 'els]	Darf es sonst noch etwas sein?	
a packet of ['pækɪt]	eine Packung …; eine Tüte …	Can I have **a packet of** crisps, please? T paket
How much (is/are) …? [ˌhaʊ 'mʌtʃ ɪz/ɑ:]	Wie viel (kostet/kosten) …?	

	... is 99p [ɪz ˌnaɪntinaɪn ˈpens]	... kostet 99 Pence	Diese Wörter am besten als Einheit lernen.
	that's £2.24 [ðæts ˌtu: paʊndz twentiˈfɔ:]	das macht 2 Pfund und 24 Pence	How much is it? – **That's £2.24.**
	You're welcome. [jɔ: ˈwelkəm]	Gern geschehen.	Thanks. – **You're welcome.**
	Here's your change. [ˌhɪəz jɔ: ˈtʃeɪndʒ]	Hier ist dein Wechselgeld.	
p. 77	**a can of** [kæn]	eine Dose ...	
	a box of [bɒks]	eine Schachtel ...	
p. 78	**CD** [ˌsi:ˈdi:]	CD	Achtung Aussprache!
	DVD [ˌdi:vi:ˈdi:]	DVD	Achtung Aussprache!
	Sorry. [ˈsɒri]	Tut mir leid.; Entschuldigung.	Do you have crisps? – No, **sorry**!
p. 79	**shopping list** [ˈʃɒpɪŋ ˌlɪst]	Einkaufszettel	Let's write a **shopping list** and go to the corner shop.
	Can you say that again, please? [kæn ju: ˌseɪ ðæt əˈgen pli:s]	Könntest du das bitte wiederholen?	Ganze Sätze am besten als Einheit lernen.
	Pardon? [ˈpɑ:dn]	Wie bitte?	

Reading corner

p. 80	**witch** [wɪtʃ]	Hexe	
	smurf [smɜ:f]	Schlumpf	**Smurfs** are blue and white.
	superman [ˈsu:pəmæn]	Superman	**Superman** wears a blue and red costume.
	alien [ˈeɪliən]	Außerirdische; Außerirdischer	
	dancer [ˈdɑ:nsə]	Tänzer; Tänzerin	**dancer** → to dance
	narrator [nəˈreɪtə]	Erzähler; Erzählerin	The **narrator** of the story is a girl.
	invitation [ˌɪnvɪˈteɪʃn]	Einladung	**invitation** → to invite
	Happy birthday! [ˌhæpi ˈbɜ:θdeɪ]	Alles Gute zum Geburtstag!	**Happy birthday**, Jay!
	happy [ˈhæpi]	glücklich; froh	
	their [ðeə]	ihr	**Their** costumes are cool.
	to **think** [θɪŋk]	denken	I **think** that's right.
	pirate [ˈpaɪrət]	Pirat; Piratin	

p. 81	to **take a photo** [ˌteɪk‿ə 'fəʊtəʊ]	ein Foto machen	Can I **take a photo** of you?
	all [ɔ:l]	alle	I invite you **all** to my party.
	to **hear** [hɪə]	hören	Can you **hear** me?
	doorbell ['dɔ:bel]	Türklingel	
	to **ring** [rɪŋ]	läuten; klingeln	The doorbell **rings**. It's Olivia.
	brilliant ['brɪliənt]	toll	I like this game. It's **brilliant**.
	to **ask** [ɑ:sk]	fragen	Who is the pirate? Let's **ask**.
	to **want (to)** ['wɒnt]	wollen	It's my birthday. I **want** to celebrate it.

Film corner

p. 83	**sleepover** ['sli:pˌəʊvə]	Übernachtung	There's a **sleepover** on Saturday night.
	snack [snæk]	Snack; Imbiss	We eat **snacks** in the cinema.

Checkpoint

to plan [plæn]	planen
What theme would you like? [ˌwɒt 'θi:m wʊd jə 'laɪk]	Welches Motto möchtest du?
I'd like (to)… (= I would like (to)) [aɪd 'laɪk (tə)]	ich möchte …; ich würde gerne …
pizza ['pi:tsə]	Pizza
p.m. [ˌpi:'em]	nachmittags *(Uhrzeit)*
come as ['kʌm æz]	komm als
everyone ['evriwʌn]	jeder
Love from … ['lʌv frɒm]	Liebe Grüße … *(am Briefende)*
It has all the information. [ɪt hæz ˌɔ:l ði‿ˌɪnfə'meɪʃn]	Sie (die Einladung) enthält alle Informationen.
I can understand it. [aɪ ˌkæn ˌʌndə'stænd ɪt]	Ich kann sie verstehen.

Writing skills

p. 88	**lots of** ['lɒts‿əv]	viel; jede Menge	We get **lots of** sweets.
	carrot pudding ['kærət ˌpʊdɪŋ]	*indische Nachspeise*	

Word bank: **Special days**

give / get presents

give / get cards or invitations

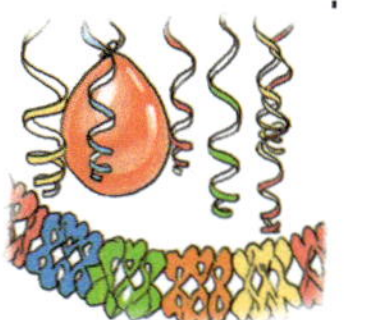
decorate the room

visit family and friends

eat special food / have a favourite meal

wear a costume or new clothes

make a cake / eat cake

have a party

play games

dance a lot

go to a restaurant

have fireworks

Christmas	Halloween	Hanukkah
Eid	Bonfire Night (GB)	Easter
Red Nose Day (GB)	Carnival	birthday

Word bank: Shopping

a bottle of

milk
water 
lemonade 

a packet of

butter
biscuits 
tea 
candles 
sugar 

a

pizza
CD 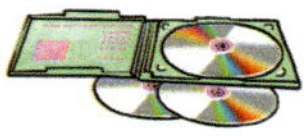
DVD 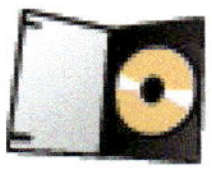
sandwich 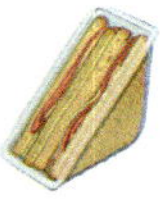

a bar of

chocolate

a kilogram of

oranges
bananas 

a box of

eggs
chocolates 

a loaf of

bread

a bag of

apples
nuts 
flour 
crisps 

a can of

peaches
pet food 
tomatoes

Unit 5 Where I live

Way in

town

flat [flæt]	Wohnung	**café** ['kæfeɪ]	Café
road [rəʊd]	Straße	**park** [pɑ:k]	Park
house [haʊs]	Haus	**station** ['steɪʃn]	Bahnhof
swimming pool ['swɪmɪŋ ˌpu:l]	Schwimmbad	**library** ['laɪbri]	Bibliothek; Bücherei
shopping centre ['ʃɒpɪŋ ˌsentə]	Einkaufszentrum	**department store** [dɪ'pɑ:tmənt ˌstɔ:]	Kaufhaus
sports shop ['spɔ:ts ˌʃɒp]	Sportgeschäft	**river** ['rɪvə]	Fluss
shop [ʃɒp]	Geschäft; Laden	**market** ['mɑ:kɪt]	Markt
post office ['pəʊst‿ˌɒfɪs]	Postamt	**museum** [mju:'zi:əm]	Museum
		supermarket ['su:pəˌmɑ:kɪt]	Supermarkt

p. 90	to **live** [lɪv]	wohnen; leben	I **live** in Greenwich. And you?
	old [əʊld]	alt	**old** ↔ new
	town [taʊn]	Stadt	Greenwich is a **town**.
	famous ['feɪməs]	berühmt	The Cutty Sark is **famous**.
	ship [ʃɪp]	Schiff	
p. 91	to **go swimming** [ˌgəʊ 'swɪmɪŋ]	schwimmen gehen	I **go swimming** at the swimming pool.

Station 1

p. 92	**morning** ['mɔ:nɪŋ]	Morgen; Vormittag	School is in the **morning**.
	tired [taɪəd]	müde	I don't want to watch TV. I'm **tired**.
	yesterday ['jestədeɪ]	gestern	I played football **yesterday**.
	was [wɒz]	simple past von *to be* (sein)	I **was** = ich war/ich bin gewesen
	exciting [ɪk'saɪtɪŋ]	spannend; aufregend	The movie was very **exciting**.
	saw [sɔ:]	simple past von *to see* (sehen)	I **saw** = ich sah/ich habe gesehen
	bought [bɔ:t]	simple past von *to buy* (kaufen)	I **bought** = ich kaufte/ich habe gekauft
	went [went]	simple past von *to go* (gehen)	I **went** = ich ging/ich bin gegangen
	had [hæd]	simple past von *to have* (haben)	I **had** = ich hatte/ich habe gehabt

	pizza ['pi:tsə]	Pizza	T pizza R пицца
	did [dɪd]	simple past von *to do* (machen)	I **did** = ich machte/ich habe gemacht
	to **do homework** [ˌdu: 'həʊmwɜ:k]	Hausaufgabe(n) machen	*homework* steht immer im Singular
	last [lɑ:st]	letzte	**Last** week I had a pizza.
	to **tell** [tel], **told** [təʊld]	erzählen; sagen	I can **tell** you at break.
p. 93	**apple** ['æpl]	Apfel	Can I have an **apple**?

Station 2

transport

train [treɪn]	Zug	**helicopter** ['helɪkɒptə]	Helikopter; Hubschrauber
car [kɑ:]	Auto	**plane** [pleɪn]	Flugzeug
ship [ʃɪp]	Schiff	**motorbike** ['məʊtəbaɪk]	Motorrad
bus [bʌs]	Bus	**boat** [bəʊt]	Boot
bike [baɪk]	Fahrrad	**skateboard** ['skeɪtbɔ:d]	Skateboard
submarine [ˌsʌbmr'i:n]	U-Boot	**underground** ['ʌndəgraʊnd]	U-Bahn
tram [træm]	Straßenbahn		

p. 96	**trip** [trɪp]	Ausflug	The day **trip** to London was fun.
	at the seaside [ət ðə 'si:saɪd]	am Meer	Margate is **at the seaside**.
	sea [si:]	Meer	sea
	to **go by (train)** [ˌgəʊ baɪ ('treɪn)]	mit (dem Zug) fahren	to **go by** train = mit dem Zug fahren to go by bike = mit dem Fahrrad fahren to go by car = mit dem Auto fahren
	to **walk** [wɔ:k]	gehen; laufen	walk
	beach [bi:tʃ]	Strand	
	frisbee ['frɪzbi]	Frisbeescheibe	We played **frisbee** on the beach.
	fish and chips [ˌfɪʃ‿ən 'tʃɪps]	Pommes mit Fisch	
	vegetarian [ˌvedʒɪ'teəriən]	Vegetarier; Vegetarierin	A **vegetarian** doesn't eat meat.
	were [wɜ:]	simple past von *to be* (sein)	we **were** = wir waren/wir sind gewesen

	postcard ['pəʊstkɑːd]	Postkarte	
	to **send** [send], **sent** [sent]	schicken; senden	I **send** postcards to my friends.
p. 97	to **go on foot** [ˌɡəʊ‿ɒn 'fʊt]	zu Fuß gehen	to **go on foot** = to walk

A postcard from Margate

with love [ˌwɪð 'lʌv]	mit lieben Grüßen	to have a cup of tea [hæv‿ə ˌkʌp‿əv 'tiː]	eine Tasse Tee trinken
I took my bags [aɪ ˌtʊk maɪ 'bæɡz]	ich nahm meine Taschen	maybe ['meɪbi]	vielleicht
I'd like (to) … (= I would like to) [aɪd 'laɪk (tə)]	ich möchte …; ich würde gerne …	lovely ['lʌvli]	schön
to visit friends [ˌvɪzɪt 'frendz]	Freunde besuchen	the best part of England [ðə ˌbest pɑːt‿əv 'ɪŋɡlənd]	der beste Teil von England
		to stay a little longer [ˌsteɪ ə ˌlɪtl 'lɒŋɡə]	ein bisschen länger bleiben

p. 99	**fantasy trip** ['fæntəsi ˌtrɪp]	Fantasieausflug	My **fantasy trip** is a day trip with the tigers from the zoo.

Reading corner

p. 100	**adventure** [əd'ventʃə]	Abenteuer	**Adventure** stories are exciting.
	attic ['ætɪk]	Dachboden	ATTIC
	a lot of [ə 'lɒt‿əv]	eine Menge; viel	I've **a lot of** friends.
	diary ['daɪəri]	Tagebuch	diary
	great-great-grandad [ˌɡreɪt ɡreɪt 'ɡrændæd]	Ururopa	My **great-great-grandad** was nice.
	today [tə'deɪ]	heute	**Today** is Monday, yesterday was Sunday.
	job [dʒɒb]	Job	**job** = work
	Australia [ɒs'treɪliə]	Australien	
	to **hate** [heɪt]	hassen; nicht mögen	I **hate** snakes, but I love bears.
	to **be sick** [bi 'sɪk]	sich übergeben	I **was sick** at the weekend.
	first mate [ˌfɜːst 'meɪt]	erster Offizier	The **first mate** is the second captain on a ship.
	awful ['ɔːfl]	schrecklich; furchtbar	The first mate is **awful**. He isn't nice.

	hungry ['hʌŋgri]	hungrig	Can I have a pizza, please? I'm **hungry**.
	potato *(sg)* [pə'teɪtəʊ], **potatoes** *(pl)* [pə'teɪtəʊz]	Kartoffel	
p. 101	**storm** [stɔ:m]	Sturm	The **storm** was awful. I was sick.
	wave [weɪv]	Welle	
	scared [skeəd]	verängstigt	The waves are very high. I'm **scared**.
	shout [ʃaʊt]	Schrei	
	Man overboard! [mæn 'əʊvəbɔ:d]	Mann über Bord!	There was a shout, "**Man overboard!**".
	man *(sg)* [mæn], **men** *(pl)* [men]	Mann	
	some [sʌm]	*hier:* einige; etwas	
	rope [rəʊp]	Seil	
	beautiful ['bju:tɪfl]	schön; hübsch	There are **beautiful** beaches in Australia.
	shark [ʃɑ:k]	Hai	
	bag [bæg]	*hier:* Sack	☺ **bag** = Sack, Tasche, Tüte
	wool [wʊl]	Wolle	
	sheep *(sg)* [ʃi:p], **sheep** *(pl)* [ʃi:p]	Schaf	
	life *(sg)* [laɪf], **lives** *(pl)* [laɪvz]	Leben	**Life** in Australia was an adventure.

Film corner

p. 103	**out and about** [ˌaʊt‿ən‿ə'baʊt]	unterwegs	
	popcorn ['pɒpkɔ:n]	Popcorn	
	Excuse me. [ɪk'skju:z mi]	Entschuldigung.	
	Can I come back for it later? [kæn aɪ kʌm ˌbæk fər‿ɪt 'leɪtə]	Kann ich später nochmal wiederkommen?	Ganze Sätze am besten als Einheit lernen.

Checkpoint

quiz [kwɪz]	Rätsel	ending ['endɪŋ]	Schluss
Good job! [ˌgʊd 'dʒɒb]	Gute Arbeit!	report [rɪ'pɔ:t]	Bericht

Speaking skills

p. 108	**asking the way** [ˌɑ:skɪŋ ðə ˈweɪ]	nach dem Weg fragen	
	tourist [ˈtʊərɪst]	Tourist; Touristin	There are lots of **tourists** in London.
	Can you tell me the way to ...? [kæn ju: ˌtel mi ðə ˈweɪ tə]	Kannst du mir sagen, wie ich ... komme?	
	Tourist Information Centre [ˌtʊərɪst‿ɪnfəˈmeɪʃn ˌsentə]	Touristeninformation	Where's the **Tourist Information Centre**?
	along [əˈlɒŋ]	entlang	Go **along** this road.
	straight on [streɪt‿ˈɒn]	geradeaus	Go **straight on**.
	to **turn right (into ...)** [ˌtɜ:n ˈraɪt]	(nach) rechts abbiegen	Go straight on, then **turn right**.
	on the left [ɒn ðə ˈleft]	auf der linken Seite; links	The Cutty Sark is **on the left**.
	on the right [ɒn ðə ˈraɪt]	auf der rechten Seite; rechts	Greenwich Market is **on the right**.
	opposite [ˈɒpəzɪt]	gegenüber	The post office is **opposite** the market.
	until [ʌnˈtɪl]	bis	Go along the road **until** the market.
	to **turn left (into ...)** [ˌtɜ:n ˈleft]	(nach) links abbiegen	Go along this road, then **turn left**.
p. 109	**hospital** [ˈhɒspɪtl]	Krankenhaus	Achtung Aussprache!
	map [mæp]	Stadtplan; Landkarte	Look at the **map**. You are here.

Word bank: **In town**

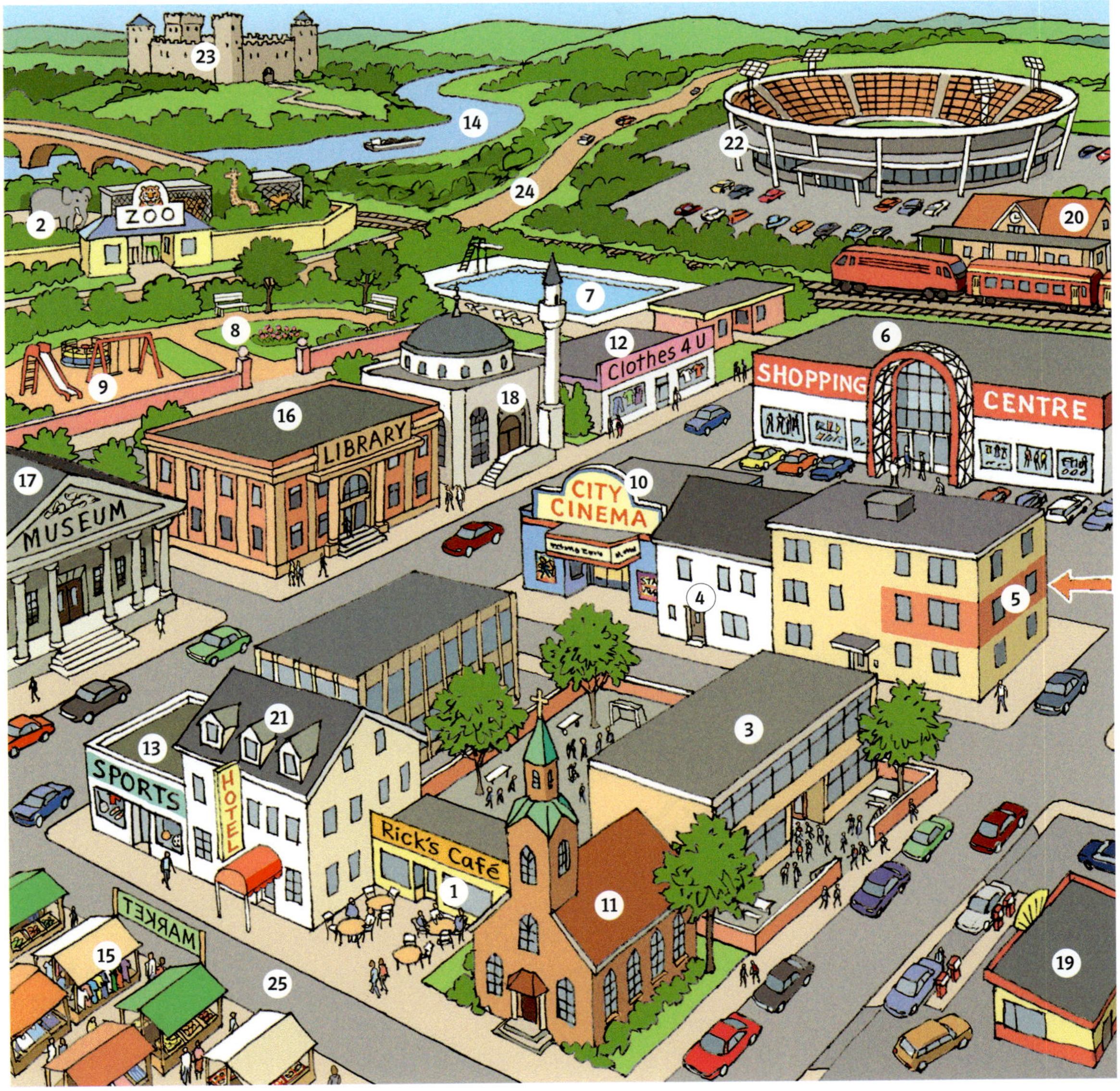

1. café
2. zoo
3. school
4. house
5. flat
6. shopping centre
7. swimming pool
8. park
9. playground
10. cinema
11. church
12. shop
13. sports shop
14. river
15. market
16. library
17. museum
18. mosque
19. petrol station
20. station
21. hotel
22. stadium
23. castle
24. road
25. street

Word bank: Activities in town

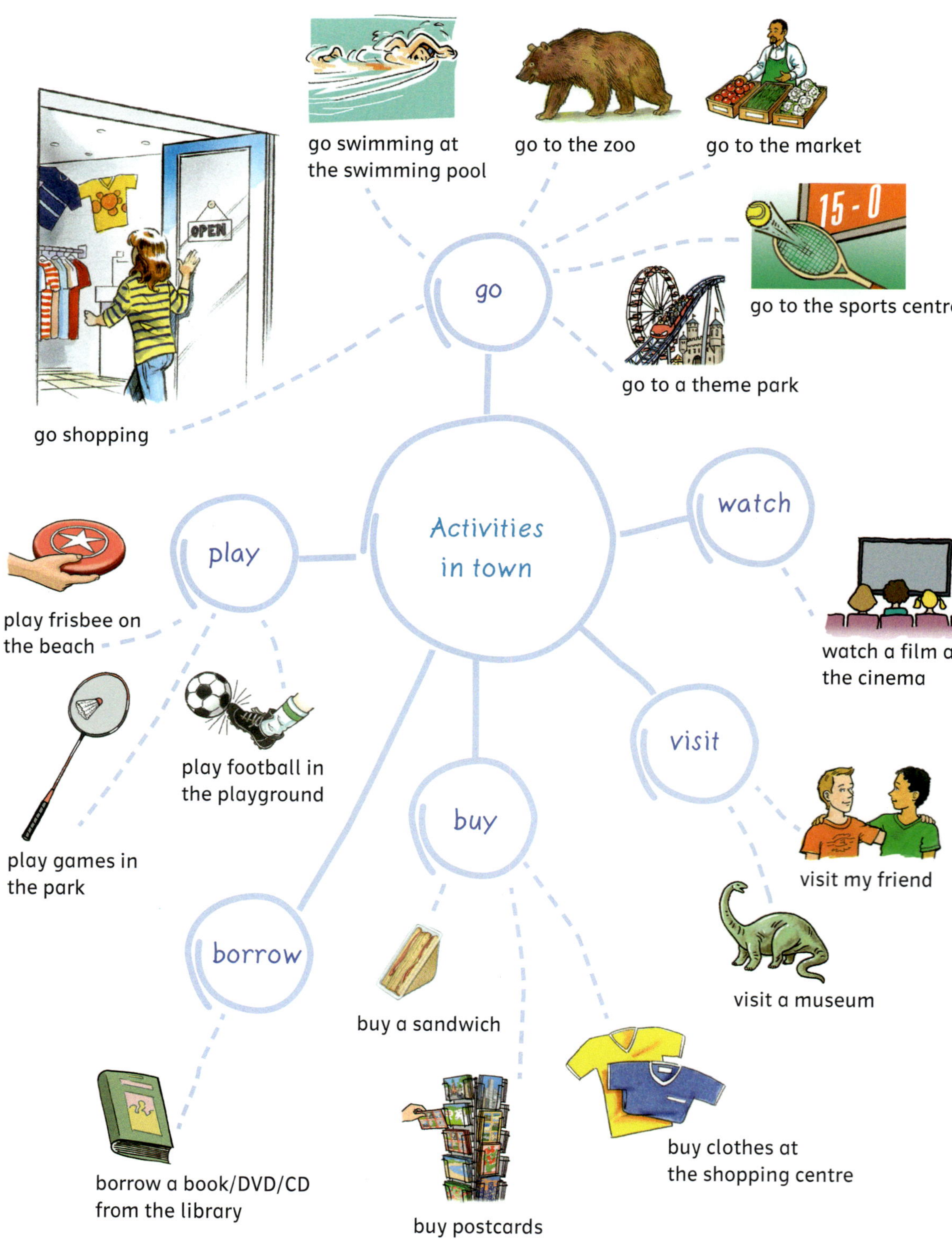
go swimming at
the swimming pool
go to the zoo
go to the market
OPEN
15 - 0
go to the sports centre
go
go to a theme park
go shopping
Activities
in town
play
watch
play frisbee on
the beach
watch a film at
the cinema
play football in
the playground
visit
buy
play games in
the park
visit my friend
borrow
visit a museum
buy a sandwich
buy clothes at
the shopping centre
borrow a book/DVD/CD
from the library
buy postcards

Unit 6 A trip to the country

Way in

p. 110	**country** ['kʌntri]	ländliche Gegend; Land	Achtung Aussprache!
	to **meet** [miːt], **met** [met]	kennen lernen	
	us [ʌs]	uns	Come and meet **us** at Highfield Farm.
	farmer ['fɑːmə]	Bauer; Bäuerin; Landwirt; Landwirtin	
	daughter ['dɔːtə]	Tochter	Olivia Fraser is Desmond's and Janet's **daughter**.
	horse [hɔːs]	Pferd	
	chicken ['tʃɪkɪn]	Huhn	
	everyone ['evriwʌn]	jeder	
	farm [fɑːm]	Bauernhof	**farm** → farmer
p. 111	**modern** ['mɒdn]	modern	**modern** ↔ old
	GPS *(Global Positioning System)* [ˌdʒiːpiː'es]	GPS *(ein satellitengestütztes System zur weltweiten Positionsbestimmung)*	
	collar ['kɒlə]	Halsband	
	tractor ['træktə]	Traktor	Achtung Schreibweise!
	near [nɪə]	in der Nähe von	I live in the country **near** a town.
	rock climbing ['rɒk ˌklaɪmɪŋ]	Klettern	Achtung Aussprache!
	canoeing [kə'nuːɪŋ]	Kanufahren	
	needn't ['niːdnt]	nicht brauchen; nicht müssen	You **needn't** do your homework. English is next week.
	to **worry** ['wʌri]	sich Sorgen machen	Don't **worry**, the food is good.
	came [keɪm]	simple past von *to come* (kommen)	I **came** = ich kam/ich bin gekommen
	to **click** [klɪk]	klicken	
p. 110	**fed** [fed]	simple past von *to feed* (füttern)	I **fed** = ich fütterte/ich habe gefüttert
	scary ['skeəri]	*hier:* beängstigend	**scary** → to be scared

p. 111	**Would you like (to)...?** [ˌwʊd jə 'laɪk (tə)]	Möchtest du ...?	**Would you like** to go to the park?
	I'd like (to) ... (= I would like to) [aɪd 'laɪk (tə)]	ich möchte ...; ich würde gerne ...	**I'd like** to go rock climbing.
	I wouldn't like (to) ... [aɪ 'wʊdnt laɪk (tə)]	ich möchte nicht ...; ich würde nicht gerne ...	**I wouldn't like to** go canoeing.
	fun [fʌn]	Freude; Spaß	Canoeing is **fun**. **fun** → funny

Station 1

clothes

coat [kəʊt]	Jacke	**T-shirt** ['ti:ʃɜ:t]	T-Shirt
trousers *(pl)* ['traʊzəz]	Hose	**trainer** ['treɪnə]	Turnschuh
sock [sɒk]	Socke	**cap** [kæp]	Kappe; Mütze
sweatshirt ['swetʃɜ:t]	Sweatshirt	**blouse** [blaʊz]	Bluse
jeans *(pl)* [dʒi:nz]	Jeans	**top** [tɒp]	Top
skirt [skɜ:t]	Rock	**shorts** *(pl)* [ʃɔ:ts]	Shorts; kurze Hose

p. 112	**phone call** ['fəʊn ˌkɔ:l]	Telefonanruf	This morning there was a **phone call** from Olivia.
	How are you? [ˌhaʊ_'ɑ: jə]	Wie geht es dir?	**How are you?** – I'm OK.
	horse riding ['hɔ:s ˌraɪdɪŋ]	Reiten	
	picnic ['pɪknɪk]	Picknick	T piknik R пикник
	wore [wɔ:]	simple past von *to wear* (tragen)	I **wore** = ich trug/ich habe getragen
	helmet ['helmət]	Helm	You wear a **helmet** for rock climbing.
	must [mʌst]	müssen	I **must** go now. See you!
	to **stop** [stɒp]	aufhören	STOP
	night walk ['naɪt wɔ:k]	Nachtwanderung	The **night walk** is at ten o'clock.
	See you soon! [ˌsi: ju: 'su:n]	Bis bald!	I must go now. **See you soon!**
p. 113	**colourful** ['kʌləfl]	bunt	colourful

chic [ʃɪk]	schick; elegant	Achtung Schreibweise! chic
pretty ['prɪti]	hübsch	**pretty** = beautiful

Station 2

weather

sunny ['sʌni]	sonnig	**warm** [wɔ:m]	warm
hot [hɒt]	heiß	**cold** [kəʊld]	kalt
to rain [reɪn]	regnen	cool [ku:l]	kühl
wet [wet]	nass	dry [draɪ]	trocken
windy ['wɪndi]	windig	mild [maɪld]	mild
cloudy ['klaʊdi]	wolkig	foggy ['fɒgi]	neblig

p. 116	**Dear ...,** [dɪə]	Liebe(r) ... *(Anrede in Briefen)*	So kann man in England Briefe und E-Mails anfangen: **Dear ...,**
	torch [tɔ:tʃ]	Taschenlampe	
	so [səʊ]	deshalb; also	
	dark [dɑ:k]	dunkel	It is **dark** at night.
	Guess what? [ges 'wɒt]	Weißt du was?	
	heard [hɜ:d]	simple past von *to hear* (hören)	I **heard** = ich hörte/ich habe gehört
	got [gɒt]	simple past von *to get* (werden)	I **got** = ich wurde/ich bin geworden
	because [bɪ'kɒz]	weil; da	Why did you get wet? – **Because** we didn't wear our coats.
	Best wishes [ˌbest 'wɪʃɪz]	Mit den besten Wünschen	So kann man eine Postkarte aufhören.
	Any idea? [ˌeni 'aɪdɪə]	Irgendeine Idee?	What was the noise? **Any idea?**
p. 117	**What's the weather like?** [ˌwɒts ðə 'weðə laɪk]	Wie ist das Wetter?	

	idea [aɪ'dɪə]	Idee	Let's play frisbee. – Good **idea**!
	to **go for a walk** [ˌɡəʊ fər͜ ə 'wɔ:k]	spazieren gehen	At the weekend my parents **went for a walk**.

Living in the countryside

living in the countryside [ˌlɪvɪŋ͜ ɪn ðə 'kʌntrisaɪd]	auf dem Lande leben	to get something done [get ˌsʌmθɪŋ 'dʌn]	etwas erledigen
out in the field [ˌaʊt͜ ɪn ðə 'fi:ld]	draußen auf dem Feld	to plough the field [ˌplaʊ ðə 'fi:ld]	das Feld pflügen
early ['ɜ:li]	früh	to climb a tree [ˌklaɪm͜ ə 'tri:]	einen Baum hinauf-klettern
until the sun goes down again [ʌntɪl ðə ˌsʌn ɡəʊz 'daʊn əgen]	bis die Sonne wieder untergeht	apple pie [ˌæpl 'paɪ]	gedeckter Apfelkuchen

p. 119	**Say hi to ...** [seɪ 'haɪ tə]	Grüße ... von mir.	**Say hi to** Mum and Dad.
	to **phone** [fəʊn]	anrufen; telefonieren	to **phone** → phone call
	to **answer** ['ɑ:nsə]	antworten; beantworten	to **answer** → answer
	text message ['tekst ˌmesɪdʒ]	Textnachricht (SMS)	In England sagt man **text message** und nicht SMS.

Reading corner

p. 120	**stuck in the mud** [ˌstʌk͜ ɪn ðə 'mʌd]	im Schlamm festgesteckt	mud
	wheelchair ['wi:ltʃeə]	Rollstuhl	Rachel is in a **wheelchair**.
	problem ['prɒbləm]	Problem	There's a **problem** on the farm. Can the students help?
	said [sed]	simple past von *to say* (sagen)	I **said** = ich sagte/ich habe gesagt
	river ['rɪvə]	Fluss	river
p. 121	**Come on!** [ˌkʌm͜ 'ɒn]	Komm jetzt!	**Come on!** Let's go!
	dirty ['dɜ:ti]	dreckig; schmutzig	dirty
	behind [bɪ'haɪnd]	hinter	I can't see you. You're **behind** the car.
	to **push** [pʊʃ]	schieben	**Push** the window and it opens.
	to **pull** [pʊl]	ziehen	to **pull** ↔ to push

foot *(sg)* [fʊt], **feet** *(pl)* [fi:t]	Fuß	
out of ['aʊt‿əv]	aus … heraus	My feet came **out of** the mud.
to **fall** [fɔ:l], **fell** [fel]	fallen; hinfallen	
face [feɪs]	Gesicht	
boring ['bɔ:rɪŋ]	langweilig	**boring** ↔ interesting
picture ['pɪktʃə]	Bild	The **picture** is nice.

Film corner

p. 123 **cache box** ['kæʃ ˌbɒks]	*Schatzkiste beim Geocaching*	What is in the blue **cache box**?
geocaching ['dʒiəʊkæʃɪŋ]	Geocaching *(eine Art elektronische Schatzsuche)*	Wird auch im Deutschen so verwendet, aber etwas anders ausgesprochen.
cache [kæʃ]	Cache *(Geheimschatz)*	Achtung Aussprache!

Checkpoint

to arrive [ə'raɪv]	ankommen	this report makes sense [ðɪs rɪˌpɔ:t meɪks 'sens]	dieser Bericht ergibt Sinn
the tense is right [ðə ˌtens ɪz 'raɪt]	die Zeitform ist richtig	it has all the facts [ɪt ˌhæz‿ɔ:l ðə 'fækts]	er beinhaltet alle Fakten
it's the simple past [ɪts ðə ˌsɪmpl 'pɑ:st]	es ist die einfache Vergangenheit	website ['websaɪt]	Website

Word bank: **How was it?**

hard
schwierig, schwer

fun
(It was fun. =
Es hat Spaß gemacht.)

funny
lustig

great
großartig

exciting
spannend, aufregend

cool
cool, super

brilliant
toll

easy
einfach, leicht

nice
schön, nett

interesting
interessant

OK
okay

bad
schlecht

awful
schrecklich, furchtbar

terrible
schrecklich, furchtbar

boring
langweilig

frightening
furchterregend

scary
gruselig,
beängstigend

crazy
verrückt

It was … .
It wasn't … .

Word bank: **In the country**

1. sheep
2. horse
3. cow
4. chickens
5. dog
6. cat
7. pig
8. go horse riding
9. have a picnic
10. play with the animals
11. play football
12. sit on the tractor
13. feed the animals
14. work on a farm
15. go rock climbing
16. go canoeing
17. go swimming
18. go walking
19. go geocaching

Im *Dictionary* kannst du Wörter nachschlagen!

How to use the dictionary

Im *Dictionary* sind alle wichtigen Wörter aus deinem Buch enthalten. Die Wörter stehen in alphabetischer Reihenfolge. Englische Wörter schlägst du auf S. 236 bis 250 nach, deutsche Wörter auf S. 251 bis 258.

Die Abkürzungen geben an, wo das Wort zum ersten Mal im Buch erscheint.

quiz	[kwɪz]	Rätsel	I	U5	104
englisches Wort	Aussprache	deutsche Übersetzung	Band 1	Unit 5	Seite

Ansonsten steht W für *Welcome* und ZI für *Zoom in*.

Die mit einem Sternchen (*) gekennzeichneten Verben sind unregelmäßige Verben (→ *List of irregular verbs*, S. 235).

Manche Wörter haben verschiedene Bedeutungen.
Am besten liest du alle, bevor du dich für eine entscheidest.

*to **get** [get] bekommen I U4, 70[1]
to get in ['get‿ɪn] hereinkommen I U3, 62[2]
to get some exercise [get sʌm 'eksəsaɪz] Sport treiben <I U3, 64>[3]
to get up [ˌget‿'ʌp] aufstehen I U3, 58

Schlagt die Wörter um die Wette nach:

scary
fancy dress
torch
Freizeitpark
Tierheim

1 Lernwortschatz für alle: schwarz; 2 Differenzierungswortschatz: blau; 3 kein Lernwortschatz: < >

List of irregular verbs

Hier findest du die unregelmäßigen Verben in der Vergangenheit, auch wenn sie noch nicht alle in den Units vorgekommen sind.

infinitive	simple past	German
be [bi:]	was, were [wɒz, wɜ:]	sein
buy [baɪ]	bought [bɔ:t]	kaufen
come [kʌm]	came [keɪm]	kommen
do [du:]	did [dɪd]	machen; tun
eat [i:t]	ate [eɪt]	essen
fall [fɔ:l]	fell [fel]	fallen; hinfallen
feed [fi:d]	fed [fed]	füttern
find [faɪnd]	found [faʊnd]	finden; herausfinden
forget [fə'get]	forgot [fə'gɒt]	vergessen
get [get]	got [gɒt]	bekommen
give [giv]	gave [geɪv]	geben
go [gəʊ]	went [went]	gehen; fahren
have [hæv]	had [hæd]	haben; besitzen
hear [hɪə]	heard [hɜ:d]	hören
know [nəʊ]	knew [nju:]	wissen; kennen
make [meɪk]	made [meɪd]	machen; tun
meet [mi:t]	met [met]	kennen lernen
read [ri:d]	read [red]	lesen
ring [rɪŋ]	rang [ræŋ]	läuten; klingeln
run [rʌn]	ran [ræn]	laufen; rennen
say [seɪ]	said [sed]	sagen; sprechen
see [si:]	saw [sɔ:]	sehen
send [send]	sent [sent]	schicken; senden
sing [sɪŋ]	sang [sæŋ]	singen
sit [sɪt]	sat [sæt]	sich setzen
sleep [sli:p]	slept [slept]	schlafen
spell [spel]	spelled/spelt [spelt]	buchstabieren
take [teɪk]	took [tʊk]	nehmen
tell [tel]	told [təʊld]	erzählen; sagen
think [θɪŋk]	thought [θɔ:t]	denken
wear [weə]	wore [wɔ:]	tragen
win [wɪn]	won [wʌn]	gewinnen; siegen
write [raɪt]	wrote [rəʊt]	schreiben

Dictionary

A

a [ə] ein; eine I ZI, 10
a **lot** [ə'lɒt] viel I U3, 52
a **lot of** [ə 'lɒt‿əv] eine Menge; viel I U5, 100
a/one **hundred** [ə/wʌn 'hʌndrəd] einhundert; hundert I U3, 55
about [ə'baʊt] über <I U1, 14>
out and about [ˌaʊt‿ən‿ə'baʊt] unterwegs I U5, 103
I'd like to know more about … [aɪd laɪk tə ˌnəʊ 'mɔː ə'baʊt] Ich würde gerne mehr wissen über … <I U1, 27>
abseiling ['æbseɪlɪŋ] Abseilen <I U6, 122>
activity [æk'tɪvəti] Aktivität I ZI, 10
to **add** [æd] hinzufügen <I U6, 113>
adjective ['ædʒɪktɪv] Adjektiv; Eigenschaftswort I U6, 113
adult ['ædʌlt] Erwachsene; Erwachsener <I U6, 122>
adventure [əd'ventʃə] Abenteuer I U5, 100
after ['ɑːftə] nach I U3, 52
after that [ˌɑːftə 'ðæt] danach I U3, 58
afternoon [ˌɑːftə'nuːn] Nachmittag I U3, 58
in the afternoon [ɪn ðiˌɑːftə'nuːn] am Nachmittag I U3, 58
again [ə'gen] noch einmal; wieder <I U1, 19>
Can you say that again, please? [kæn juː ˌseɪ ðæt ə'gen pliːs] Könntest du das bitte wiederholen? I U4, 79
age [eɪdʒ] Alter I U3, 54
ago [ə'gəʊ] vor *(zeitlich)* <I U5, 102>
alarm clock [ə'lɑːm ˌklɒk] Wecker I U1, 19
alien ['eɪliən] Außerirdische; Außerirdischer I U4, 80
all [ɔːl] alle I U4, 81
along [ə'lɒŋ] entlang I U5, 108
alphabet ['ælfəbet] Alphabet I U2, 39
always ['ɔːlweɪz] immer I U4, 72
am [æm] bin I W, 8
a.m. [ˌeɪ'em] vormittags *(Uhrzeit)* <I U2, 44>
an [ən] ein; eine I U2, 35
and [ænd] und I W, 8
animal ['ænɪml] Tier I W, 8
animal rescue shelter [ˌænɪml 'reskjuː ˌʃeltə] Tierheim I U3, 53
answer ['ɑːnsə] Antwort I U2, 36
to **answer** ['ɑːnsə] antworten; beantworten I U6, 119
any ['eni] jedem <I U2, 44>; irgendeine <I U6, 122>
Any idea? [ˌeni 'aɪdɪə] Irgendeine Idee? I U6, 116
Anything else? [ˌeniθɪŋ 'els] Darf es sonst noch etwas sein? I U4, 76
anything unusual ['eniθɪŋ ˌʌnjuːʒl] etwas Ungewöhnliches <I U5, 104>
apple ['æpl] Apfel I U5, 93
April ['eɪprl] April I U4, 71
are [ɑː] bist; sind I U1, 13
around the house [əˌraʊnd ðə 'haʊs] zu Hause I U1, 25
to **arrive** [ə'raɪv] ankommen <I U6, 125>
Art [ɑːt] Kunst I U2, 39
to **ask** [ɑːsk] fragen I U4, 81
asking the way [ˌɑːskɪŋ ðə 'weɪ] nach dem Weg fragen I U5, 108
assembly hall [ə'sembli ˌhɔːl] Aula <I U2, 202>
at [ət] am; an; auf; bei; in; um I U3, 53
at 8.50 a.m. [ət 'eɪt fɪfti ˌeɪ'em] um 8.50 Uhr <I U2, 44>
at break [ət 'breɪk] in der Pause I U2, 38
at home [ət 'həʊm] zu Hause I U1, 18
at school [ət 'skuːl] in der Schule I U2, 32
at the seaside [ət ðə 'siːsaɪd] am Meer I U5, 96
at the weekend [ət ðə ˌwiːk'end] am Wochenende I U3, 53
attic ['ætɪk] Dachboden I U5, 100
August ['ɔːgəst] August I U4, 71
in August [ɪn 'ɔːgəst] im August I U4, 70
aunt [ɑːnt] Tante I U1, 15
awful ['ɔːfl] furchtbar; schrecklich I U5, 100

B

*to **babysit** ['beɪbɪsɪt] babysitten <I U3, 209>
badminton ['bædmɪntən] Badminton <I U3, 64>
bag [bæg] Tasche; Tüte I U2, 35; Sack I U5, 101
balloon [bə'luːn] Luftballon I U4, 76
banana [bə'nɑːnə] Banane I U3, 57
band [bænd] Band; Musikgruppe <I U4, 82>
a **bar** of chocolate [bɑːr‿əv 'tʃɒklət] eine Tafel Schokolade I U4, 76
barbecue ['bɑːbɪkjuː] Grill I U4, 72
basketball ['bɑːskɪtbɔːl] Basketball <I U3, 209>
bat [bæt] Fledermaus I W, 8
bathroom ['bɑːθrʊm] Bad(ezimmer) I U1, 25
*to **be** [biː] sein I U1, 16
to be good at [bi 'gʊd‿ət] gut sein bei; gut sein in I U2, 38
to be sick [bi 'sɪk] sich übergeben I U5, 100
beach [biːtʃ] Strand I U5, 96
beautiful ['bjuːtɪfl] hübsch; schön I U5, 101
because [bɪ'kɒz] da; weil I U6, 116
bed [bed] Bett I U1, 18
to go to bed [ˌgəʊ tə 'bed] ins Bett gehen I U3, 59
bedroom ['bedrʊm] Kinderzimmer; Schlafzimmer I U1, 18
behind [bɪ'haɪnd] hinter I U6, 121
Best wishes [ˌbest 'wɪʃɪz] Mit den besten Wünschen I U6, 116
big [bɪg] groß I U4, 72
biggest ['bɪgɪst] größte <I U6, 122>
bike [baɪk] Fahrrad I U1, 12
Biology [baɪ'ɒlədʒi] Biologie I U2, 39
birthday ['bɜːθdeɪ] Geburtstag I U4, 72

Happy birthday! [ˌhæpi 'bɜ:θdeɪ] Alles Gute zum Geburtstag! I U4, 80

biscuit ['bɪskɪt] Keks <I U4, 219>

black [blæk] schwarz I W, 9

blazer ['bleɪzə] Blazer <I U2, 50>

blouse [blaʊz] Bluse I U6, 113

blue [blu:] blau I W, 9

board [bɔ:d] Tafel I U2, 34

boat [bəʊt] Boot I U5, 97

book [bʊk] Buch; Heft I U1, 18

exercise book ['eksəsaɪz ˌbʊk] Übungsheft I U2, 34

boring ['bɔ:rɪŋ] langweilig I U6, 121

to **borrow** ['bɒrəʊ] ausleihen <I U5, 226>

a **bottle** of ['bɒtl] eine Flasche … I U4, 76

bought [bɔ:t] simple past von *to buy* I U5, 92

box [bɒks] Box; Kiste I U1, 18

a box of [bɒks] eine Schachtel … I U4, 77

boy [bɔɪ] Junge I ZI, 10

a loaf of **bread** [ə ˌləʊf‿əv 'bred] Brotlaib <I U4, 219>

at **break** [ət 'breɪk] in der Pause I U2, 38

*to **break** into, **broke** into [ˌbreɪk‿'ɪntə; ˌbrəʊk‿'ɪntə] einbrechen in <I U5, 104>

breakfast ['brekfəst] Frühstück I U3, 58

to have breakfast [ˌhæv 'brekfəst] frühstücken I U3, 58

brilliant ['brɪliənt] toll I U4, 81

brother ['brʌðə] Bruder I U1, 14

brown [braʊn] braun I W, 9

burger ['bɜ:gə] Hamburger I U4, 73

bus [bʌs] Bus I ZI, 11

busy ['bɪzi] beschäftigt I U1, 22

a busy day [ə ˌbɪzi 'deɪ] ein ausgefüllter Tag I U3, 58

but [bʌt] aber I U4, 72

butter ['bʌtə] Butter I U4, 77

*to **buy** [baɪ] kaufen I ZI, 11

by [baɪ] bis <I U2, 44>

to go by (train) [ˌgəʊ baɪ ('treɪn)] mit (dem Zug) fahren I U5, 96

Bye! [baɪ] Tschüss! I W, 8

C

cache [kæʃ] Cache *(Geheimschatz)* I U6, 123

cache box ['kæʃ ˌbɒks] *Schatzkiste beim Geocaching* I U6, 123

café ['kæfeɪ] Café I U3, 62

cafeteria [kæfə'tɪəriə] Cafeteria; Mensa I U2, 33

cage [keɪdʒ] Käfig I U3, 58

cake [keɪk] Kuchen I U4, 72

calculator ['kælkjəleɪtə] (Taschen-) Rechner I U2, 35

phone **call** ['fəʊn ˌkɔ:l] Telefonanruf I U6, 112

to **call** [kɔ:l] anrufen; rufen I U3, 59

call me ['kɔ:l ˌmi] nenne mich I U2, 34

came [keɪm] simple past von *to come* I U6, 111

camel ['kæml] Kamel I U3, 54

a **can** of [kæn] eine Dose … I U4, 77

can [kæn; kən] können I ZI, 11

Can I come back for it later? [kæn aɪ kʌm ˌbæk fər‿ɪt 'leɪtə] Kann ich später nochmal wiederkommen? I U5, 103

Can you say that again, please? [kæn ju: ˌseɪ ðæt ə'gen pli:s] Könntest du das bitte wiederholen? I U4, 79

Can you tell me the way to …? [kæn ju: ˌtel mi ðə 'weɪ tə] Kannst du mir sagen, wie ich … komme? I U5, 108

can't [kɑ:nt] nicht können I U1, 18

I can't find … [aɪ kɑ:nt 'faɪnd] ich kann … nicht finden I U1, 18

candle ['kændl] Kerze I U4, 76

canoeing [kə'nu:ɪŋ] Kanufahren I U6, 111

cap [kæp] Kappe; Mütze I U6, 113

captain ['kæptɪn] Kapitän; Kapitänin I U3, 53

car [kɑ:] Auto I U5, 96

car park ['kɑ: ˌpɑ:k] Parkplatz <I U6, 122>

card [kɑ:d] Karte <I W, 9>

caretaker ['keəˌteɪkə] Hausmeister; Hausmeisterin I U2, 33

carnival ['kɑ:nɪvl] Fasching; Karneval I U4, 70

carpet ['kɑ:pɪt] Teppich I U1, 19

carrot pudding ['kærət ˌpʊdɪŋ] *indische Nachspeise* I U4, 88

pencil **case** ['pensl ˌkeɪs] Federmäppchen I U2, 35

castle ['kɑ:sl] Burg; Schloss <I U5, 225>; <I U6, 122>

cat [kæt] Katze I U1, 13

CD [ˌsi:'di:] CD I U4, 78

ceiling ['si:lɪŋ] Zimmerdecke <I U1, 195>; I U3, 62

to **celebrate** ['seləbreɪt] feiern I U4, 70

centimetre (cm) ['sentɪˌmi:tə] Zentimeter (cm) I U3, 54

shopping **centre** ['ʃɒpɪŋ ˌsentə] Einkaufszentrum I U5, 90

chair [tʃeə] Stuhl I U1, 18

chameleon [kə'mi:liən] Chamäleon <I U3, 210>

checklist ['tʃeklɪst] Checkliste <I U1, 26>

checkpoint ['tʃekpɔɪnt] Kontrollpunkt <I U1, 13>

cheese [tʃi:z] Käse I U4, 77

Chemistry ['kemɪstri] Chemie <I U2, 203>

chess [tʃes] Schach <I U3, 64>

chewing gum ['tʃu:ɪŋ ˌgʌm] Kaugummi I U2, 45

chic [ʃɪk] elegant; schick I U6, 113

chicken ['tʃɪkɪn] Huhn I U6, 110

only **child** [ˌəʊnli 'tʃaɪld] Einzelkind <I U1, 194>

children *(pl)* ['tʃɪldrn] Kinder <I U6, 122>

chips *(pl)* [tʃɪps] Pommes I U5, 96

fish and chips [ˌfɪʃ‿ən 'tʃɪps] Pommes mit Fisch I U5, 96

chocolate ['tʃɒklət] Schokolade I U4, 72; Praline <I U4, 219>

choir ['kwaɪə] Chor <I U3, 209>

*to **choose** [tʃu:z] auswählen; wählen <I U1, 23>

What do you choose? ['wɒt dʊ ju: ˌtʃu:z] Was nimmst du? <I U4, 77>
chorus ['kɔ:rəs] Refrain <I U1, 15>
Christmas ['krɪsməs] Weihnachten I U4, 70
church [tʃɜ:tʃ] Kirche <I U5, 225>
cinema ['sɪnəmə] Kino I U3, 53
circus ['sɜ:kəs] Zirkus <I U2, 46>
class [klɑ:s] Unterricht <I U2, 44>
classical ['klæsɪkl] klassisch <I U4, 82>
classroom ['klɑ:srʊm] Klassenzimmer I U2, 33
to **clean** [kli:n] putzen; sauber machen I U3, 58
That was very **clear.** [ðæt wɒz veri 'klɪə] Das war sehr klar. <I U3, 67>
to **click** [klɪk] klicken I U6, 111
clock [klɒk] Uhr I U5, 102
alarm clock [ə'lɑ:m ˌklɒk] Wecker I U1, 19
o'clock [ə'klɒk] Uhr *(Zeitangabe bei vollen Stunden)* I U3, 58
to **close** [kləʊz] schließen; zumachen I U2, 34
closed [kləʊzd] geschlossen <I U6, 122>
clothes *(pl)* [kləʊðz] Kleider *(Pl.)*; Kleidung I U4, 70
cloudy ['klaʊdi] wolkig I U6, 117
club [klʌb] Klub; Schul-AG <I U2, 46>
clue [klu:] Hinweis; Spur I U3, 62
coat [kəʊt] Jacke I U6, 113
coke [kəʊk] Cola I U4, 76
cold [kəʊld] kalt I U6, 117
collar ['kɒlə] Halsband I U6, 111
to **collect** [kə'lekt] sammeln I U4, 70
colour ['kʌlə] Farbe I ZI, 10
colourful ['kʌləfl] bunt I U6, 113
*to **come** [kʌm] kommen I U3, 54
come as ['kʌm æz] komm als <I U4, 85>
Come in. [ˌkʌm‿'ɪn] Komm herein. <I U6, 122>
Come on! [ˌkʌm‿'ɒn] Komm jetzt! I U6, 121
computer [ˌkəm'pju:tə] Computer I W, 8
computer game [ˌkəm'pju:tə geɪm] Computerspiel I U1, 31
cool [ku:l] cool; super I U1, 12; kühl I U6, 117
corner shop ['kɔ:nə ˌʃɒp] Tante-Emma-Laden I U4, 76
film corner ['fi:lm ˌkɔ:nə] Filmecke <I U1, 13>
reading corner ['ri:dɪŋ ˌkɔ:nə] Leseecke <I U1, 13>
costume ['kɒstju:m] Kostüm I U4, 70
country ['kʌntri] Land; ländliche Gegend I U6, 110
cousin ['kʌzn] Cousin; Cousine <I U1, 194>
cow [kaʊ] Kuh <I U6, 233>
crazy ['kreɪzi] verrückt I U2, 34
creative [kri'eɪtɪv] kreativ <I U3, 64>
crisp [krɪsp] Kartoffelchip I U4, 76
crocodile ['krɒkədaɪl] Krokodil I U3, 54
culture ['kʌltʃə] Kultur <I U1, 25>

D

dad [dæd] Papa; Vati I U1, 14
daily news [ˌdeɪli 'nju:z] Nachrichten des Tages <I U5, 104>
dance [dɑ:ns] Tanz <I U3, 64>
to **dance** [dɑ:ns] tanzen I U4, 70
dancer ['dɑ:nsə] Tänzer; Tänzerin I U4, 80
dark [dɑ:k] dunkel I U6, 116
date [deɪt] Datum; Zeitpunkt I U4, 73
daughter ['dɔ:tə] Tochter I U6, 110
day [deɪ] Tag I U2, 38
a busy day [ə ˌbɪzi 'deɪ] ein ausgefüllter Tag I U3, 58
day visitors ['deɪ ˌvɪzɪtəz] Tagesbesucher <I U6, 122>
four hours a day [ˌfɔ:r aʊəz‿ə 'deɪ] vier Stunden täglich I U3, 54
Dear ..., [dɪə] Liebe(r) ... *(Anrede in Briefen)* I U6, 116
December [dɪ'sembə] Dezember I U4, 70
to **decorate** ['dekreɪt] schmücken <I U4, 218>
department store [dɪ'pɑ:tmənt ˌstɔ:] Kaufhaus I U5, 93
to **describe** [dɪ'skraɪb] beschreiben <I U6, 113>
Design Technology (DT) [dɪˌzaɪn tek'nɒlədʒi] Technik I U2, 38
detective [dɪ'tektɪv] Detektiv; Detektivin <I U1, 16>
dialogue ['daɪəlɒg] Dialog; Gespräch <I U1, 25>
diary ['daɪəri] Tagebuch I U5, 100
did [dɪd] simple past von *to do* I U5, 92
difficult ['dɪfɪklt] schwierig I U2, 39
dining room ['daɪnɪŋ ˌrʊm] Esszimmer I U1, 31
dirty ['dɜ:ti] dreckig; schmutzig I U6, 121
divorced [dɪ'vɔ:st] geschieden <I U1, 194>
*to **do** [du:] machen; tun I U2, 34
to do experiments [ˌdu: ɪk'sperɪmənts] Experimente machen; Versuche machen <I U2, 202>
to do homework [ˌdu: 'həʊmwɜ:k] Hausaufgabe(n) machen I U5, 92
to do sport [du: 'spɔ:t] Sport machen <I U2, 202>
Do you have ...? [du ju: 'hæv] Hast du ...? <I U1, 24>
dog [dɒg] Hund I ZI, 10
to take the dog for a walk [ˌteɪk ðə dɒg fɔ:r‿ə 'wɔ:k] den Hund ausführen I U3, 62
door [dɔ:] Tür <I U1, 195>
doorbell ['dɔ:bel] Türklingel I U4, 81
*to **draw** a picture [drɔ: ə 'pɪktʃə] ein Bild malen <I U2, 202>
fancy dress [ˌfænsi 'dres] Kostüm; Verkleidung I U4, 72
*to **drink** [drɪŋk] trinken <I U2, 202>
dry [draɪ] trocken I U6, 117
DVD [ˌdi:vi:'di:] DVD I U4, 78

E

in the east [ɪn ði‿ˈi:st] im Osten <I U5, 102>
Easter [ˈi:stə] Ostern <I U4, 218>
easy [ˈi:zi] einfach; leicht I U2, 38
*to **eat** [i:t] essen I U2, 33
egg [eg] Ei I U4, 77
Eid [i:d] *muslimisches Fest* I U4, 70
eight [eɪt] acht I W, 9
eighteen [ˌeɪˈti:n] achtzehn I U3, 55
eighty [ˈeɪti] achtzig I U3, 55
elephant [ˈelɪfənt] Elefant I U3, 54
eleven [ɪˈlevn] elf I U1, 12
ending [ˈendɪŋ] Schluss <I U5, 105>
English [ˈɪŋglɪʃ] Englisch I W, 8
eraser [ɪˈreɪzə] Radiergummi I U2, 35
evening [ˈi:vnɪŋ] Abend I U4, 70
every [ˈevri] jede I U3, 62
everyone [ˈevriwʌn] jeder I U6, 110
exciting [ɪkˈsaɪtɪŋ] aufregend; spannend I U5, 92
Excuse me. [ɪkˈskju:z mi] Entschuldigung. I U5, 103
exercise book [ˈeksəsaɪz ˌbʊk] Übungsheft I U2, 34
to get some **exercise** [get sʌm ˈeksəsaɪz] Sport treiben <I U3, 64>
extra practice [ˌekstrə ˈpræktɪs] Zusatzübungen <I U1, 13>

F

face [feɪs] Gesicht I U6, 121
it has all the **facts** [ɪt ˌhæz‿ɔ:l ðə ˈfækts] es beinhaltet alle Fakten <I U6, 125>
school **fair** [ˌsku:l ˈfeə] Schulfest <I U3, 64>
*to **fall** [fɔ:l] fallen; hinfallen I U6, 121
family [ˈfæmli] Familie I U1, 14
famous [ˈfeɪməs] berühmt I U5, 90
fan [fæn] Fan I U1, 12
fancy dress [ˌfænsi ˈdres] Kostüm; Verkleidung I U4, 72
fantasy trip [ˈfæntəsi ˌtrɪp] Fantasieausflug I U5, 99
farm [fɑ:m] Bauernhof I U6, 110
farmer [ˈfɑ:mə] Bauer; Bäuerin; Landwirt; Landwirtin I U6, 110
fashion [ˈfæʃn] Mode <I U2, 50>
fast food restaurant [ˌfɑ:st fu:d ˈrestrɒnt] Fastfood-Restaurant I U4, 73
the **fastest** [ðə ˈfɑ:stɪst] der/die/das schnellste I U3, 65
father [ˈfɑ:ðə] Vater I U1, 14
favourite [ˈfeɪvrɪt] Lieblings- I U2, 32
February [ˈfebruri] Februar I U4, 71
fed [fed] simple past von *to feed* I U6, 110
*to **feed** [fi:d] füttern I U3, 58
foot *(sg)* [fʊt], **feet** *(pl)* [fi:t] Fuß I U6, 121
fell [fel] simple past von *to fall* I U6, 121
felt-tip [ˌfeltˈtɪp] Filzstift I U2, 35
summer **festival** [ˌsʌmə ˈfestɪvl] Sommerfest <I U4, 82>
science **fiction** [ˌsaɪəns ˈfɪkʃn] Science-Fiction I U3, 53
fifteen [ˌfɪfˈti:n] fünfzehn I U3, 55
fifty [ˈfɪfti] fünfzig I U3, 55
film [fɪlm] Film I U2, 45
film corner [ˈfi:lm ˌkɔ:nə] Filmecke <I U1, 13>
*to **find** [faɪnd] finden; herausfinden I U1, 18
I can't **find** … [aɪ kɑ:nt ˈfaɪnd] ich kann … nicht finden I U1, 18
to **finish** [ˈfɪnɪʃ] aufhören; enden <I U2, 44>
fireworks *(pl)* [ˈfaɪəwɜ:ks] Feuerwerk <I U4, 218>
first [fɜ:st] als Erstes; zuerst I U3, 58; erste I U4, 73
first mate [ˌfɜ:st ˈmeɪt] erster Offizier I U5, 100
the **first** time [ðə ˌfɜ:st ˈtaɪm] das erste Mal I U3, 62
fish *(sg)* [fɪʃ], **fish** *(pl)* [fɪʃ] Fisch I U3, 57
fish and chips [ˌfɪʃ‿ən ˈtʃɪps] Pommes mit Fisch I U5, 96
five [faɪv] fünf I W, 9
flamingo [fləˈmɪŋgəʊ] Flamingo I U3, 54
flat [flæt] Wohnung I U5, 90
floor [flɔ:] Fußboden <I U1, 195>
flour [flaʊə] Mehl I U4, 77
foggy [ˈfɒgi] neblig I U6, 117
food [fu:d] Essen; Lebensmittel I U2, 33
Food Technology [ˌfu:d ˈteknɒlədʒi] Hauswirtschaft <I U2, 203>
foot *(sg)* [fʊt], **feet** *(pl)* [fi:t] Fuß I U6, 121
to go on **foot** [ˌgəʊ‿ɒn ˈfʊt] zu Fuß gehen I U5, 97
football [ˈfʊtbɔ:l] Fußball I ZI, 11
for [fɔ:] für I U2, 34
for five months [fə ˌfaɪv ˈmʌnθs] fünf Monate lang I U3, 54
for sale [fə ˈseɪl] zu verkaufen <I U6, 122>
*to **forget** [fəˈget] vergessen I U4, 72
forty [ˈfɔ:ti] vierzig I U3, 55
found [faʊnd] *simple past von to find* <I U5, 105>
four [fɔ:] vier I W, 9
fourteen [ˌfɔ:ˈti:n] vierzehn I U3, 55
fourth [fɔ:θ] vierte I U4, 73
free [fri:] kostenlos <I U4, 82>
free time [ˌfri: ˈtaɪm] Freizeit I U3, 52
French [frenʃ] Französisch I U2, 39
fresh [freʃ] frisch <I U6, 122>
Friday [ˈfraɪdeɪ] Freitag I U2, 39
friend [frend] Freund; Freundin I U1, 14
to make **friends** [ˌmeɪk ˈfrendz] Freundschaften schließen I U2, 45
to see **friends** [si: ˈfrendz] sich mit Freunden treffen <I U3, 66>
frightening [ˈfraɪtnɪŋ] furchterregend <I U6, 232>
frisbee [ˈfrɪzbi] Frisbeescheibe I U5, 96
from [frɒm] aus; von I U1, 12
from … to [frəm ˈtə] von … bis <I U2, 44>
I'm **from** … [ˈaɪm ˌfrɒm] ich komme aus … I U1, 12

Where are you from? [ˌweər‿ə ju ˈfrɒm] Woher kommst du? I U1, 13
fruit [fru:t] Frucht; Obst I U3, 54
full day [ˌfʊl ˈdeɪ] ganztägig <I U6, 122>
fun [fʌn] Freude; Spaß I U6, 111
funny [ˈfʌni] komisch; merkwürdig I U1, 23; lustig; witzig I U2, 38

G

game [geɪm] Spiel I U2, 32
computer game [ˌkəmˈpju:tə geɪm] Computerspiel I U1, 31
garden [ˈgɑ:dn] Garten I U1, 14
geocaching [ˈdʒiəʊkæʃɪŋ] Geocaching *(eine Art elektronische Schatzsuche)* I U6, 123
Geography [dʒiˈɒgrəfi] Erdkunde; Geografie I U2, 39
German [ˈdʒɜ:mən] Deutsch I U2, 39
*to **get** [get] bekommen I U4, 70
to get in [ˈget‿ɪn] hereinkommen I U3, 62
to get some exercise [get sʌm ˈeksəsaɪz] Sport treiben <I U3, 64>
to get up [ˌget‿ˈʌp] aufstehen I U3, 58
giraffe [dʒɪˈrɑ:f] Giraffe I U3, 54
girl [gɜ:l] Mädchen I U2, 34
*to **give** [gɪv] geben I U4, 72
gave back [ˌgeɪv ˈbæk] gab zurück <I U5, 105>
glue [glu:] Klebstoff I U2, 35
*to **go** [gəʊ] gehen I U2, 32; fahren I U5, 96
to go by (train) [ˌgəʊ baɪ (ˈtreɪn)] mit (dem Zug) fahren I U5, 96
to go for a walk [ˌgəʊ fər‿ə ˈwɔ:k] spazieren gehen I U6, 117
to go on foot [ˌgəʊ‿ɒn ˈfʊt] zu Fuß gehen I U5, 97
to go swimming [ˌgəʊ ˈswɪmɪŋ] schwimmen gehen I U5, 91
to go to bed [ˌgəʊ tə ˈbed] ins Bett gehen I U3, 59
to go to the toilet [ˌgəʊ tə ðə ˈtɔɪlət] zur Toilette gehen <I U2, 202>
good [gʊd] gut I U2, 34
to be good at [bi ˈgʊd‿ət] gut sein bei; gut sein in I U2, 38
Good job! [ˌgʊd ˈdʒɒb] Gute Arbeit! <I U5, 105>
Goodbye. [gʊdˈbaɪ] Auf Wiedersehen. I W, 8
gorilla [gəˌrɪlə] Gorilla <I U3, 210>
got [gɒt] simple past von *to get* I U6, 116
GPS *(Global Positioning System)* [ˌdʒi:pi:ˈes] GPS *(ein satellitengestütztes System zur weltweiten Positionsbestimmung)* I U6, 111
grammar [ˈgræmə] Grammatik <I U1, 17>
grandfather [ˈgrænˌfɑ:ðə] Großvater I U1, 15
grandmother [ˈgrænˌmʌðə] Großmutter I U1, 15
great [greɪt] großartig; toll I U4, 72
great-great-grandad [ˌgreɪt greɪt ˈgrændæd] Ururopa I U5, 100
green [gri:n] grün I W, 9
grey [greɪ] grau I W, 9
group [gru:p] Gruppe I U2, 37
group skills [ˈgru:p ˌskɪlz] Fertigkeit Kooperatives Lernen <I U1, 27>
tutor group [ˈtju:tə ˌgru:p] Klasse I U2, 33
Guess what? [ges ˈwɒt] Weißt du was? I U6, 116

H

had [hæd] simple past von *to have* I U5, 92
hair straightener [ˈheə ˌstreɪtnə] Haarglätter I U1, 25
half day [ˌhɑ:f ˈdeɪ] halbtägig <I U6, 122>
half past (two) [ˌhɑ:f ˈpɑ:st] halb (drei) I U3, 59
half-sister [ˈhɑ:fˌsɪstə] Halbschwester <I U1, 194>
Halloween [ˌhæləʊˈi:n] **Halloween** I U4, 70
Put your **hands** up. [pʊt jɔ: ˌhændz‿ˈʌp] Meldet euch. I U2, 34
handball [ˈhændbɔ:l] Handball <I U3, 209>
Hanukkah [ˈhʌnʊkə] Chanukka *(jüdisches Fest)* <I U4, 218>
happy [ˈhæpi] froh; glücklich I U4, 80
Happy birthday! [ˌhæpi ˈbɜ:θdeɪ] Alles Gute zum Geburtstag! I U4, 80
hard [hɑ:d] schwer; schwierig <I U6, 232>
to **hate** [heɪt] hassen; nicht mögen I U5, 100
*to **have** [hæv] besitzen; haben I U1, 14
to have breakfast [ˌhæv ˈbrekfəst] frühstücken I U3, 58
Have a look. [ˌhæv‿ə ˈlʊk] Schau dich um. <I U6, 122>
he [hi:] er I U1, 14
he has [hi: ˈhæz] er hat <I U1, 24>
he's (= he is) [hi:z] er ist I U1, 14
*to **hear** [hɪə] hören I U4, 81
heard [hɜ:d] simple past von *to hear* I U6, 116
helicopter [ˈhelɪkɒptə] Helikopter; Hubschrauber I U5, 97
Hello. [həˈləʊ] Hallo. I W, 8
helmet [ˈhelmət] Helm I U6, 112
to **help** [help] helfen I U3, 53
How can I help you? [ˌhaʊ kæn aɪ ˈhelp‿ju:] Was kann ich für dich tun? I U4, 76
her [hɜ:] ihr I U1, 14
here [hɪə] hier I ZI, 11
Here you are. [ˌhɪə ju‿ˈɑ:] Bitte schön. I U2, 35
Here's your change. [ˌhɪəz jɔ: ˈtʃeɪndʒ] Hier ist dein Wechselgeld. I U4, 76
Hi. [haɪ] Hallo.; Hi. I W, 8
Say hi to … [seɪ ˈhaɪ tə] Grüße … von mir. I U6, 119
high [haɪ] groß; hoch I U3, 54

him [hɪm] ihm; ihn I U4, 72
his [hɪz] sein I U1, 14
History ['hɪstri] Geschichte I U2, 39
hole [həʊl] Loch I U3, 62
home [həʊm] Heim; Zuhause I U1, 18
at home [ət 'həʊm] zu Hause I U1, 18
*to do **homework** [ˌdu: 'həʊmwɜ:k] Hausaufgabe(n) machen I U5, 92
horse [hɔ:s] Pferd I U6, 110
horse riding ['hɔ:s ˌraɪdɪŋ] Reiten I U6, 112
hospital ['hɒspɪtl] Krankenhaus I U5, 109
hot [hɒt] heiß I U6, 117
hotel [həʊ'tel] Hotel <I U5, 225>
hour [aʊə] Stunde <I U3, 211>
40 kilometres an hour [kɪ'lɒmi:təz‿ən‿'aʊə] 40 Kilometer pro Stunde I U3, 54
four hours a day [ˌfɔ:r aʊəz‿ə 'deɪ] vier Stunden täglich I U3, 54
house [haʊs] Haus I U1, 22
around the house [əˌraʊnd ðə 'haʊs] zu Hause I U1, 25
tree house ['tri: ˌhaʊs] Baumhaus I U1, 22
how [haʊ] wie I U3, 62
How are you? [ˌhaʊ‿'ɑ: jə] Wie geht es dir? I U6, 112
How can I help you? [ˌhaʊ kæn aɪ 'help‿ju:] Was kann ich für dich tun? I U4, 76
How much (is/are) …? [ˌhaʊ 'mʌtʃ‿ɪz/ɑ:] Wie viel (kostet/kosten) …? I U4, 76
How old are you? [haʊ‿'əʊld‿ə ju:] Wie alt bist du? I U1, 12
How was my presentation? [ˌhaʊ wɒz maɪ ˌprezn'teɪʃn] Wie war meine Präsentation? <I U1, 27>
a/one **hundred** [ə/wʌn 'hʌndrəd] einhundert; hundert I U3, 55
hungry ['hʌŋgri] hungrig I U5, 100

I

I [aɪ] ich I W, 8
I don't know! [ˌaɪ dəʊnt 'nəʊ] Ich weiß (es) nicht! I U3, 62
I don't like [aɪ ˌdəʊnt 'laɪk] gefällt mir nicht; ich mag nicht I U2, 32
I like [aɪ 'laɪk] gefällt mir; ich mag I W, 8
I spy with my little eye … [aɪ spaɪ wɪð ˌmaɪ lɪtl 'aɪ] Ich sehe was, was du nicht siehst … I ZI, 11
I wouldn't like (to) … [aɪ 'wʊdnt laɪk (tə)] ich möchte nicht …; ich würde nicht gerne … I U6, 111
I'd like (to) … (= I would like to) [aɪd 'laɪk (tə)] ich möchte …; ich würde gerne … I U6, 111
I'd like to know more about … [aɪd laɪk tə ˌnəʊ 'mɔ: ə'baʊt] Ich würde gerne mehr wissen über … <I U1, 27>
I'm (= I am) [aɪm] ich bin I W, 8
I'm from … ['aɪm ˌfrɒm] ich komme aus … I U1, 12
ice cream [ˌaɪs 'kri:m] Eis(creme) I U4, 73
idea [aɪ'dɪə] Idee I U6, 117
Any idea? [ˌeni 'aɪdɪə] Irgendeine Idee? I U6, 116
if [ɪf] wenn <I U4, 82>
in [ɪn] im; in I ZI, 10
in August [ɪn 'ɔ:gəst] im August I U4, 70
in the world [ɪn ðə 'wɜ:ld] auf der Welt <I U5, 102>
information [ˌɪnfə'meɪʃn] Information; Informationen <I U2, 44>
It has all the information. [ɪt hæz ˌɔ:l ði‿ˌɪnfə'meɪʃn] Es enthält alle Informationen. <I U4, 85>
with the same **interests** [wɪð ðə 'seɪm ˌɪntrəsts] mit denselben Interessen <I U3, 64>
interesting ['ɪntrəstɪŋ] interessant I U2, 38
It was very interesting! [ɪt wɒz veri 'ɪntrəstɪŋ] Es war sehr interessant! <I U1, 27>
internet ['ɪntənet] Internet <I U4, 82>
to **interview** ['ɪntəvju:] befragen; interviewen I U3, 58
are **investigating** [ˌɑ: ɪn'vestɪgeɪtɪŋ] ermitteln <I U5, 104>
invitation [ˌɪnvɪ'teɪʃn] Einladung I U4, 80
to **invite** [ɪn'vaɪt] einladen I U4, 72
is [ɪz] ist I ZI, 11
… is 99p [ɪz ˌnaɪntinaɪn 'pens] … kostet 99 Pence I U4, 76
it [ɪt] es I ZI, 11
it's (= it is) [ɪts] es ist I ZI, 11
It's me! [ɪts 'mi:] Ich bin es! I U1, 18
It's time to go. [ɪts ˌtaɪm tə 'gəʊ] Es ist Zeit, zu gehen. I W, 8
IT (Information Technology) [ˌaɪ'ti:] Informatik; Informationstechnik I U2, 39
item ['aɪtəm] Artikel; Ding <I U2, 44>

J

January ['dʒænjuri] Januar I U4, 71
jeans *(pl)* [dʒi:nz] Jeans I U2, 45
job [dʒɒb] Job I U5, 100
jogging ['dʒɒgɪŋ] Joggen <I U3, 209>
to **join** [dʒɔɪn] beitreten <I U3, 64>
joke [dʒəʊk] Witz I U2, 38
judo ['dʒu:dəʊ] Judo <I U3, 209>
July [dʒʊ'laɪ] Juli I U4, 71
on 7th July [ɒn ðə ˌsevnθ əv 'dʒʊlaɪ] am 7. Juli I U4, 72
June [dʒu:n] Juni I U4, 71

K

7 **kilograms** a day [ˌkɪləgræmz ə 'deɪ] sieben Kilogramm täglich I U3, 54
40 **kilometres** an hour [kɪ'lɒmi:təz‿ən‿'aʊə] 40 Kilometer pro Stunde I U3, 54
kitchen ['kɪtʃɪn] Küche I U1, 25
*to **know** [nəʊ] kennen; wissen I U3, 62

I don't know! [ˌaɪ dəʊnt ˈnəʊ] Ich weiß (es) nicht! I U3, 62
I'd like to know more about … [aɪd laɪk tə ˌnəʊ ˈmɔː əˈbaʊt] Ich würde gerne mehr wissen über … <I U1, 27>

L

ladder [ˈlædə] Leiter I U1, 22
lamp [læmp] Lampe I U1, 19
language tip [ˌlæŋgwɪdʒ ˈtɪp] Grammatikhinweis <I U1, 15>
laptop [ˈlæptɒp] Laptop <I U5, 104>
last [lɑːst] letzte I U5, 92
later [ˈleɪtə] später I U1, 22
leaf *(sg)* [liːf], **leaves** *(pl)* [liːvz] Blatt <I U3, 210>
leaflet [ˈliːflət] Broschüre; Prospekt <I U2, 46>
to turn **left** (into …) [ˌtɜːn ˈleft] (nach) links abbiegen I U5, 108
on the left [ɒn ðə ˈleft] auf der linken Seite; links I U5, 108
lemonade [ˌleməˈneɪd] Limonade I U4, 78
lesson [ˈlesn] Schulstunde; Unterricht I U2, 38
let's (= let us) [lets] lass(t) uns I U2, 42
letter [ˈletə] Buchstabe <I U2, 39>
library [ˈlaɪbri] Bibliothek; Bücherei I U5, 93
life *(sg)* [laɪf], **lives** *(pl)* [laɪvz] Leben I U5, 101
school **life** [ˈskuː‿laɪf] Schulalltag <I U2, 41>
to **like** [laɪk] gern haben; mögen I W, 8
I don't like [aɪ ˌdəʊnt ˈlaɪk] gefällt mir nicht; ich mag nicht I U2, 32
I like [aɪ ˈlaɪk] gefällt mir; ich mag I W, 8
I wouldn't like (to) … [aɪ ˈwʊdnt laɪk (tə)] ich möchte nicht …; ich würde nicht gerne … I U6, 111
I'd like (to) … (= I would like to) [aɪd ˈlaɪk (tə)] ich möchte …; ich würde gerne … I U6, 111
What theme would you like? [ˌwɒt ˈθiːm wʊd jə laɪk] Welches Motto möchtest du? <I U4, 84>
Would you like (to)…? [ˌwʊd jə ˈlaɪk (tə)] Möchtest du? I U6, 111
like that [laɪk ˈðæt] so I U2, 38
line [laɪn] Linie <I U5, 102>; Zeile <I U6, 113>
lion [ˈlaɪən] Löwe I U3, 54
shopping **list** [ˈʃɒpɪŋ ˌlɪst] Einkaufszettel I U4, 79
to **listen** (to) [ˈlɪsn (tə)] anhören; hören; zuhören I U3, 52
listening [ˈlɪsnɪŋ] Hörverstehen <I ZI, 10>
listening skills [ˈlɪsnɪŋ ˌskɪlz] Fertigkeit Hören <I U1, 30>
to **live** [lɪv] leben; wohnen I U5, 90
living room [ˈlɪvɪŋ ˌrʊm] Wohnzimmer I U1, 25
a **loaf** of bread [ə ˌləʊf‿əv ˈbred] Brotlaib <I U4, 219>
logo [ˈləʊgəʊ] Firmenzeichen; Logo <I U2, 44>
long [lɒŋ] lang I U3, 54
Have a **look**. [ˌhæv‿ə ˈlʊk] Schau dich um. <I U6, 122>
to **look** [lʊk] (nach)schauen I U1, 25
to look after [lʊk‿ˈɑːftə] aufpassen; hüten <I U3, 209>
to look at [ˈlʊk‿ət] anschauen I U2, 34
to look for [ˈlʊk ˌfə] suchen I U3, 62
Well, look … [wel ˈlʊk] Na ja, schau mal … nach. I U1, 25
a **lot** [əˈlɒt] viel I U3, 52
a lot of [ə ˈlɒt‿əv] eine Menge; viel I U5, 100
lots more [ˌlɒts ˈmɔː] viel mehr <I U4, 82>
lots of [ˈlɒts‿əv] jede Menge; viel I U4, 88
Love from … [ˈlʌv frɒm] Liebe Grüße … *(am Briefende)* <I U4, 85>
to **love** [lʌv] gern mögen; lieben I U3, 52
lunch [lʌnʃ] Mittagessen I U2, 42
lunchtime [ˈlʌnʃtaɪm] Mittagspause; Mittagszeit I U3, 53

M

magazine [ˌmægəˈziːn] Zeitschrift I U3, 58
main hall [ˌmeɪn ˈhɔːl] Schulaula <I U3, 64>
*to **make** [meɪk] machen; tun I U4, 72
to make friends [ˌmeɪk ˈfrendz] Freundschaften schließen I U2, 45
man *(sg)* [mæn], **men** *(pl)* [men] Mann I U5, 101
Man overboard! [mæn ˈəʊvəbɔːd] Mann über Bord! I U5, 101
map [mæp] Landkarte; Stadtplan I U5, 109
map of the world [ˌmæp‿əv ðə ˈwɜːld] Weltkarte <I U5, 102>
March [mɑːtʃ] März I U4, 71
market [ˈmɑːkɪt] Markt I U5, 93
marmalade [ˈmɑːməleɪd] *Marmelade aus Zitrusfrüchten* <I U6, 122>
married [ˈmærid] verheiratet <I U1, 194>
first **mate** [ˌfɜːst ˈmeɪt] erster Offizier I U5, 100
Maths [mæθs] Mathe I U2, 33
May [meɪ] Mai I U4, 71
me [miː] ich I U1, 14; mich I U2, 34; mir I U4, 72
Excuse me. [ɪkˈskjuːz mi] Entschuldigung. I U5, 103
call me [ˈkɔːl ˌmi] nenne mich I U2, 34
It's me! [ɪts ˈmiː] Ich bin es! I U1, 18
meal [miːl] Essen; Mahlzeit I U4, 73
meat [miːt] Fleisch I U3, 54
mediation [ˌmiːˈdiˈeɪʃn] Sprachmittlung <I U1, 13>
mediation skills [ˌmiːdiˈeɪʃn ˌskɪlz] Fertigkeit Sprachmitteln <I U1, 24>
*to **meet** [miːt] kennen lernen I U6, 110
meridian line [məˈrɪdiən ˌlaɪn] Längenkreis; *Nullmeridian in Greenwich* <I U5, 102>

mess [mes] Durcheinander; Unordnung I U1, 18
text **message** ['tekst ˌmesɪdʒ] Textnachricht (SMS) I U6, 119
met [met] simple past von *to meet* I U6, 110
metre ['mi:tə] Meter I U3, 54
Miaow! [ˌmi:'aʊ] Miau! <I U5, 101>
mouse *(sg)* [maʊs], **mice** *(pl)* [maɪs] Maus I U3, 54
mild [maɪld] mild I U6, 117
milk [mɪlk] Milch I U4, 77
minute ['mɪnɪt] Minute <I U3, 211>
missing ['mɪsɪŋ] verschwunden <I U5, 104>
mobile (phone) ['məʊbaɪl (ˌfəʊn)] Handy I U1, 18
modern ['mɒdn] modern I U6, 111
Monday ['mʌndeɪ] Montag I U2, 39
money ['mʌni] Geld I U4, 70
monkey ['mʌŋki] Affe I U3, 54
month [mʌnθ] Monat I U3, 54
for five months [fə ˌfaɪv 'mʌnθs] fünf Monate lang I U3, 54
more [mɔ:] mehr <I U1, 13>
lots more [ˌlɒts 'mɔ:] viel mehr <I U4, 82>
morning ['mɔ:nɪŋ] Morgen; Vormittag I U5, 92
mosque [mɒsk] Moschee <I U5, 225>
mother ['mʌðə] Mutter I U1, 14
motorbike ['məʊtəbaɪk] Motorrad I U5, 97
mountain biking ['maʊntɪn ˌbaɪkɪŋ] Mountainbike fahren <I U6, 122>
mouse *(sg)* [maʊs], **mice** *(pl)* [maɪs] Maus I U3, 54
movie ['mu:vi] Film I U3, 53
Mr ['mɪstə] Herr *(Anrede)* I U2, 33
Mrs ['mɪsɪz] Frau *(Anrede)* I U2, 33
Ms [mɪz] Frau *(Anrede)* I U2, 38
much [mʌtʃ] viel I U3, 54
How much (is/are) ...? [ˌhaʊ 'mʌtʃ‿ɪz/ɑ:] Wie viel (kostet/kosten) ...? I U4, 76
mud [mʌd] Matsch; Schlamm I U6, 120
stuck in the mud [ˌstʌk‿ɪn ðə 'mʌd] im Schlamm festgesteckt I U6, 120
mum [mʌm] Mama; Mutti I U1, 14
museum [mju:'zi:əm] Museum I U5, 93
music ['mju:zɪk] Musik I W, 8
Muslim ['mʊzlɪm] Muslim; Muslimin I U4, 70
must [mʌst] müssen I U6, 112
my [maɪ] mein I U1, 12
My name is ... [maɪ 'neɪm‿ɪz] Ich heiße ... I W, 8
mystery ['mɪstri] Geheimnis; Rätsel I U3, 62

N

name [neɪm] Name I U1, 14
My name is ... [maɪ 'neɪm‿ɪz] Ich heiße ... I W, 8
narrator [nə'reɪtə] Erzähler; Erzählerin I U4, 80
naval college ['neɪvl ˌkɒlɪdʒ] Marineakademie <I U4, 82>
near [nɪə] in der Nähe von I U6, 111
needn't ['ni:dnt] nicht brauchen; nicht müssen I U6, 111
netball ['netbɔ:l] Korbball I U3, 52
never ['nevə] nie; niemals I U4, 72
new [nju:] neu I U1, 18
daily **news** [ˌdeɪli 'nju:z] Nachrichten des Tages <I U5, 104>
newspaper ['nju:sˌpeɪpə] Zeitung <I U5, 104>
next [nekst] nächste I U2, 34
next to ['nekst tə] neben I U1, 18
nice [naɪs] nett; schön I U1, 13
Nice to meet you. [ˌnaɪs tə 'mi:t ju:] Nett, dich kennen zu lernen. I W, 8
night [naɪt] Nacht I U1, 23
night walk ['naɪt wɔ:k] Nachtwanderung I U6, 112
nine [naɪn] neun I W, 9
nineteen [ˌnaɪn'ti:n] neunzehn I U3, 55
ninety ['naɪnti] neunzig I U3, 55
no [nəʊ] kein; keine I U1, 14; nein I U1, 18
no one ['nəʊ wʌn] niemand I U1, 23
noise [nɔɪz] Geräusch I U1, 23
in the **north** of [ɪn ðe 'nɔ:θ‿əv] im Norden von <I U1, 24>
nose [nəʊz] Nase I U4, 70
not [nɒt] nicht I U2, 38
nothing else ['nʌθɪŋ ˌels] nichts anderes <I U5, 104>
notice board ['nəʊtɪs bɔ:d] Pinnwand <I U1, 195>; <I U2, 50>
noun [naʊn] Hauptwort; Nomen <I U6, 113>
November [nə'vembə] November I U4, 71
now [naʊ] jetzt; nun I U2, 34
number ['nʌmbə] Nummer; Zahl I ZI, 10; Anzahl <I U3, 66>
nut [nʌt] Nuss I U3, 62

O

o'clock [ə'klɒk] Uhr *(Zeitangabe bei vollen Stunden)* I U3, 58
October [ɒk'təʊbə] Oktober I U4, 70
a photo **of** [ə 'fəʊtəʊ‿əv] ein Foto von I U1, 14
post **office** ['pəʊst‿ɒfɪs] Postamt I U5, 103
police **officer** [pə'li:s‿ɒfɪsə] Polizeibeamter; Polizeibeamtin I U3, 62
often ['ɒfn] häufig; oft I U4, 72
oh [əʊ] null *(bei Uhrzeiten und Telefonnummern)* I U3, 59
OK [əʊ'keɪ] okay I W, 8
old [əʊld] alt I U5, 90
How old are you? [haʊ‿'əʊld‿ə ˌju:] Wie alt bist du? I U1, 12
on [ɒn] auf I U1, 18; am; an I U2, 38
on Monday, 15th September [ɒn 'mʌndeɪ ˌfɪfti:nθ 'septembə] am Montag, den 15. September <I U3, 64>
on Saturdays [ɒn 'sætədeɪz] samstags I U3, 52
on 7th July [ɒn ðə ˌsevnθ əv 'dʒʊlaɪ] am 7. Juli I U4, 72
on Tuesday [ˌɒn 'tju:zdeɪ] am Dienstag I U2, 38

on the left [ɒn ðə 'left] auf der linken Seite; links I U5, 108

on the right [ɒn ðə 'raɪt] auf der rechten Seite; rechts I U5, 108

one [wʌn] eins I W, 9

a/one hundred [ə/wʌn 'hʌndrəd] einhundert; hundert I U3, 55

no one ['nəʊ wʌn] niemand I U1, 23

one of our [wʌn‿əv 'aʊə] einen von unseren <I U3, 64>

only child [ˌəʊnli 'tʃaɪld] Einzelkind <I U1, 194>

to **open** ['əʊpn] aufmachen; öffnen I U2, 34

open ['əʊpn] geöffnet <I U2, 44>

opposite ['ɒpəzɪt] gegenüber I U5, 108

or [ɔ:] oder I U1, 23

orange ['ɒrɪndʒ] orange I ZI, 10; Orange I U4, 77

orchestra ['ɔ:kɪstrə] Orchester <I U4, 82>

ordinal number [ˌɔ:dɪnəl 'nʌmbə] Ordinalzahl I U4, 73

other ['ʌðə] andere I U4, 70

our [aʊə] unser I U1, 14

out and about [ˌaʊt‿ən‿ə'baʊt] unterwegs I U5, 103

out of ['aʊt‿əv] aus … heraus I U6, 121

Man **overboard**! [mæn 'əʊvəbɔ:d] Mann über Bord! I U5, 101

own [əʊn] eigene <I U2, 37>

P

a **packet** of ['pækɪt] eine Packung …; eine Tüte … I U4, 76

Panda ['pændə] Pandabär <I U3, 210>

Pardon? ['pɑ:dn] Wie bitte? I U4, 79

parents *(pl)* ['peərnts] Eltern I U1, 15

park [pɑ:k] Park I ZI, 10

theme park ['θi:m ˌpɑ:k] Freizeitpark I U4, 73

partner ['pɑ:tnə] Partner; Partnerin <I W, 8>

party ['pɑ:ti] Feier; Party I U4, 72

past [pɑ:st] nach *(bei Uhrzeitangaben)* I U3, 59

half past (two) [ˌhɑ:f 'pɑ:st] halb (drei) I U3, 59

quarter past ['kwɔ:tə pɑ:st] Viertel nach I U3, 59

pasta ['pæstə] Nudeln; Pasta I U4, 78

PE (Physical Education) [ˌpi:'i:, ˌfɪzɪkl edʒʊ'keɪʃn] Sportunterricht I U2, 39

peach [pi:tʃ] Pfirsich I U4, 77

pen [pen] Füller; Stift I U2, 34

pence *(pl)* [pens:], **penny** *(sg)* ['peni] Pence *(brit. Währungseinheit)* I U4, 76

… is 99p [ɪz ˌnaɪntinaɪn 'pens] … kostet 99 Pence I U4, 76

pencil ['pensl] Bleistift I U2, 35

pencil case ['pensl ˌkeɪs] Federmäppchen I U2, 35

pencil sharpener ['pensl ˌʃɑ:pnə] Anspitzer I U2, 35

penguin ['peŋgwɪn] Pinguin I U3, 54

people ['pi:pl] Leute; Menschen I ZI, 10

pet [pet] Haustier I U1, 13

pet food ['pet ˌfu:d] Haustiernahrung <I U4, 219>

petrol station ['petrl ˌsteɪʃn] Tankstelle <I U5, 225>

Phew! [fju:] Puh! <I U1, 14>

phone call ['fəʊn ˌkɔ:l] Telefonanruf I U6, 112

to **phone** [fəʊn] anrufen; telefonieren I U6, 119

photo ['fəʊtəʊ] Foto I U1, 12

to take a photo [ˌteɪk‿ə 'fəʊtəʊ] ein Foto machen I U4, 81

Physics ['fɪzɪks] Physik <I U2, 203>

picnic ['pɪknɪk] Picknick I U6, 112

picture ['pɪktʃə] Bild I U6, 121

pig [pɪg] Schwein <I U6, 233>

pink [pɪŋk] pink; rosa I W, 9

pirate ['paɪrət] Pirat; Piratin I U4, 80

pizza ['pi:tsə] Pizza I U5, 92

place [pleɪs] Ort; Platz; Stelle I U2, 32

to take place [ˌteɪk 'pleɪs] statt-finden <I U4, 82>

to **plan** [plæn] planen <I U4, 84>

plane [pleɪn] Flugzeug I U5, 97

play [pleɪ] Theaterstück <I U4, 82>

to **play** [pleɪ] spielen I ZI, 11

to play games [pleɪ 'geɪmz] Spiele spielen <I U2, 202>

playground ['pleɪgraʊnd] Pausenhof; Schulhof; Spielplatz I U2, 32

please [pli:z] bitte I U2, 34

p.m. [ˌpi:'em] nachmittags *(Uhrzeit)* <I U2, 44>; <I U4, 84>

poem ['pəʊɪm] Gedicht <I U6, 113>

police officer [pə'li:s‿ɒfɪsə] Polizeibeamter; Polizeibeamtin I U3, 62

polo shirt [ˌpəʊləʊ 'ʃɜ:t] Polohemd <I U2, 44>

swimming **pool** ['swɪmɪŋ ˌpu:l] Schwimmbad I U5, 91

popcorn ['pɒpkɔ:n] Popcorn I U5, 103

post office ['pəʊst‿ɒfɪs] Postamt I U5, 103

postcard ['pəʊstkɑ:d] Postkarte I U5, 96

poster ['pəʊstə] Poster I U1, 18

potato *(sg)* [pə'teɪtəʊ], **potatoes** *(pl)* [pə'teɪtəʊz] Kartoffel I U5, 100

pound [paʊnd] Pfund *(brit. Währungseinheit)* I U4, 76

practice ['præktɪs] Training; Übung I U3, 53

present ['preznt] Geschenk I U4, 70

to **present** [prɪ'zent] präsentieren <I U1, 26>

presentation [ˌprezn'teɪʃn] Präsentation; Vortrag <I U1, 26>

How was my presentation? [ˌhaʊ wɒz maɪ ˌprezn'teɪʃn] Wie war meine Präsentation? <I U1, 27>

pretty ['prɪti] hübsch I U6, 113

problem ['prɒbləm] Problem I U6, 120

profile ['prəʊfaɪl] Profil; Steckbrief <I U3, 57>

pudding ['pʊdɪŋ] Nachspeise <I U6, 122>

to **pull** [pʊl] ziehen I U6, 121

pullover ['pʊləʊvə] Pullover <I U2, 44>

purple ['pɜ:pl] lila; violett I ZI, 10

to **push** [pʊʃ] schieben I U6, 121

Put your hands up. [pʊt jɔ: ˌhændz‿'ʌp] Meldet euch. I U2, 34

Alicia put it in there. [ə'lɪʃə pʊt‿ɪt ɪn ˌðeə] Alicia hat es dort hinein getan. I U2, 45

Q

quarter past ['kwɔ:tə pɑ:st] Viertel nach I U3, 59
quarter to ['kwɔ:tə tə] Viertel vor I U3, 59
question ['kwestʃən] Frage I U2, 36
quiz [kwɪz] Rätsel <I U5, 104>

R

raccoon [rə'ku:n] Waschbär I U3, 62
race [reɪs] Wettrennen I U3, 65
to **rain** [reɪn] regnen I U6, 116
rap [ræp] Rap <I U2, 39>
*to **read** [ri:d] lesen I U2, 36
reading ['ri:dɪŋ] Lesen <I U1, 14>
reading corner ['ri:dɪŋ ˌkɔ:nə] Leseecke <I U1, 13>
reading skills ['ri:dɪŋ ˌskɪlz] Fertigkeit Lesen <I U1, 22>
ready ['redi] bereit; fertig I U1, 18
really ['rɪəli] sehr <I U2, 50>
Really? ['rɪəli] Wirklich? I U2, 34
recording studio [rɪ'kɔ:dɪŋ ˌstju:dəʊ] Tonstudio <I U2, 202>
red [red] rot I W, 9
registration [ˌredʒɪ'streɪʃn] Überprüfung der Anwesenheit I U2, 38
RE (= Religious Education) [ˌɑ:‿'ri:, rɪˌlɪdʒəs‿edʒʊ'keɪʃn] Religionsunterricht I U2, 39
report [rɪ'pɔ:t] Bericht <I U5, 104>
this report makes sense [ðɪs rɪˌpɔ:t meɪks 'sens] dieser Bericht ergibt Sinn <I U6, 125>
animal **rescue** shelter [ˌænɪml 'reskju: ˌʃeltə] Tierheim I U3, 53
fast food **restaurant** [ˌfɑ:st fu:d 'restrɒnt] Fastfood-Restaurant I U4, 73
*to **ride** my bike [ˌraɪd maɪ 'baɪk] Fahrrad fahren <I U3, 209>

horse **riding** ['hɔ:s ˌraɪdɪŋ] Reiten I U6, 112
right [raɪt] korrekt; richtig I U1, 19
to turn right (into …) [ˌtɜ:n 'raɪt] (nach) rechts abbiegen I U5, 108
on the right [ɒn ðə 'raɪt] auf der rechten Seite; rechts I U5, 108
You're right. [jɔ:‿'raɪt] Du hast Recht. I U2, 38
*to **ring** [rɪŋ] klingeln; läuten I U4, 81
river ['rɪvə] Fluss I U6, 120
road [rəʊd] Straße I U5, 90
rock [rɒk] Rock *(Musik)* <I U4, 82>
rock climbing ['rɒk ˌklaɪmɪŋ] Klettern I U6, 111
room [ru:m] Raum; Zimmer I U1, 18
dining room ['daɪnɪŋ ˌrʊm] Esszimmer I U1, 31
rope [rəʊp] Seil I U5, 101
ruin ['ru:ɪn] Ruine <I U6, 122>
ruler ['ru:lə] Lineal I U2, 35
*to **run** [rʌn] laufen; rennen I U3, 54

S

said [sed] simple past von *to say* I U6, 120
salad ['sæləd] Salat <I U4, 82>
for **sale** [fə 'seɪl] zu verkaufen <I U6, 122>
with the **same** interests [wɪð ðə 'seɪm ˌɪntrəsts] mit denselben Interessen <I U3, 64>
sandwich ['sænwɪdʒ] belegtes Brot; Sandwich I U4, 77
on **Saturdays** [ɒn 'sætədeɪz] samstags I U3, 52
Saturday ['sætədeɪ] Samstag I U1, 18
sausage ['sɒsɪdʒ] (Brat-)Wurst <I U2, 50>; <I U4, 82>
saw [sɔ:] simple past von *to see* I U5, 92
saxophone ['sæksəfəʊn] Saxophon I U2, 42
*to **say** [seɪ] sagen; sprechen I U2, 37
Can you say that again, please? [kæn ju: ˌseɪ ðæt ə'gen pli:s] Könntest du das bitte wiederholen? I U4, 79
Say hi to … [seɪ 'haɪ tə] Grüße … von mir. I U6, 119
scared [skeəd] verängstigt I U5, 101
scarf *(sg)* [skɑ:f], **scarves** *(pl)* [skɑ:vz] Schal; Tuch I U1, 19
scary ['skeəri] gruselig I U4, 70; beängstigend I U6, 110
school [sku:l] Schule I U2, 32
at school [ət 'sku:l] in der Schule I U2, 32
school fair [ˌsku:l 'feə] Schulfest <I U3, 64>
school life ['sku:‿ˌlaɪf] Schulalltag <I U2, 41>
Science [saɪəns] Naturwissenschaft; Wissenschaft I U2, 39
science fiction [ˌsaɪəns 'fɪkʃn] Science-Fiction I U3, 53
science lab ['saɪəns ˌlæb] Labor <I U2, 202>
screen [skri:n] Leinwand <I U4, 82>
sea [si:] Meer I U5, 96
seal [si:l] Robbe; Seehund <I U3, 210>
search [sɜ:tʃ] Suche <I U2, 50>
at the **seaside** [ət ðə 'si:saɪd] am Meer I U5, 96
second ['seknd] Sekunde <I U3, 211>; zweite I U4, 73
*to **see** [si:] sehen I U2, 42
to see friends [si: 'frendz] sich mit Freunden treffen <I U3, 66>
See you! ['si: ju:] Bis bald!; Tschüss! I W, 8
See you soon! [ˌsi: ju: 'su:n] Bis bald! I U6, 112
*to **send** [send] schicken; senden I U5, 96
sent [sent] simple past von *to send* I U5, 96
sentence ['sentəns] Satz <I U1, 13>
September [sep'tembə] September I U4, 71
seven ['sevn] sieben I W, 9
seventeen [ˌsevn'ti:n] siebzehn I U3, 55
seventy ['sevnti] siebzig I U3, 55

shark [ʃɑ:k] Hai I U5, 101
pencil **sharpener** ['pensl ˌʃɑ:pnə] Anspitzer I U2, 35
she [ʃi:] sie I U1, 14
she's (= she is) [ʃi:z] sie ist I U1, 14
sheep *(sg)* [ʃi:p], **sheep** *(pl)* [ʃi:p] Schaf I U5, 101
shelf *(sg)* [ʃelf], **shelves** *(pl)* [ʃelvz] Regal; Regalbrett I U1, 19
animal rescue **shelter** [ˌænɪml 'reskju: ˌʃeltə] Tierheim I U3, 53
ship [ʃɪp] Schiff I U5, 90
polo **shirt** [ˌpəʊləʊ 'ʃɜ:t] Polohemd <I U2, 44>
shoe [ʃu:] Schuh <I U2, 44>
shop [ʃɒp] Geschäft; Laden I U4, 76
corner shop ['kɔ:nə ˌʃɒp] Tante-Emma-Laden I U4, 76
sports shop ['spɔ:ts ˌʃɒp] Sportgeschäft I U5, 92
shopping ['ʃɒpɪŋ] Einkaufen I U4, 76
shopping centre ['ʃɒpɪŋ ˌsentə] Einkaufszentrum I U5, 90
shopping list ['ʃɒpɪŋ ˌlɪst] Einkaufszettel I U4, 79
shorts *(pl)* [ʃɔ:ts] kurze Hose; Shorts I U6, 113
shout [ʃaʊt] Schrei I U5, 101
talent **show** ['tælənt ˌʃəʊ] Talentwettbewerb I U2, 34
*to be **sick** [bi 'sɪk] sich übergeben I U5, 100
side [saɪd] Seite <I U5, 102>
sight [saɪt] Sehenswürdigkeit <I U5, 102>
sign [saɪn] Schild <I U6, 122>
it's the **simple** past [ɪts ðə ˌsɪmpl 'pɑ:st] es ist die einfache Vergangenheit <I U6, 125>
*to **sing** [sɪŋ] singen I U2, 34
singer ['sɪŋə] Sänger; Sängerin I U2, 34
sister ['sɪstə] Schwester I U1, 14
half-sister ['hɑ:fˌsɪstə] Halbschwester <I U1, 194>
*to **sit** (down) [ˌsɪt 'daʊn] sich (hin) setzen I U2, 34
six [sɪks] sechs I W, 9
sixteen [ˌsɪk'sti:n] sechzehn I U3, 55
sixty ['sɪksti] sechzig I U3, 55
skateboard ['skeɪtbɔ:d] Skateboard I U5, 97
skateboarding ['skeɪtbɔ:dɪŋ] Skateboardfahren <I U3, 209>
skating ['skeɪtɪŋ] Inlineskaten; Schlittschuhlaufen <I U3, 209>
skirt [skɜ:t] Rock I U6, 113
*to **sleep** [sli:p] schlafen I U3, 54
sleepover ['sli:pˌəʊvə] Übernachtung I U4, 83
smurf [smɜ:f] Schlumpf I U4, 80
snack [snæk] Imbiss; Snack I U4, 83
snake [sneɪk] Schlange I U3, 54
so [səʊ] also; deshalb I U6, 116
Social Studies ['səʊʃl ˌstʌdiz] Gesellschaftslehre; Sozialkunde <I U2, 203>
sock [sɒk] Socke I U6, 113
to **solve** [sɒlv] lösen I U3, 62
some [sʌm] etwas; einige I U5, 101
somebody ['sʌmbədi] jemand <I U5, 104>
something ['sʌmθɪŋ] etwas I ZI, 11
son [sʌn] Sohn <I U1, 194>
song [sɒŋ] Lied <I W, 9>
See you **soon**! [ˌsi: ju: 'su:n] Bis bald! I U6, 112
Sorry. ['sɒri] Entschuldigung.; Tut mir leid. I U4, 78
sounds [saʊndz] Laute <I U1, 15>
speaking ['spi:kɪŋ] Sprechen <I W, 8>
speaking skills ['spi:kɪŋ ˌskɪlz] Fertigkeit Sprechen <I U1, 26>
special ['speʃl] besonders; speziell I U4, 70
*to **spell** [spel] buchstabieren I U2, 38
spelling ['spelɪŋ] Rechtschreibung I U2, 38
sport [spɔ:t] Sport I W, 8
sports hall ['spɔ:ts ˌhɔ:l] Sporthalle <I U2, 202>
sports shop ['spɔ:ts ˌʃɒp] Sportgeschäft I U5, 92
I **spy** with my little eye … [aɪ spaɪ wɪð ˌmaɪ lɪtl 'aɪ] Ich sehe was, was du nicht siehst … I ZI, 11
stadium ['steɪdiəm] Stadion <I U5, 225>
stage [steɪdʒ] Bühne <I U4, 82>
street **stall** ['stri:t stɔ:l] Verkaufsstand auf der Straße <I U4, 82>
star [stɑ:] Star I U2, 43
to **start** [stɑ:t] beginnen <I U2, 44>
station ['steɪʃn] Haltestelle; Station <I U1, 13>; Bahnhof I U5, 93
*to **steal**, **stole** [sti:l; stəʊl] stehlen <I U5, 104>
step [step] Schritt <I U1, 26>
stepbrother ['stepˌbrʌðə] Stiefbruder <I U1, 194>
stepfather ['stepˌfɑ:ðə] Stiefvater <I U1, 194>
stepmother ['stepˌmʌðə] Stiefmutter <I U1, 194>
to **stop** [stɒp] aufhören I U6, 112
department **store** [dɪ'pɑ:tmənt ˌstɔ:] Kaufhaus I U5, 93
storm [stɔ:m] Sturm I U5, 101
story ['stɔ:ri] Geschichte I U3, 62
straight on [streɪt‿'ɒn] geradeaus I U5, 108
hair **straightener** ['heə ˌstreɪtnə] Haarglätter I U1, 25
strawberry ['strɔ:bri] Erdbeere I U4, 73
street [stri:t] Straße <I U5, 225>
street stall ['stri:t stɔ:l] Verkaufsstand auf der Straße <I U4, 82>
strict diet [strɪkt 'daɪət] strenge Diät <I U6, 122>
*to be **stuck** [bi 'stʌk] feststecken; nicht weg können I U6, 120
stuck in the mud [ˌstʌk‿ɪn ðə 'mʌd] im Schlamm festgesteckt I U6, 120
student ['stju:dnt] Schüler; Schülerin I U2, 33
study skills [ˌstʌdi 'skɪlz] Fertigkeit Lern- und Arbeitstechniken <I U1, 16>
subject ['sʌbdʒɪkt] Schulfach I U2, 38
submarine [ˌsʌbmr'i:n] U-Boot I U5, 97
sugar ['ʃʊgə] Zucker <I U4, 219>
summer ['sʌmə] Sommer <I U6, 122>
summer festival [ˌsʌmə 'festɪvl] Sommerfest <I U4, 82>

Sunday ['sʌndeɪ] Sonntag I U2, 39
sunny ['sʌni] sonnig I U6, 117
superman ['su:pəmæn] Superman I U4, 80
supermarket ['su:pəˌmɑ:kɪt] Supermarkt I U5, 93
surprise [sə'praɪz] Überraschung I U4, 72
survey ['sɜ:veɪ] Umfrage <I U3, 66>
sweatshirt ['swetʃɜ:t] Sweatshirt I U6, 113
sweet [swi:t] Bonbon; Süßigkeit I U4, 70
*to go **swimming** [ˌgəʊ 'swɪmɪŋ] schwimmen gehen I U5, 91
swimming pool ['swɪmɪŋ ˌpu:l] Schwimmbad I U5, 91
to **switch off** [ˌswɪtʃ'ɒf] ausschalten <I U2, 44>

T

table ['teɪbl] Tisch I U1, 18
*to **take** a photo [ˌteɪk‿ə 'fəʊtəʊ] ein Foto machen I U4, 81
to take out [ˌteɪk'aʊt] herausnehmen I U2, 34
to take place [ˌteɪk 'pleɪs] stattfinden <I U4, 82>
to take the dog for a walk [ˌteɪk ðə dɒg fɔ:r‿ə 'wɔ:k] den Hund ausführen I U3, 62
talent show ['tælənt ˌʃəʊ] Talentwettbewerb I U2, 34
What's your talent? [wɒts jɔ: 'tæ‿lənt] Was ist dein Talent? I U2, 42
to **talk** (to) [tɔ:k] reden (mit); sprechen (mit) I U2, 32
don't talk [ˌdəʊnt 'tɔ:k] rede nicht; sei still I U2, 34
task [tɑ:sk] Aufgabe; Auftrag <I U1, 26>
tea [ti:] (frühes) Abendessen; Tee I U3, 59
teacher ['ti:tʃə] Lehrer; Lehrerin I U2, 33
team [ti:m] Gruppe; Team I U3, 52

Design **Technology** (DT) [dɪˌzaɪn tek'nɒlədʒi] Technik I U2, 38
*to **tell** [tel] erzählen; sagen I U5, 92
Can you tell me the way to …? [kæn ju: ˌtel mi ðə 'weɪ tə] Kannst du mir sagen, wie ich … komme? I U5, 108
ten [ten] zehn I W, 9
tennis ['tenɪs] Tennis I ZI, 10
the **tense** is right [ðə ˌtens ɪz 'raɪt] die Zeitform ist richtig <I U6, 125>
tent [tent] Zelt <I U4, 82>
terrible ['terəbl] furchtbar; schrecklich <I U6, 232>
text [tekst] Text <I U2, 33>
text message ['tekst ˌmesɪdʒ] Textnachricht (SMS) I U6, 119
Textiles ['tekstaɪlz] Textilunterricht <I U2, 203>
Thank you. ['θæŋk ju] Danke. I U2, 35
Thanks. [θæŋks] Danke. I U1, 25
that [ðæt] das I U1, 13
after that [ˌɑ:ftə 'ðæt] danach I U3, 58
that's (= that is) [ðæts] das ist I U1, 13
that's £2.24 [ðæts ˌtu: paʊndz twenti'fɔ:] das macht 2 Pfund und 24 Pence I U4, 76
the [ðə] das; der; die I W, 8
theatre ['θɪətə] Theater <I U4, 82>
their [ðeə] ihr I U4, 80
theme park ['θi:m ˌpɑ:k] Freizeitpark I U4, 73
What theme would you like? [ˌwɒt 'θi:m wʊd jə laɪk] Welches Motto möchtest du? <I U4, 84>
then [ðen] danach; dann I U1, 23
there [ðeə] da; dort I U1, 18
there are [ðeər‿'ɑ:] da sind; es gibt I U1, 18
there is (= there's) [ðeə‿'ɪz] da ist; es gibt I U1, 18
these [ði:z] diese (hier) <I U2, 44>
they [ðeɪ] sie *(Pl.)* I U1, 13
they're (= they are) [ðeə] sie sind I U1, 13

thief *(sg)* [θi:f], **thieves** *(pl)* [θi:vz] Dieb; Diebin <I U5, 105>
thing [θɪŋ] Ding; Sache <I U1, 19>
*to **think** [θɪŋk] denken I U4, 80
third [θɜ:d] dritte I U4, 73
thirteen [θɜ:'ti:n] dreizehn I U3, 55
thirty ['θɜ:ti] dreißig I U3, 55
this [ðɪs] das; dies I U1, 12
three [θri:] drei I W, 9
Thursday ['θɜ:zdeɪ] Donnerstag I U2, 39
tiger ['taɪgə] Tiger I U3, 54
time [taɪm] Uhrzeit; Zeit I U3, 52
free time [ˌfri: 'taɪm] Freizeit I U3, 52
It's time to go. [ɪts ˌtaɪm tə 'gəʊ] Es ist Zeit, zu gehen. I W, 8
the first time [ðə ˌfɜ:st 'taɪm] das erste Mal I U3, 62
What time is it? [ˌwɒt 'taɪm‿ɪz‿ɪt] Wie spät ist es?; Wie viel Uhr ist es? I U3, 58
timetable ['taɪmˌteɪbl] Stundenplan I U2, 38
tip [tɪp] Ratschlag; Tipp <I U1, 13>
language tip [ˌlæŋgwɪdʒ 'tɪp] Grammatikhinweis <I U1, 15>
tired [taɪəd] müde I U5, 92
to [tu:] in; nach; zu I U2, 32; vor *(bei Uhrzeitangaben)* I U3, 59
from … to [frəm 'tə] von … bis <I U2, 44>
quarter to ['kwɔ:tə tə] Viertel vor I U3, 59
today [tə'deɪ] heute I U5, 100
together [tə'geðə] gemeinsam; zusammen I U4, 70
toilet ['tɔɪlət] Toilette <I U2, 202>
to go to the toilet [ˌgəʊ tə ðə 'tɔɪ‿lət] zur Toilette gehen <I U2, 202>
told [təʊld] simple past von *to tell* I U5, 92
tomato [tə'mɑ:təʊ] Tomate <I U4, 219>
too [tu:] auch I U1, 14
top [tɒp] Top I U6, 113
torch [tɔ:tʃ] Taschenlampe I U6, 116
tourist ['tʊərɪst] Tourist; Touristin I U5, 108

Tourist Information Centre [ˌtʊərɪst‿ɪnfəˈmeɪʃn ˌsentə] Touristeninformation I U5, 108
town [taʊn] Stadt I U5, 90
tractor [ˈtræktə] Traktor I U6, 111
train [treɪn] Zug I U5, 96
to go by (train) [ˌgəʊ baɪ (ˈtreɪn)] mit (dem Zug) fahren I U5, 96
trainer [ˈtreɪnə] Turnschuh I U6, 113
tram [træm] Straßenbahn I U5, 97
Trick or **treat**! [ˌtrɪk‿ə ˈtri:t] Süßes, sonst gibt's Saures! I U4, 71
tree [tri:] Baum I U1, 22
tree house [ˈtri: ˌhaʊs] Baumhaus I U1, 22
trick [trɪk] Streich; Trick I U2, 42
Trick or treat! [ˌtrɪk‿ə ˈtri:t] Süßes, sonst gibt's Saures! I U4, 71
trip [trɪp] Ausflug I U5, 96
trousers *(pl)* [ˈtraʊzəz] Hose I U6, 113
to **try** [traɪ] probieren <I U4, 82>
to try something different [ˈtraɪ ˌsʌmθɪŋ ˈdɪfrnt] etw. anderes ausprobieren <I U3, 64>
T-shirt [ˈti:ʃɜ:t] T-Shirt I U1, 18
Tuesday [ˈtju:zdeɪ] Dienstag I U2, 39
on Tuesday [ˌɒn ˈtju:zdeɪ] am Dienstag I U2, 38
Your **turn**. [jɔ: ˈtɜ:n] Du bist dran. <I U1, 13>
to **turn** left (into ...) [ˌtɜ:n ˈleft] (nach) links abbiegen I U5, 108
to turn right (into ...) [ˌtɜ:n ˈraɪt] (nach) rechts abbiegen I U5, 108
tutor [ˈtju:tə] Klassenlehrer; Klassenlehrerin I U2, 33
tutor group [ˈtju:tə ˌgru:p] Klasse I U2, 33
TV [ti:ˈvi:] Fernseher I U3, 52
to watch TV [ˌwɒtʃ ti:ˈvi:] fernsehen I U3, 52
twelve [twelv] zwölf I U1, 13
twenty [ˈtwenti] zwanzig I U3, 55
twenty-one [ˌtwentiˈwʌn] einundzwanzig I U3, 55
two [tu:] zwei I W, 9

U

uncle [ˈʌŋkl] Onkel I U1, 15
under [ˈʌndə] unter I U1, 18
underground [ˈʌndəgraʊnd] U-Bahn I U5, 97
I can **understand** it. [aɪ ˌkæn ˌʌndəˈstænd ɪt] Ich kann sie verstehen. <I U4, 85>
I don't understand [aɪ dəʊnt ˌʌndəˈstænd] ich verstehe nicht <I U2, 46>
uniform [ˈju:nɪfɔ:m] Uniform I U2, 32
unit [ˈju:nɪt] Kapitel; Lektion <I U1, 12>
until [ʌnˈtɪl] bis I U5, 108
anything **unusual** [ˈeniθɪŋ ˌʌnju:ʒl] etwas Ungewöhnliches <I U5, 104>
us [ʌs] uns I U6, 110
to **use** [ju:z] benutzen <I U2, 44>

V

vegetarian [ˌvedʒɪˈteəriən] Vegetarier; Vegetarierin I U5, 96
very [ˈveri] sehr I U2, 38
viewing [ˈvju:ɪŋ] Hör-/Sehverstehen <I U1, 25>
viewing skills [ˈvju:ɪŋ ˌskɪlz] Fertigkeit Hör-/Sehverstehen <I U1, 25>
day **visitors** [ˈdeɪ ˌvɪzɪtəz] Tagesbesucher <I U6, 122>
volleyball [ˈvɒlibɔ:l] Volleyball <I U3, 209>

W

*to go for a **walk** [ˌgəʊ fər‿ə ˈwɔ:k] spazieren gehen I U6, 117
night walk [ˈnaɪt wɔ:k] Nachtwanderung I U6, 112
to take the dog for a walk [ˌteɪk ðə dɒg fɔ:r‿ə ˈwɔ:k] den Hund ausführen I U3, 62
to **walk** [wɔ:k] gehen; laufen I U5, 96
to **want** (to) [ˈwɒnt] wollen I U4, 81
wardrobe [ˈwɔ:drəʊb] Kleiderschrank I U1, 19
warm [wɔ:m] warm I U6, 112
was [wɒz] simple past von *to be* I U5, 92
to **watch** [wɒtʃ] ansehen <I U2, 50>
to watch TV [ˌwɒtʃ ti:ˈvi:] fernsehen I U3, 52
water [ˈwɔ:tə] Wasser I U4, 78
wave [weɪv] Welle I U5, 101
asking the **way** [ˌɑ:skɪŋ ðə ˈweɪ] nach dem Weg fragen I U5, 108
way in [ˌweɪ ˈɪn] Einstieg <I U1, 13>
Can you tell me the way to ...? [kæn ju: ˌtel mi ðə ˈweɪ tə] Kannst du mir sagen, wie ich ... komme? I U5, 108
we [wi:; wi] wir I U1, 14
we're (= we are) [wɪə] wir sind I U1, 14
*to **wear** [weə] tragen I U4, 70
weather [ˈweðə] Wetter I U6, 117
What's the weather like? [ˌwɒts ðə ˈweðə laɪk] Wie ist das Wetter? I U6, 117
website [ˈwebsaɪt] Website <I U6, 125>
Wednesday [ˈwenzdeɪ] Mittwoch I U2, 34
week [wi:k] Woche I U2, 34
weekend [ˈwi:kend] Wochenende I U3, 53
at the weekend [ət ðə ˌwi:kˈend] am Wochenende I U3, 53
You're **welcome**. [jɔ: ˈwelkəm] Gern geschehen. I U4, 76
welcome (to) [ˈwelkəm tʊ] willkommen (bei/in) I W, 8
Well done! [ˌwel ˈdʌn] Gut gemacht! I U2, 43
well [wel] na ja I U1, 25
Well, look ... [wel ˈlʊk] Na ja, schau mal ... nach. I U1, 25
went [went] simple past von *to go* I U5, 92
were [wɜ:] simple past von *to be* I U5, 96
in the **west** [ɪn ðə ˈwest] im Westen <I U5, 102>
wet [wet] nass I U6, 116
what [wɒt] was I U1, 18; welche <I U2, 34>

What about you? [ˌwɒt‿əbaʊt ˈjuː] Und du? <I U1, 24>
What time is it? [ˌwɒt ˈtaɪm‿ɪz‿ɪt] Wie spät ist es?; Wie viel Uhr ist es? I U3, 58
what's (= what is) [wɒts] was ist I U1, 18
What's the weather like? [ˌwɒts ðə ˈweðə laɪk] Wie ist das Wetter? I U6, 117
What's your name? [ˌwɒts jə ˈneɪm] Wie heißt du? I W, 8
wheelchair [ˈwiːltʃeə] Rollstuhl I U6, 120
when [wen] wann I U3, 58
where [weə] wo; woher; wohin I U1, 18
Where are you from? [ˌweər‿ə ju ˈfrɒm] Woher kommst du? I U1, 13
white [waɪt] weiß I W, 9
who [huː] wer I U1, 18
why [waɪ] warum <I U2, 50>
***to win** [wɪn] gewinnen; siegen I U3, 52
wind [wɪnd] Wind I U1, 23
window [ˈwɪndəʊ] Fenster I U2, 34
windy [ˈwɪndi] windig I U6, 117
winner [ˈwɪnə] Gewinner; Gewinnerin I U2, 42
winter [ˈwɪntə] Winter I U3, 54
Best wishes [ˌbest ˈwɪʃɪz] Mit den besten Wünschen I U6, 116
witch [wɪtʃ] Hexe I U4, 80
with [wɪð] mit I U1, 14
with the same interests [wɪð ðə ˈseɪm ˌɪntrəsts] mit denselben Interessen <I U3, 64>
wood [wʊd] Holz I U1, 22
wool [wʊl] Wolle I U5, 101
word [wɜːd] Wort <I U1, 15>
wore [wɔː] simple past von *to wear* I U6, 112
work [wɜːk] Arbeit I U3, 58
to work [wɜːk] arbeiten I U3, 58
in the world [ɪn ðə ˈwɜːld] auf der Welt <I U5, 102>
to worry [ˈwʌri] sich Sorgen machen I U6, 111
Would you like (to)…? [ˌwʊd jə ˈlaɪk (tə)] Möchtest du? I U6, 111
I wouldn't like (to) … [aɪ ˈwʊdnt laɪk (tə)] ich möchte nicht …; ich würde nicht gerne … I U6, 111
Wow! [waʊ] Toll!; Wow! <I U2, 42>
***to write** [raɪt] schreiben I U2, 36
writing [ˈraɪtɪŋ] Schreiben <I U1, 15>
wrong [rɒŋ] falsch I U1, 19

Y

year [jɪə] Jahr; Jahrgangsstufe; Klasse I U2, 32
yellow [ˈjeləʊ] gelb I ZI, 10
yes [jes] ja I W, 8
yesterday [ˈjestədeɪ] gestern I U5, 92
you [juː] dich; dir; du; euch; Ihnen; ihr; Sie I W, 8
Would you like (to)…? [ˌwʊd jə ˈlaɪk (tə)] Möchtest du? I U6, 111
you're (= you are) [jɔː] du bist I U1, 17
You're right. [jɔː‿ˈraɪt] Du hast Recht. I U2, 38
You're welcome. [jɔː ˈwelkəm] Gern geschehen. I U4, 76
your [jɔː] dein; euer I U1, 18
Your turn. [ˌjɔː ˈtɜːn] Du bist dran. <I U1, 13>
Yuck! [jʌk] Igitt! <I U5, 100>
Yum! [jʌm] Lecker! <I U5, 100>

Z

zebra [ˈzebrə] Zebra I U3, 54
zero [ˈzɪərəʊ] null I W, 9
zoo [zuː] Tierpark; Zoo I U3, 54
at the zoo [ət ðə ˈzuː] im Zoo I U3, 54
zookeeper [ˈzuːˌkiːpə] Tierpfleger; Tierpflegerin I U3, 58
to zoom in [ˈzuːm‿ɪn] heranzoomen <I ZI, 10>

Boys' names

Barry [ˈbæri] I U6, 110
Ben [ben] I W, 8
Bert [bɜːt] I U5, 100
Dave [deɪv] I U1, 13
Desmond [ˈdezmənd] I U1, 14
Edgar [ˈedgə] I U3, 54
Frank [fræŋk] I U6, 110
Fred [fred] I U3, 58
Jahangir [ˈdʒəhæŋgɪr] I U2, 34
Jamie [ˈdʒeɪmi] I U1, 28
Jay [dʒeɪ] I U2, 34
Jayden [ˈdʒeɪdn] <I U1, 24>
Jim [dʒɪm] I U5, 100
Jinsoo [ˈdʒɪnsuː] I U2, 45
Luke [luːk] I U1, 12
Marley [ˈmɑːli] I U2, 45
Nathan [ˈneɪθn] I U1, 25
Rodney [ˈrɒdni] I U5, 100
Sam [sæm] I U3, 55
Shahid [ˈʃɑːhɪd] I U4, 81
Sid [sɪd] I U1, 13
Simon [ˈsaɪmən] I U2, 37
Tim [tɪm] I U3, 57
Tom [tɒm] I U3, 54

Girls' names

Alicia [əˈlɪʃə] I U2, 45
Claire [kleə] I U1, 14
Hannah [ˈhænə] I U4, 75
Holly [ˈhɒli] I U1, 13
Irina [ɪˈriːnə] I U1, 20
Janet [ˈdʒænɪt] I U1, 14
Jessica [ˈdʒesɪkə] <I U1, 24>
Laura [ˈlɔːrə] I U1, 25
Lizzy [ˈlɪzi] I U3, 54
Lucy [ˈluːsi] I U1, 14
Mary [ˈmeəri] I U3, 57
Olivia [ɒlˈɪviə] I U1, 12
Parule [ˈpəruːl] I U1, 25
Rachel [ˈreɪtʃl] I U6, 110
Rosie [rəʊzi] I U6, 113
Sally [ˈsæli] I U3, 55

Surnames

Abrihim [æ'brəhi:m] I U3, 62
Azad ['æzæd] I U2, 34
Elliot ['eliət] I U1, 12
Fraser ['freɪzə] I U1, 12
Kapoor ['kæpɔ:] I U2, 38
Miller ['mɪlə] I U5, 105
Preston ['prestən] I U1, 13
Richardson ['rɪtʃədsn] I U1, 13
Safi ['sæfi] I U4, 76
Swindon ['swɪndən] I U2, 33
Turner ['tɜ:nə] I U6, 110
Warren ['wɒrn] I U2, 33
Welch [weltʃ] I U5, 105

Place names

Africa ['æfrɪkə] Afrika I U3, 57
Antarctica [æn'tɑ:ktɪkə] Antarktis <I U3, 210>
Asia ['eɪʒə] Asien <I U3, 210>
Australia [ɒs'treɪliə] Australien I U5, 100
Devon ['devn] *Grafschaft in Südwestengland* I U6, 116
England ['ɪŋglənd] England I U1, 13
Europe ['jʊərəp] Europa <I U3, 210>
Germany ['dʒɜ:məni] Deutschland I U1, 13
Greenwich ['grenɪdʒ] *Stadtteil im Südosten Londons* I U1, 12
Greenwich Market ['grenɪdʒ ˌmɑ:kɪt] *überdachter Markt in Greenwich* I U5, 103
Greenwich Park ['grenɪdʒ ˌpɑ:k] *Park in Greenwich* I U5, 103
India ['ɪndiə] Indien I U3, 54
London ['lʌndən] *Hauptstadt von England* I U4, 70
Manchester ['mæntʃɪstə] *Stadt im Norden von England* <I U1, 24>
Margate ['mɑ:geɪt] *Ausflugsort in England* I U5, 96
North America [ˌnɔ:θ‿ə'merɪkə] Nordamerika <I U3, 210>
South America [ˌsaʊθ‿ə'merɪkə] Südamerika <I U3, 210>

Other names

Baker Street ['beɪkə ˌstri:t] *Straßenname* I U5, 104
Begbie Road [ˌbegbi 'rəʊd] *Straßenname* I U6, 116
Bonfire night ['bɒnfaɪə ˌnaɪt] *Festtag am 5. November in England* <I U4, 218>
Brook Lane [ˌbrʊk 'leɪn] *Straßenname* I U5, 90
Cutty Sark [ˌkʌti 'sɑ:k] *Museumsschiff in Greenwich* I U5, 90
Fluff [flʌf] *Tiername* I U1, 13
Highfield Farm [ˌhaɪfi:ld 'fɑ:m] *Name eines Bauernhofs* I U6, 110
Honey ['hʌni] *Tiername* I U1, 13
King William Walk [kɪŋ 'wɪljəm ˌwɔ:k] *Straßenname* I U5, 108
Notting Hill Carnival [ˌnɒtɪŋ hɪl 'kɑ:nɪvl] *jährlicher Karneval im Londoner Stadtteil Notting Hill* I U4, 70
Okehampton Castle [ˌəʊkhæmtn 'kɑ:sl] *Burgruine in Devon* <I U6, 122>
Ray-B [ˌreɪ 'bi:] *Musiker* I U5, 92
Red Nose Day [red nəʊz 'deɪ] *Spendenmarathon* I U4, 70
Royal Observatory [ˌrɔɪəl‿əb'zɜ:vətri] *Museum in Greenwich (alte Uhren und Sternwarte)* <I U5, 102>
Sherlock ['ʃɜ:lɒk] *Tiername* I U1, 12
Superstars ['su:pəstɑ:z] *Name einer Talentshow* I U3, 52
Thomas Tallis School [ˌtɒməs 'tælɪs ˌsku:l] *Schulname* I U2, 32
Uplands Outdoor Centre [ˌʌpləndz 'aʊtdɔ: ˌsentə] *Natursportzentrum* <I U6, 122>

A

(nach) links **abbiegen** to turn left (into ...) I U5, 108
Abend evening I U4, 70
(frühes) **Abendessen** tea I U3, 59
Abenteuer adventure I U5, 100
aber but I U4, 72
acht eight I W, 9
achtzehn eighteen I U3, 55
achtzig eighty I U3, 55
Affe monkey I U3, 54
Aktivität activity I ZI, 10
alle all I U4, 81
Alphabet alphabet I U2, 39
also so I U6, 116
alt old I U5, 90
Wie alt bist du? How old are you? I U1, 12
Alter age I U3, 54
am on I U2, 38; at I U3, 53
am 7. Juli on 7th July I U4, 72
am Dienstag on Tuesday I U2, 38
am Wochenende at the weekend I U3, 53
an on I U2, 38; at I U3, 53
andere other I U4, 70
anhören to listen (to) I U3, 52
anrufen to call I U3, 59; to phone I U6, 119
anschauen to look at I U2, 34
Anspitzer pencil sharpener I U2, 35
Antwort answer I U2, 36
antworten to answer I U6, 119
Apfel apple I U5, 93
April April I U4, 71
Arbeit work I U3, 58
arbeiten to work I U3, 58
auch too I U1, 14
auf on I U1, 18; at I U3, 53
Auf Wiedersehen. Goodbye. I W, 8
aufhören to stop I U6, 112
aufmachen to open I U2, 34
aufregend exciting I U5, 92
aufstehen *to get up I U3, 58
August August I U4, 71
im August in August I U4, 70
aus from I U1, 12
Ausflug trip I U5, 96
den Hund **ausführen** to take the dog for a walk I U3, 62
ein **ausgefüllter** Tag a busy day I U3, 58
Außerirdische alien I U4, 80
Außerirdischer alien I U4, 80
Auto car I U5, 96

B

Bad(ezimmer) bathroom I U1, 25
Bahnhof station I U5, 93
Bis **bald**! See you! I W, 8; See you soon! I U6, 112
Banane banana I U3, 57
Bauer farmer I U6, 110
Bäuerin farmer I U6, 110
Bauernhof farm I U6, 110
Baum tree I U1, 22
Baumhaus tree house I U1, 22
beängstigend scary I U6, 110
beantworten to answer I U6, 119
befragen to interview I U3, 58
bei at I U3, 53
bekommen *to get I U4, 70
bereit ready I U1, 18
berühmt famous I U5, 90
beschäftigt busy I U1, 22
besitzen *to have I U1, 14
besonders special I U4, 70
Bett bed I U1, 18
ins Bett gehen *to go to bed I U3, 59
Bibliothek library I U5, 93
Bild picture I U6, 121
Biologie Biology I U2, 39
Bis bald! See you! I W, 8; See you soon! I U6, 112
bis until I U5, 108
bitte please I U2, 34
Bitte schön. Here you are. I U2, 35
blau blue I W, 9
Bleistift pencil I U2, 35
Bluse blouse I U6, 113
Bonbon sweet I U4, 70
Boot boat I U5, 97
Box box I U1, 18
nicht **brauchen** needn't I U6, 111
braun brown I W, 9
belegtes **Brot** sandwich I U4, 77
Bruder brother I U1, 14
Buch book I U1, 18
Bücherei library I U5, 93
buchstabieren *to spell I U2, 38
bunt colourful I U6, 113
Bus bus I ZI, 11
Butter butter I U4, 77

C

Cache *(Geheimschatz)* cache I U6, 123
Café café I U3, 62
Cafeteria cafeteria I U2, 33
Cola coke I U4, 76
Computer computer I W, 8
Computerspiel computer game I U1, 31
cool cool I U1, 12

D

da there I U1, 18
da because I U6, 116
Dachboden attic I U5, 100
danach then I U1, 23; after that I U3, 58
Danke. Thanks. I U1, 25; Thank you. I U2, 35
dann then I U1, 23
das the I W, 8
das this I U1, 12; that I U1, 13
das ist that's (= that is) I U1, 13
Datum date I U4, 73
dein your I U1, 18
denken *to think I U4, 80
der the I W, 8
deshalb so I U6, 116
Deutsch German I U2, 39
Deutschland Germany I U1, 13
Dezember December I U4, 70
dich you I W, 8
die the I W, 8
Dienstag Tuesday I U2, 39
am Dienstag on Tuesday I U2, 38
dies this I U1, 12

dir you I W, 8
Donnerstag Thursday I U2, 39
dort there I U1, 18
eine **Dose** ... a can of I U4, 77
dreckig dirty I U6, 121
drei three I W, 9
dreißig thirty I U3, 55
dreizehn thirteen I U3, 55
dritte third I U4, 73
du you I W, 8
dunkel dark I U6, 116
Durcheinander mess I U1, 18

E

Ei egg I U4, 77
ein a I ZI, 10; an I U2, 35
eine a I ZI, 10; an I U2, 35
einfach easy I U2, 38
einhundert a/one hundred I U3, 55
einige some I U5, 101
Einkaufen shopping I U4, 76
Einkaufszentrum shopping centre I U5, 90
Einkaufszettel shopping list I U4, 79
einladen to invite I U4, 72
Einladung invitation I U4, 80
eins one I W, 9
einundzwanzig twenty-one I U3, 55
Eis(creme) ice cream I U4, 73
Elefant elephant I U3, 54
elegant chic I U6, 113
elf eleven I U1, 12
Eltern parents *(pl)* I U1, 15
Englisch English I W, 8
entlang along I U5, 108
Entschuldigung. Sorry. I U4, 78; Excuse me. I U5, 103
er he I U1, 14
Erdbeere strawberry I U4, 73
Erdkunde Geography I U2, 39
erste first I U4, 73
  das erste Mal the first time I U3, 62
erster Offizier first mate I U5, 100
als **Erstes** first I U3, 58
erzählen *to tell I U5, 92
Erzähler narrator I U4, 80
Erzählerin narrator I U4, 80
es it I ZI, 11
es gibt there are; there is (= there's) I U1, 18
Essen food I U2, 33; meal I U4, 73
essen *to eat I U2, 33
Esszimmer dining room I U1, 31
etwas something I ZI, 11; some I U5, 101
euch you I W, 8
euer your I U1, 18

F

fahren *to go I U5, 96
  mit (dem Zug) fahren *to go by (train) I U5, 96
Fahrrad bike I U1, 12
fallen *to fall I U6, 121
falsch wrong I U1, 19
Familie family I U1, 14
Fan fan I U1, 12
Fantasieausflug fantasy trip I U5, 99
Farbe colour I ZI, 10
Fasching carnival I U4, 70
Fastfood-Restaurant fast food restaurant I U4, 73
Februar February I U4, 71
Federmäppchen pencil case I U2, 35
Feier party I U4, 72
feiern to celebrate I U4, 70
Fenster window I U2, 34
fernsehen to watch TV I U3, 52
Fernseher TV I U3, 52
fertig ready I U1, 18
feststecken *to be stuck I U6, 120
  im Schlamm festgesteckt stuck in the mud I U6, 120
Film film I U2, 45; movie I U3, 53
Filzstift felt-tip I U2, 35
finden *to find I U1, 18
  ich kann ... nicht finden I can't find ... I U1, 18
Fisch fish *(sg)*, fish *(pl)* I U3, 57
  Pommes mit Fisch fish and chips I U5, 96
Flamingo flamingo I U3, 54
eine **Flasche** ... a bottle of I U4, 76
Fledermaus bat I W, 8
Fleisch meat I U3, 54
Flugzeug plane I U5, 97
Fluss river I U6, 120
Foto photo I U1, 12
  ein Foto machen *to take a photo I U4, 81
Frage question I U2, 36
fragen to ask I U4, 81
Französisch French I U2, 39
Frau *(Anrede)* Mrs I U2, 33; Ms I U2, 38
Freitag Friday I U2, 39
Freizeit free time I U3, 52
Freizeitpark theme park I U4, 73
Freude fun I U6, 111
Freund friend I U1, 14
Freundin friend I U1, 14
Freundschaften schließen *to make friends I U2, 45
Frisbeescheibe frisbee I U5, 96
froh happy I U4, 80
Frucht fruit I U3, 54
Frühstück breakfast I U3, 58
frühstücken *to have breakfast I U3, 58
Füller pen I U2, 34
fünf five I W, 9
fünfzehn fifteen I U3, 55
fünfzig fifty I U3, 55
für for I U2, 34
furchtbar awful I U5, 100
Fuß foot *(sg)*, feet *(pl)* I U6, 121
  zu Fuß gehen *to go on foot I U5, 97
Fußball football I ZI, 11
füttern *to feed I U3, 58

G

Garten garden I U1, 14
es **gibt** there are; there is (= there's) I U1, 18
geben *to give I U4, 72
Geburtstag birthday I U4, 72
  Alles Gute zum Geburtstag! Happy birthday! I U4, 80
gefällt mir I like I W, 8

gefällt mir nicht I don't like | U2, 32
gegenüber opposite | U5, 108
Geheimnis mystery | U3, 62
gehen *to go | U2, 32; to walk | U5, 96
ins Bett gehen *to go to bed | U3, 59
spazieren gehen *to go for a walk | U6, 117
zu Fuß gehen *to go on foot | U5, 97
Es ist Zeit, zu gehen. It's time to go. | W, 8
Wie geht es dir? How are you? | U6, 112
gelb yellow | ZI, 10
Geld money | U4, 70
gemeinsam together | U4, 70
Schatzkiste beim Geocaching cache box | U6, 123
Geografie Geography | U2, 39
geradeaus straight on | U5, 108
Geräusch noise | U1, 23
gern haben to like | W, 8
Gern geschehen. You're welcome. | U4, 76
ich würde gerne ... I'd like (to) ... (= I would like to) | U6, 111
Geschäft shop | U4, 76
Geschenk present | U4, 70
Geschichte History | U2, 39; story | U3, 62
Gesicht face | U6, 121
gestern yesterday | U5, 92
gewinnen *to win | U3, 52
Gewinner winner | U2, 42
Gewinnerin winner | U2, 42
Giraffe giraffe | U3, 54
glücklich happy | U4, 80
GPS *(ein satellitengestütztes System zur weltweiten Positionsbestimmung)* GPS *(Global Positioning System)* | U6, 111
grau grey | W, 9
Grill barbecue | U4, 72
groß high | U3, 54; big | U4, 72
großartig great | U4, 72
Großmutter grandmother | U1, 15
Großvater grandfather | U1, 15
grün green | W, 9
Gruppe group | U2, 37; team | U3, 52
gruselig scary | U4, 70
Grüße ... von mir. Say hi to ... | U6, 119
gut good | U2, 34
Gut gemacht! Well done! | U2, 43
gut sein in *to be good at | U2, 38
gut sein bei *to be good at | U2, 38

H

Haarglätter hair straightener | U1, 25
haben *to have | U1, 14
Du hast Recht. You're right. | U2, 38
Hai shark | U5, 101
halb (drei) half past (two) | U3, 59
Hallo. Hello.; Hi. | W, 8
Halsband collar | U6, 111
Hamburger burger | U4, 73
Handy mobile (phone) | U1, 18
hassen to hate | U5, 100
häufig often | U4, 72
Haus house | U1, 22
zu Hause at home | U1, 18; around the house | U1, 25
Hausaufgabe(n) **machen** *to do homework | U5, 92
Hausmeister caretaker | U2, 33
Hausmeisterin caretaker | U2, 33
Haustier pet | U1, 13
Heft book | U1, 18
Heim home | U1, 18
heiß hot | U6, 117
Ich **heiße** ... My name is ... | W, 8
Wie heißt du? What's your name? | W, 8
helfen to help | U3, 53
Helikopter helicopter | U5, 97
Helm helmet | U6, 112
herausfinden *to find | U1, 18
herausnehmen *to take out | U2, 34
hereinkommen *to get in | U3, 62
Herr *(Anrede)* Mr | U2, 33
heute today | U5, 100
Hexe witch | U4, 80
hier here | ZI, 11
hinfallen *to fall | U6, 121
hinter behind | U6, 121
Hinweis clue | U3, 62
hoch high | U3, 54
Holz wood | U1, 22
hören to listen (to) | U3, 52; *to hear | U4, 81
Hose trousers *(pl)* | U6, 113
kurze Hose shorts *(pl)* | U6, 113
hübsch beautiful | U5, 101; pretty | U6, 113
Hubschrauber helicopter | U5, 97
Huhn chicken | U6, 110
Hund dog | ZI, 10
den Hund ausführen to take the dog for a walk | U3, 62
hundert a/one hundred | U3, 55
hungrig hungry | U5, 100

I

ich I | W, 8; me | U1, 14
ich mag I like | W, 8
ich möchte ... I'd like (to) ... (= I would like to) | U6, 111
ich würde gerne ... I'd like (to) ... (= I would like to) | U6, 111
ich würde nicht gerne ... I wouldn't like (to) ... | U6, 111
Idee idea | U6, 117
Irgendeine Idee? Any idea? | U6, 116
ihm him | U4, 72
ihn him | U4, 72
Ihnen you | W, 8
ihr you | W, 8; her | U1, 14; their | U4, 80
im in | ZI, 10
im August in August | U4, 70
Imbiss snack | U4, 83
immer always | U4, 72
in in | ZI, 10; to | U2, 32; at | U3, 53
in der Schule at school | U2, 32
Indien India | U3, 54
Informatik IT (Information Technology) | U2, 39
Informationstechnik IT (Information Technology) | U2, 39
interessant interesting | U2, 38

interviewen to interview I U3, 58
Irgendeine Idee? Any idea? I U6, 116

J

ja yes I W, 8
Jacke coat I U6, 113
Jahr year I U2, 32
Jahrgangsstufe year I U2, 32
Januar January I U4, 71
Jeans jeans *(pl)* I U2, 45
jede every I U3, 62
jeder everyone I U6, 110
jetzt now I U2, 34
Job job I U5, 100
Juli July I U4, 71
am 7. Juli on 7th July I U4, 72
Junge boy I ZI, 10
Juni June I U4, 71

K

Käfig cage I U3, 58
kalt cold I U6, 117
Kamel camel I U3, 54
Kanufahren canoeing I U6, 111
Kapitän captain I U3, 53
Kapitänin captain I U3, 53
Kappe cap I U6, 113
Karneval carnival I U4, 70
Kartoffel potato *(sg)*, potatoes *(pl)* I U5, 100
Kartoffelchip crisp I U4, 76
Käse cheese I U4, 77
Katze cat I U1, 13
kaufen *to buy I ZI, 11
Kaufhaus department store I U5, 93
Kaugummi chewing gum I U2, 45
kein no I U1, 14
keine no I U1, 14
kennen lernen *to **meet** I U6, 110
Kerze candle I U4, 76
sieben **Kilogramm** täglich 7 kilograms a day I U3, 54
40 **Kilometer** pro Stunde 40 kilometres an hour I U3, 54
Kinderzimmer bedroom I U1, 18
Kino cinema I U3, 53
Kiste box I U1, 18
Klasse year I U2, 32; tutor group I U2, 33
Klassenlehrer tutor I U2, 33
Klassenlehrerin tutor I U2, 33
Klassenzimmer classroom I U2, 33
Klebstoff glue I U2, 35
Kleider *(Pl.)* clothes *(pl)* I U4, 70
Kleiderschrank wardrobe I U1, 19
Kleidung clothes *(pl)* I U4, 70
Klettern rock climbing I U6, 111
klicken to click I U6, 111
klingeln *to ring I U4, 81
komisch funny I U1, 23
kommen *to come I U3, 54
ich komme aus ... I'm from ... I U1, 12
Kannst du mir sagen, wie ich ... komme? Can you tell me the way to ...? I U5, 108
Komm jetzt! Come on! I U6, 121
Woher kommst du? Where are you from? I U1, 13
können can I ZI, 11
nicht können can't I U1, 18
ich kann ... nicht finden I can't find ... I U1, 18
Kannst du mir sagen, wie ich ... komme? Can you tell me the way to ...? I U5, 108
Könntest du das bitte wiederholen? Can you say that again, please? I U4, 79
nicht weg **können** *to be stuck I U6, 120
Korbball netball I U3, 52
korrekt right I U1, 19
Wie viel (kostet/**kosten**) ...? How much (is/are) ...? I U4, 76
... kostet 99 Pence ... is 99p I U4, 76
Kostüm costume I U4, 70; fancy dress I U4, 72
Krankenhaus hospital I U5, 109
Krokodil crocodile I U3, 54
Küche kitchen I U1, 25
Kuchen cake I U4, 72
kühl cool I U6, 117
Kunst Art I U2, 39
kurze Hose shorts *(pl)* I U6, 113

L

Laden shop I U4, 76
Tante-Emma-Laden corner shop I U4, 76
Lampe lamp I U1, 19
Land country I U6, 110
Landkarte map I U5, 109
ländliche Gegend country I U6, 110
Landwirt farmer I U6, 110
Landwirtin farmer I U6, 110
lang long I U3, 54
fünf Monate lang for five months I U3, 54
langweilig boring I U6, 121
lass(t) uns let's (= let us) I U2, 42
laufen *to run I U3, 54; to walk I U5, 96
läuten *to ring I U4, 81
Leben life *(sg)*, lives *(pl)* I U5, 101
leben to live I U5, 90
Lebensmittel food I U2, 33
Lehrer teacher I U2, 33
Lehrerin teacher I U2, 33
leicht easy I U2, 38
Tut mir **leid**. Sorry. I U4, 78
Leiter ladder I U1, 22
lesen *to read I U2, 36
letzte last I U5, 92
Leute people I ZI, 10
Liebe(r) ... *(Anrede in Briefen)* Dear ..., I U6, 116
lieben to love I U3, 52
Lieblings- favourite I U2, 32
lila purple I ZI, 10
Limonade lemonade I U4, 78
Lineal ruler I U2, 35
links on the left I U5, 108
(nach) links abbiegen to turn left (into ...) I U5, 108
auf der linken Seite on the left I U5, 108
Loch hole I U3, 62
lösen to solve I U3, 62
Löwe lion I U3, 54

Luftballon balloon I U4, 76
lustig funny I U2, 38

M

machen *to do I U2, 34; *to make I U4, 72
ein Foto machen *to take a photo I U4, 81
Hausaufgabe(n) machen *to do homework I U5, 92
Mädchen girl I U2, 34
Mahlzeit meal I U4, 73
Mai May I U4, 71
das erste **Mal** the first time I U3, 62
Mama mum I U1, 14
Mann man *(sg)*, men *(pl)* I U5, 101
Markt market I U5, 93
März March I U4, 71
Mathe Maths I U2, 33
Matsch mud I U6, 120
Maus mouse *(sg)*, mice *(pl)* I U3, 54
Meer sea I U5, 96
am Meer at the seaside I U5, 96
Mehl flour I U4, 77
mein my I U1, 12
eine **Menge** a lot of I U5, 100
jede Menge lots of I U4, 88
Mensa cafeteria I U2, 33
merkwürdig funny I U1, 23
Meter metre I U3, 54
mich me I U2, 34
nenne mich call me I U2, 34
Milch milk I U4, 77
mild mild I U6, 117
mir me I U4, 72
mit with I U1, 14
Mit den besten Wünschen Best wishes I U6, 116
Mittagessen lunch I U2, 42
Mittagspause lunchtime I U3, 53
Mittagszeit lunchtime I U3, 53
Mittwoch Wednesday I U2, 34
modern modern I U6, 111
mögen to like I W, 8
gern mögen to love I U3, 52
nicht mögen to hate I U5, 100
ich mag I like I W, 8
ich mag nicht I don't like I U2, 32
ich möchte nicht … I wouldn't like (to) … I U6, 111
ich möchte … I'd like (to) … (= I would like to) I U6, 111
Möchtest du? Would you like (to)…? I U6, 111
Monat month I U3, 54
fünf Monate lang for five months I U3, 54
Montag Monday I U2, 39
Morgen morning I U5, 92
Motorrad motorbike I U5, 97
müde tired I U5, 92
Museum museum I U5, 93
Musik music I W, 8
Muslim Muslim I U4, 70
Muslimin Muslim I U4, 70
müssen must I U6, 112
nicht müssen needn't I U6, 111
Mutter mother I U1, 14
Mutti mum I U1, 14
Mütze cap I U6, 113

N

na ja well I U1, 25
Na ja, schau mal … nach. Well, look … I U1, 25
nach to I U2, 32; after I U3, 52
nach *(bei Uhrzeitangaben)* past I U3, 59
Nachmittag afternoon I U3, 58
am Nachmittag in the afternoon I U3, 58
nächste next I U2, 34
Nacht night I U1, 23
Nachtwanderung night walk I U6, 112
in der **Nähe** von near I U6, 111
Name name I U1, 14
Nase nose I U4, 70
nass wet I U6, 116
Naturwissenschaft Science I U2, 39
neben next to I U1, 18
neblig foggy I U6, 117
nein no I U1, 18
nenne mich call me I U2, 34
nett nice I U1, 13
Nett, dich kennen zu lernen. Nice to meet you. I W, 8
neu new I U1, 18
neun nine I W, 9
neunzehn nineteen I U3, 55
neunzig ninety I U3, 55
nicht not I U2, 38
nicht können can't I U1, 18
nicht mögen to hate I U5, 100
ich kann … nicht finden I can't find … I U1, 18
nie never I U4, 72
niemals never I U4, 72
niemand no one I U1, 23
November November I U4, 71
Nudeln pasta I U4, 78
null zero I W, 9
null *(bei Uhrzeiten und Telefonnummern)* oh I U3, 59
Nummer number I ZI, 10
nun now I U2, 34
Nuss nut I U3, 62

O

Obst fruit I U3, 54
oder or I U1, 23
erster **Offizier** first mate I U5, 100
öffnen to open I U2, 34
oft often I U4, 72
okay OK I W, 8
Oktober October I U4, 70
Onkel uncle I U1, 15
Orange orange I U4, 77
orange orange I ZI, 10
Ordinalzahl ordinal number I U4, 73
Ort place I U2, 32

P

eine **Packung** … a packet of I U4, 76
Papa dad I U1, 14
Park park I ZI, 10
Party party I U4, 72
Pasta pasta I U4, 78
in der **Pause** at break I U2, 38
Pausenhof playground I U2, 32

Pence *(brit. Währungseinheit)* pence *(pl)*, penny *(sg)* I U4, 76
... kostet 99 Pence ... is 99p I U4, 76
das macht 2 Pfund und 24 Pence that's £2.24 I U4, 76
Pferd horse I U6, 110
Pfirsich peach I U4, 77
Pfund *(brit. Währungseinheit)* pound I U4, 76
das macht 2 Pfund und 24 Pence that's £2.24 I U4, 76
Picknick picnic I U6, 112
Pinguin penguin I U3, 54
pink pink I W, 9
Pirat pirate I U4, 80
Piratin pirate I U4, 80
Pizza pizza I U5, 92
Platz place I U2, 32
Polizeibeamter police officer I U3, 62
Polizeibeamtin police officer I U3, 62
Pommes chips *(pl)* I U5, 96
Pommes mit Fisch fish and chips I U5, 96
Popcorn popcorn I U5, 103
Postamt post office I U5, 103
Poster poster I U1, 18
Postkarte postcard I U5, 96
Problem problem I U6, 120
putzen to clean I U3, 58

R

Radiergummi eraser I U2, 35
Rätsel mystery I U3, 62
Raum room I U1, 18
(Taschen-) **Rechner** calculator I U2, 35
Du hast **Recht**. You're right. I U2, 38
rechts on the right I U5, 108
(nach) rechts abbiegen to turn right (into ...) I U5, 108
auf der rechten Seite on the right I U5, 108
Rechtschreibung spelling I U2, 38
reden (mit) to talk (to) I U2, 32
Regal shelf *(sg)*, shelves *(pl)* I U1, 19
Regalbrett shelf *(sg)*, shelves *(pl)* I U1, 19
regnen to rain I U6, 116
Reiten horse riding I U6, 112
Religionsunterricht RE (= Religious Education) I U2, 39
rennen *to run I U3, 54
Fastfood-**Restaurant** fast food restaurant I U4, 73
richtig right I U1, 19
Rock skirt I U6, 113
Rollstuhl wheelchair I U6, 120
rosa pink I W, 9
rot red I W, 9
rufen to call I U3, 59

S

Sack bag I U5, 101
sagen *to say I U2, 37; *to tell I U5, 92
sammeln to collect I U4, 70
Samstag Saturday I U1, 18
samstags on Saturdays I U3, 52
Sandwich sandwich I U4, 77
Sänger singer I U2, 34
Sängerin singer I U2, 34
sauber machen to clean I U3, 58
Süßes, sonst gibt's **Saures**! Trick or treat! I U4, 71
Saxophon saxophone I U2, 42
eine **Schachtel** ... a box of I U4, 77
Schaf sheep *(sg)*, sheep *(pl)* I U5, 101
Schal scarf *(sg)*, scarves *(pl)* I U1, 19
(nach)**schauen** to look I U1, 25
Na ja, schau mal ... nach. Well, look ... I U1, 25
schick chic I U6, 113
schicken *to send I U5, 96
schieben to push I U6, 121
Schiff ship I U5, 90
schlafen *to sleep I U3, 54
Schlafzimmer bedroom I U1, 18
Schlamm mud I U6, 120
im Schlamm festgesteckt stuck in the mud I U6, 120
Schlange snake I U3, 54
schließen to close I U2, 34
Schlumpf smurf I U4, 80
schmutzig dirty I U6, 121
der/die/das **schnellste** the fastest I U3, 65
Schokolade chocolate I U4, 72
eine Tafel Schokolade a bar of chocolate I U4, 76
schön nice I U1, 13; beautiful I U5, 101
schrecklich awful I U5, 100
Schrei shout I U5, 101
schreiben *to write I U2, 36
Schule school I U2, 32
in der Schule at school I U2, 32
Schüler student I U2, 33
Schülerin student I U2, 33
Schulfach subject I U2, 38
Schulhof playground I U2, 32
Schulstunde lesson I U2, 38
schwarz black I W, 9
Schwester sister I U1, 14
schwierig difficult I U2, 39
Schwimmbad swimming pool I U5, 91
schwimmen gehen *to go swimming I U5, 91
Science-Fiction science fiction I U3, 53
sechs six I W, 9
sechzehn sixteen I U3, 55
sechzig sixty I U3, 55
sehen *to see I U2, 42
sehr very I U2, 38
Seil rope I U5, 101
sein *to be I U1, 16
sei still don't talk I U2, 34
sein his I U1, 14
senden *to send I U5, 96
September September I U4, 71
sich (hin)**setzen** *to sit (down) I U2, 34
Shorts shorts *(pl)* I U6, 113
Sie you I W, 8
sie she I U1, 14
sie *(Pl.)* they I U1, 13
sieben seven I W, 9
siebzehn seventeen I U3, 55
siebzig seventy I U3, 55
siegen *to win I U3, 52
singen *to sing I U2, 34
Skateboard skateboard I U5, 97
Textnachricht (**SMS**) text message I U6, 119

Snack snack | U4, 83
so like that | U2, 38
Socke sock | U6, 113
sonnig sunny | U6, 117
Sonntag Sunday | U2, 39
sich **Sorgen** machen to worry | U6, 111
spannend exciting | U5, 92
Spaß fun | U6, 111
Wie **spät** ist es? What time is it? | U3, 58
später later | U1, 22
spazieren gehen *to go for a walk | U6, 117
speziell special | U4, 70
Spiel game | U2, 32
spielen to play | ZI, 11
Spielplatz playground | U2, 32
Sport sport | W, 8
Sportgeschäft sports shop | U5, 92
Sportunterricht PE (Physical Education) | U2, 39
sprechen *to say | U2, 37
sprechen (mit) to talk (to) | U2, 32
Spur clue | U3, 62
Stadt town | U5, 90
Stadtplan map | U5, 109
Star star | U2, 43
Stelle place | U2, 32
Stift pen | U2, 34
Strand beach | U5, 96
Straße road | U5, 90
Straßenbahn tram | U5, 97
Streich trick | U2, 42
Stuhl chair | U1, 18
40 Kilometer pro **Stunde** 40 kilometres an hour | U3, 54
vier Stunden täglich four hours a day | U3, 54
Stundenplan timetable | U2, 38
Sturm storm | U5, 101
suchen to look for | U3, 62
super cool | U1, 12
Superman superman | U4, 80
Supermarkt supermarket | U5, 93
Süßes, sonst gibt's Saures! Trick or treat! | U4, 71
Süßigkeit sweet | U4, 70
Sweatshirt sweatshirt | U6, 113

T

Tafel board | U2, 34
eine Tafel Schokolade a bar of chocolate | U4, 76
Tag day | U2, 38
ein ausgefüllter Tag a busy day | U3, 58
Tagebuch diary | U5, 100
Was ist dein **Talent**? What's your talent? | U2, 42
Talentwettbewerb talent show | U2, 34
Tante aunt | U1, 15
tanzen to dance | U4, 70
Tänzer dancer | U4, 80
Tänzerin dancer | U4, 80
Tasche bag | U2, 35
Taschenlampe torch | U6, 116
Team team | U3, 52
Technik Design Technology (DT) | U2, 38
Tee tea | U3, 59
Telefonanruf phone call | U6, 112
telefonieren to phone | U6, 119
Tennis tennis | ZI, 10
Teppich carpet | U1, 19
Textnachricht (SMS) text message | U6, 119
Tier animal | W, 8
Tierheim animal rescue shelter | U3, 53
Tierpark zoo | U3, 54
Tierpfleger zookeeper | U3, 58
Tierpflegerin zookeeper | U3, 58
Tiger tiger | U3, 54
Tisch table | U1, 18
Tochter daughter | U6, 110
toll great | U4, 72; brilliant | U4, 81
Top top | U6, 113
Tourist tourist | U5, 108
Touristin tourist | U5, 108
Touristeninformation Tourist Information Centre | U5, 108
tragen *to wear | U4, 70
Training practice | U3, 53
Traktor tractor | U6, 111
Trick trick | U2, 42
trocken dry | U6, 117
Tschüss! Bye!; See you! | W, 8
T-Shirt T-shirt | U1, 18
Tuch scarf *(sg)*, scarves *(pl)* | U1, 19
tun *to do | U2, 34; *to make | U4, 72
Tut mir leid. Sorry. | U4, 78
Was kann ich für dich tun? How can I help you? | U4, 76
Türklingel doorbell | U4, 81
Turnschuh trainer | U6, 113
eine **Tüte** … a packet of | U4, 76
Tüte bag | U2, 35

U

U-Bahn underground | U5, 97
sich **übergeben** *to be sick | U5, 100
Übernachtung sleepover | U4, 83
Überraschung surprise | U4, 72
U-Boot submarine | U5, 97
Übung practice | U3, 53
Übungsheft exercise book | U2, 34
Uhr *(Zeitangabe bei vollen Stunden)* o'clock | U3, 58
Wie viel Uhr ist es? What time is it? | U3, 58
Uhrzeit time | U3, 52
um at | U3, 53
und and | W, 8
Uniform uniform | U2, 32
Unordnung mess | U1, 18
uns us | U6, 110
unser our | U1, 14
unter under | U1, 18
Unterricht lesson | U2, 38
unterwegs out and about | U5, 103
Ururopa great-great-grandad | U5, 100

V

Vater father | U1, 14
Vati dad | U1, 14
Vegetarier vegetarian | U5, 96
Vegetarierin vegetarian | U5, 96

verängstigt scared I U5, 101
vergessen *to forget I U4, 72
Verkleidung fancy dress I U4, 72
verrückt crazy I U2, 34
viel much I U3, 54; lots of I U4, 88; a lot of I U5, 100
vier four I W, 9
vierte fourth I U4, 73
Viertel nach quarter past I U3, 59
Viertel vor quarter to I U3, 59
vierzehn fourteen I U3, 55
vierzig forty I U3, 55
violett purple I ZI, 10
von from I U1, 12
ein Foto von a photo of I U1, 14
vor *(bei Uhrzeitangaben)* to I U3, 59
Vormittag morning I U5, 92

W

wann when I U3, 58
warm warm I U6, 112
was what I U1, 18
was ist what's (= what is) I U1, 18
Was kann ich für dich tun? How can I help you? I U4, 76
Waschbär raccoon I U3, 62
Wasser water I U4, 78
Hier ist dein **Wechselgeld.** Here's your change. I U4, 76
Wecker alarm clock I U1, 19
nach dem **Weg** fragen asking the way I U5, 108
nicht **weg** können *to be stuck I U6, 120
Weihnachten Christmas I U4, 70
weil because I U6, 116
weiß white I W, 9
Welle wave I U5, 101
wer who I U1, 18
Wetter weather I U6, 117
Wie ist das Wetter? What's the weather like? I U6, 117
Wettrennen race I U3, 65
wie how I U3, 62
Wie alt bist du? How old are you? I U1, 12
Wie bitte? Pardon? I U4, 79
Wie geht es dir? How are you? I U6, 112
Wie heißt du? What's your name? I W, 8
Wie ist das Wetter? What's the weather like? I U6, 117
Wie spät ist es? What time is it? I U3, 58
Wie viel (kostet/kosten) ...? How much (is/are) ...? I U4, 76
Wie viel Uhr ist es? What time is it? I U3, 58
Könntest du das bitte **wiederholen?** Can you say that again, please? I U4, 79
Auf **Wiedersehen.** Goodbye. I W, 8
willkommen (bei/in) welcome (to) I W, 8
Wind wind I U1, 23
windig windy I U6, 117
Winter winter I U3, 54
wir we I U1, 14
Wirklich? Really? I U2, 34
Ich **weiß** (es) nicht! I don't know! I U3, 62
Weißt du was? Guess what? I U6, 116
Wissenschaft Science I U2, 39
Witz joke I U2, 38
witzig funny I U2, 38
wo where I U1, 18
Woche week I U2, 34
Wochenende weekend I U3, 53
am Wochenende at the weekend I U3, 53
woher where I U1, 18
Woher kommst du? Where are you from? I U1, 13
wohin where I U1, 18
wohnen to live I U5, 90
Wohnung flat I U5, 90
Wohnzimmer living room I U1, 25
wolkig cloudy I U6, 117
Wolle wool I U5, 101
wollen to want (to) I U4, 81
Mit den besten **Wünschen** Best wishes I U6, 116
ich **würde** gerne ... I'd like (to) ... (= I would like to) I U6, 111
ich würde nicht gerne ... I wouldn't like (to) ... I U6, 111

Z

Zahl number I ZI, 10
Zebra zebra I U3, 54
zehn ten I W, 9
Zeit time I U3, 52
Es ist Zeit, zu gehen. It's time to go. I W, 8
Zeitpunkt date I U4, 73
Zeitschrift magazine I U3, 58
Zentimeter (cm) centimetre (cm) I U3, 54
ziehen to pull I U6, 121
Zimmer room I U1, 18
Zimmerdecke ceiling I U3, 62
Zoo zoo I U3, 54
im Zoo at the zoo I U3, 54
zu to I U2, 32
zuerst first I U3, 58
Zug train I U5, 96
mit (dem Zug) fahren *to go by (train) I U5, 96
Zuhause home I U1, 18
zuhören to listen (to) I U3, 52
zumachen to close I U2, 34
zusammen together I U4, 70
zwanzig twenty I U3, 55
zwei two I W, 9
zweite second I U4, 73
zwölf twelve I U1, 13

L

Lösungen Extra practice

Seite 28

1 Write the answers.
Hi! My name is (Markus). I'm (ten). I'm from (Berlin).

2 Write the words.
1. sister 2. mother 3. father 4. brother
5. family

3 Find the words.
1. It's 2. I'm 3. She's 4. He's 5. She's
6. He's

4 Say the colours.
Number 1 is red. Number 2 is blue. Number 3 is green. Number 4 is yellow. Number 5 is white. Number 6 is black.

5 Make questions.
1. Where is Holly?
2. Where are Fluff and Honey?
3. Where is the mobile?
4. Where is Dave?
5. Where are Luke and Sherlock?
6. Where is Olivia?

6 Find ten words.
one, night, busy, garden, house, tree, what, dog, there, cool

Seite 48

1 Complete Holly's sentences.
1. I go to Thomas Tallis School.
2. I'm in Year 7.
3. Students can eat in the cafteria.
4. My favourite place is the playground.
5. I'm in tutor group 7 RS.
6. My tutor is Mr Swindon.

2 What is it?
1. Number 1 is a pencil.
2. Number 2 is an eraser.
3. Number 3 is a ruler.
4. Number 4 is a pen.
5. Number 5 is a chair.

3 What can Mr Swindon say?
1. F 2. D 3. E 4. B 5. C 6. A

4 What are the words?
1. English 2. Music 3. DT 4. PE 5. Art
6. Maths

5 Match the sentences with the pictures.
1. C 2. B 3. E 4. F 5. A 6. D

6 Write the words.
1. school 2. teacher 3. talent show
4. playground 5. caretaker 6. classroom

Seite 68

1 Complete the sentences.
1. music 2. netball 3. cinema 4. football
5. help

2 Match the numbers with the words.
a) 1. That's thirty-eight.
2. That's twenty-one.
3. That's forty-two.
4. That's one hundred/a hundred.
5. That's fifteen.
6. That's sixty-four.

b) fifty

3 Match!
1. Tom, the tiger runs 40 kilometres an hour.
2. Tigers eat meat.
3. Edgar, the elephant comes from India.
4. Elephants like fruit.
5. Holly Richardson loves animals.
6. She helps at an animal rescue shelter.

4 What time is it?
1. It's ten forty-five.
2. It's four o'clock.
3. It's seven fifteen.
4. It's twelve thirty.
5. It's three twenty-five.
6. It's nine forty.

5 Match the questions with the answers.
1. C 2. E 3. F 4. A 5. B 6. D

6 Put the words into two groups.
Animals: tiger, giraffe, penguin, snake, monkey
Free time: netball, football, music, cinema, café

Seite 86

1 Match the pictures with the days.
1. It's Halloween. 2. It's the Notting Hill Carnival.
3. It's Eid. 4. It's Christmas. 5. It's Red Nose Day.

2 Write the next month.
1. June 2. December 3. March 4. February
5. July 6. October

3 Find the words.
1. July 2. barbecue 3. card 4. cake 5. nice
6. cinema

4 What does Holly do on Sundays?
1. often 2. always 3. always 4. never
5. often 6. often

5 Write a shopping list.
a) chocolate, crisps, coke, balloons
b) Yes.

6 Find ten words.
birthday, friend, party, brilliant, costume, think, scary, sorry, invitation, happy

Seite 106

1 Match the words.
1. old town
2. shopping centre
3. Cutty Sark
4. swimming pool
5. Brook Lane
6. favourite place

2 What did they do?
1. did 2. played 3. watched 4. played
5. went 6. saw

3 How do they go there?
1. by bike 2. by train 3. by bus 4. on foot
5. by car

4 Match the questions with the answers.
1. F 2. C 3. E 4. A 5. D 6. B

5 Put the words into two groups.
places in town: café, beach, park, shop
I can go by ...: ship, bus, car, train, bike

Seite 126

1 Make two mind maps.
animals:
farm dog, sheep, horses, chickens
activities:
rock climbing, canoeing, horse riding

2 Match the pictures with the words.
1. sweatshirt 2. trainers 3. coat 4. socks
5. trousers 6. skirt

3 Put in was or were.
1. were 2. was 3. were 4. was
5. was 6. were 7. were

4 What's the weather like?
1. hot 2. cloudy 3. wet 4. sunny
5. windy 6. cold

5 Put the words in the right order.
1. Jay didn't eat an English breakfast.
2. He didn't like the chickens.
3. Holly didn't have trainers.
4. She didn't play football.
5. The students didn't have torches.
6. Mr Swindon didn't see the bats.

6 Match the words.
1. mud – Matsch
2. it's stuck – es steckt fest
3. he pushed – er schob
4. dirty – dreckig
5. river – Fluss
6. he pulled – er zog

Bildquellennachweis

Cover.1 February Films (Elke Bock), London; **Cover.2** Thinkstock (iStockphoto), München; **Cover.3** iStockphoto (MARK BOND), Calgary, Alberta; **Vorsatz.1** February Films, London; **Vorsatz.2** February Films, London; **Vorsatz.3** February Films, London; **Vorsatz.4** February Films, London; **Vorsatz.5** February Films, London; **2.1** Fotolia.com (Sport Moments), New York; **3.1** February Films, London; **3.2** iStockphoto (majaiva), Calgary, Alberta; **4.1** Thinkstock (Photodisc), München; **4.2** iStockphoto (ilbusca), Calgary, Alberta; **5.1** Fotolia.com (Tyler Olson), New York; **8.1** Weccard, Thomas, Ludwigsburg; **9.1** Weccard, Thomas, Ludwigsburg; **12.2** February Films, London; **12.3** February Films, London; **13.1** February Films, London; **13.2** February Films, London; **13.3** Klett-Archiv, Stuttgart; **13.4** Getty Images, München; **14.1** February Films, London; **14.2** February Films, London; **14.3** February Films, London; **16.1** February Films, London; **16.2** February Films, London; **16.3** February Films, London; **17.1** Thinkstock (iStockphoto), München; **17.1** February Films, London; **17.2** Thinkstock (Hemera), München; **17.3** Thinkstock (iStockphoto), München; **17.4** Avenue Images GmbH (Stockbyte RF, George Doyle), Hamburg; **17.5** Thinkstock (Lifesize/ Ryan McVay), München; **24.1** Weccard, Thomas, Ludwigsburg; **25.1** February Films, London; **25.1** February Films, London; **25.2** February Films, London; **25.3** February Films, London; **25.4** February Films, London; **25.5** February Films, London; **26.1** Fotolia.com (ElisabethM), New York; **26.2** Avenue Images GmbH (Stockbyte RF, George Doyle), Hamburg; **26.3** MEV Verlag GmbH, Augsburg; **27.1** Weccard, Thomas, Ludwigsburg; **27.2** Weccard, Thomas, Ludwigsburg; **28.1** Thinkstock (Wavebreak Media), München; **28.2** February Films, London; **28.3** Thinkstock (Jupiterimages), München; **28.4** shutterstock (Monkey Business Images), New York, NY; **28.5** February Films, London; **28.6** Avenue Images GmbH (Photo Alto), Hamburg; **28.7** Getty Images, München; **32.1** February Films, London; **32.2** February Films, London; **33.1** February Films, London; **33.2** February Films, London; **33.4** February Films, London; **34.1** February Films, London; **34.2** February Films, London; **34.3** February Films, London; **34.4** February Films, London; **36.1** February Films, London; **36.2** February Films, London; **38.1** February Films, London; **44.1** February Films, London; **44.2** Logo, Stuttgart; **45.1** February Films, London; **45.2** February Films, London; **45.3** February Films, London; **45.4** February Films, London; **45.5** February Films, London; **45.6** February Films, London; **45.7** February Films, London; **47.1** Weccard, Thomas, Ludwigsburg; **47.2** Weccard, Thomas, Ludwigsburg; **48.1** February Films, London; **48.2** February Films, London; **48.3** February Films, London; **51.1** Weccard, Thomas, Ludwigsburg; **52.1** February Films, London; **52.2** February Films, London; **53.1** February Films, London; **53.2** February Films, London; **53.3** February Films, London; **54.1** Fotolia.com (Gama-Déborah), New York; **54.2** Thinkstock (iStockphoto), München; **54.3** shutterstock (Matt Jeppson), New York, NY; **54.4** Thinkstock (iStockphoto), München; **54.5** Fotolia.com (arolina66), New York; **54.6** Thinkstock (iStockphoto), München; **58.1** February Films, London; **60.1** February Films, London; **64.3** Alamy Images (ALAN EDWARDS), Abingdon, Oxon; **64.4** Alamy Images (keith morris), Abingdon, Oxon; **64.5** Avenue Images GmbH (Alamy RF), Hamburg; **64.6** Mauritius Images (Alamy), Mittenwald; **65.1** February Films, London; **65.2** February Films, London; **65.3** February Films, London; **65.4** February Films, London; **65.5** February Films, London; **66.1** Thinkstock (iStockphoto), München; **66.2** Fotolia.com (erikdegraaf), New York; **68.1** February Films, London; **68.2** February Films, London; **68.3** February Films, London; **68.4** February Films, London; **68.5** February Films, London; **69.1** February Films, London; **69.2** February Films, London; **70.1** Avenue Images GmbH (PhotoAlto), Hamburg; **70.2** Getty Images (ADEK BERRY/AFP), München; **70.3** February Films (Andrew Kemp), London; **70.4** Getty Images, München; **71.1** Getty Images (Cultura), München; **71.2** Getty Images (Oli Scarff), München; **72.1** February Films (Andrew Kemp), London; **72.2** Thinkstock (iStock), München; **72.3** February Films (Andrew Kemp), London; **72.6** Thinkstock (iStockphoto), München; **74.1** February Films, London; **75.1** February Films (Andrew Kemp), London; **75.2** February Films (Andrew Kemp), London; **75.3** February Films (Andrew Kemp), London; **75.4** February Films (Andrew Kemp), London; **75.6** February Films (Andrew Kemp), London; **75.7** February Films (Andrew Kemp), London; **75.7** February Films (Andrew Kemp), London; **76.1** February Films (Andrew Kemp), London; **76.2** February Films (Andrew Kemp), London; **80.1** February Films (Andrew Kemp), London; **82.1** dreamstime.com (Alessandro0770), Brentwood, TN; **82.2** Getty Images (Andy Sheppard/Redferns), München; **82.3** Thinkstock (iStockphoto), München; **82.4** Thinkstock, München; **83.1** February Films, London; **83.2** February Films, London; **83.3** February Films, London; **83.4** February Films, London; **83.5** February Films, London; **84.1** Weccard, Thomas, Ludwigsburg; **85.1** Weccard, Thomas, Ludwigsburg; **85.2** shutterstock (Ramona Kaulitzki), New York, NY; **85.3** MEV Verlag GmbH, Augsburg; **85.4** Fotolia.com (Ruth Black), New York; **85.5** iStockphoto (Vasko Miokovic/RF), Calgary, Alberta; **85.6** Weccard, Thomas, Ludwigsburg; **86.1** Getty Images (Cultura), München; **86.2** Getty Images (Oli Scarff), München; **86.3** Getty Images (ADEK BERRY/AFP), München; **86.4** Getty Images, München; **86.5** February Films (Andrew Kemp), London; **87.4** February Films, London; **90.1** Fotosearch Stock Photography, Waukesha, WI; **90.2** February Films (Andrew Kemp), London; **90.3** Corbis (Steven Vidler), Düsseldorf; **91.1** Corbis (Glowimages), Düsseldorf; **91.2** plainpicture GmbH & Co. KG (Image Source), Hamburg; **91.3** February Films, London; **91.4** Getty Images (Riser), München; **92.1** February Films (Andrew Kemp), London; **96.1** shutterstock (Tomas Urbelionis), New York, NY; **96.2** Alamy Images (Monica Wells), Abingdon, Oxon; **96.3** Alamy Images (Maurice Crooks), Abingdon, Oxon; **98.1** February Films, London; **98.2** February Films, London; **101.1** Thinkstock (iStockphoto), München; **102.2** iStockphoto (Michael_at_isp), Calgary, Alberta; **102.3** Robert Harding Picture Library Ltd. (RF), Maidenhead, Berkshire; **102.4** dreamstime.com (Biserko), Brentwood, TN; **103.1** February Films, London; **103.2** February Films, London; **103.3** February Films, London; **103.4** February Films, London; **103.5** February Films, London; **106.1** February Films, London; **106.2** February Films, London; **106.3** February Films, London; **106.4** February Films, London; **106.5** February Films, London; **106.6** February Films, London; **107.1** February Films, London; **110.1** February Films (Andrew Kemp), London; **110.2** plainpicture GmbH & Co. KG (Siegfried Kuttig), Hamburg; **111.1** Getty Images (Cultura), München; **111.2** Thinkstock (Jupiterimages), München; **111.3** Thinkstock (Lifesize), München; **111.4** iStockphoto (travellinglight), Calgary, Alberta; **113.1** shutterstock (Karkas), New York, NY; **113.2** Thinkstock (iStock), München; **113.4** iStockphoto (Digital Paws Inc.), Calgary, Alberta; **113.5** Thinkstock (Photodisc), München; **113.6** shutterstock (jocic), New York, NY; **113.6** iStockphoto (George Pchemyan), Calgary, Alberta; **114.1** February Films (Andrew Kemp), London; **114.2** February Films (Andrew Kemp), London; **115.1** February Films, London; **115.2** Weccard, Thomas, Ludwigsburg; **116.1** shutterstock (R. Fassbind), New York, NY; **116.2** shutterstock (MarkauMark), New York, NY; **116.3** Thinkstock (iStockphoto), München; **118.1** February Films (Andrew Kemp), London; **118.2** February Films (Andrew Kemp), London; **120.1** February Films (Andrew Kemp), London; **121.2** February Films (Andrew Kemp), London; **122.1** shutterstock (BESTWEB), New York, NY; **122.2** Thinkstock (iStockphoto), München; **122.3** Getty Images (Britain On View), München; **122.4** Thinkstock (iStockphoto), München; **122.5** shutterstock (Stephen Coburn), New York, NY; **122.6** Thinkstock (iStockphoto), München; **122.7** Thinkstock (Hemera), München; **122.8** Thinkstock (iStockphoto), München; **123.1** February Films, London; **123.2** February Films, London; **123.3** February Films, London; **123.4** February Films, London; **123.5** February Films, London; **124.1** Weccard, Thomas, Ludwigsburg; **125.1** Thinkstock (iStockphoto), München; **128.1** February Films, London; **130.1** February Films, London; **130.3** February Films, London; **130.4** February Films, London;

131.2 February Films, London; **137.1** February Films, London; **137.2** February Films, London; **137.3** February Films, London; **137.4** February Films, London; **138.1** February Films (Andrew Kemp), London; **138.2** February Films (Andrew Kemp), London; **138.3** February Films (Andrew Kemp), London; **138.4** February Films (Andrew Kemp), London; **138.5** February Films (Andrew Kemp), London; **138.6** February Films (Andrew Kemp), London; **139.1** February Films (Andrew Kemp), London; **139.2** February Films (Andrew Kemp), London; **144.1** Alamy Images (Maurice Crooks), Abingdon, Oxon; **148.1** February Films, London; **148.2** shutterstock (MarkauMark), New York, NY; **148.3** Thinkstock (iStockphoto), München; **154.1** Okapia (NAS/Merlin Tuttle), Frankfurt; **154.3** Thinkstock (iStockphoto), München; **155.1** Thinkstock (iStockphoto), München; **156.1** akg-images, Berlin; **156.2** Thinkstock (iStockphoto), München; **156.3** Alamy Images (Christine Osborne Pictures), Abingdon, Oxon; **157.1** Picture-Alliance (dpa), Frankfurt; **194.1** Thinkstock (Digital Vision), München; **194.2** Thinkstock (Photodisc), München; **194.3** Thinkstock (Photos.com), München; **194.4** Thinkstock (iStockphoto), München; **194.5** Thinkstock (iStockphoto), München; **194.6** Thinkstock (iStockphoto), München; **194.7** Thinkstock (Purestock), München; **194.8** Thinkstock (Digital Vision), München; **194.9** Thinkstock (Wavebreak Media), München; **194.10** Thinkstock (iStockphoto), München; **194.11** iStockphoto (rarpia), Calgary, Alberta; **194.12** Thinkstock (FogStock), München; **194.13** Thinkstock (iStockphoto), München; **202.1** Fotolia.com (Dawn Hudson), New York

Sollte es in einem Einzelfall nicht gelungen sein, den korrekten Rechteinhaber ausfindig zu machen, so werden berechtigte Ansprüche selbstverständlich im Rahmen der üblichen Regelungen abgegolten.

Textquellennachweis

S. 89: PONS – Red Line Wörterbuch, Englisch – Deutsch, Deutsch – Englisch, Neuentwicklung 2006
S. 151: © Jürg Obrist: Case Closed? 40 Mini-mysteries for you to solve. New York: Millbrook Press, 2003.
© für die englische Übersetzung: Jürg Obrist. Deutsches Original: Jürg Obrist: Klarer Fall? 40 Minikrimis zum Mitraten.
© 1999 Deutscher Taschenbuchverlag, München

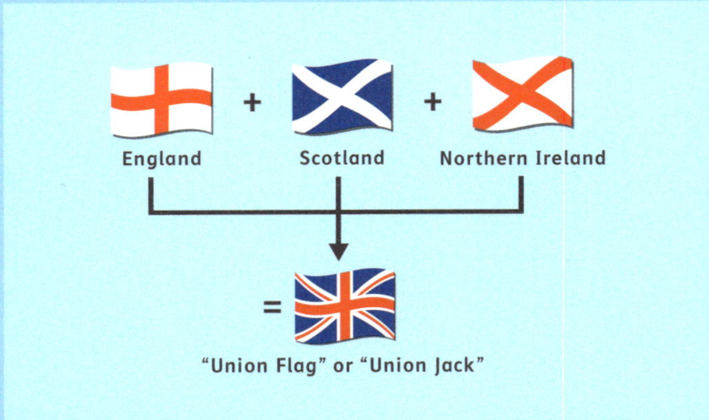
England
Scotland
Northern Ireland
=
"Union Flag" or "Union Jack"

Atlantic Ocean

Galway
Cork